Hiking Colorado's Weminuche and South San Juan Wilderness Areas

Third Edition

Donna Ikenberry

FALCON GUIDES

GUILFORD, CONNECTICUT
HELENA, MONTANA

AN IMPRINT OF GLOBE PEQUOT PRESS

FALCONGUIDES®

Copyright © 2014 by Morris Book Publishing, LLC
Previously published by Falcon Publishing, Inc.

FalconGuides is an imprint of Globe Pequot Press.
Falcon, FalconGuides, and Outfit Your Mind are registered trademarks of Morris Book Publishing, LLC.

All photos by the author unless otherwise indicated.

Project Editor: Lauren Brancato
Layout Artist: Sue Murray
Maps updated by Daniel Lloyd © Morris Book Publishing, LLC

Library of Congress Cataloging-in-Publication data is available on file.

ISBN 978-0-7627-8244-4

Printed in the United States of America

10 9 8 7 6 5 4 3 2 1

In memory of my dad, Donald Dean Ikenberry, who passed away on May 17, 2012. It was way too soon, Dad—not a day goes by that I don't miss you.

Contents

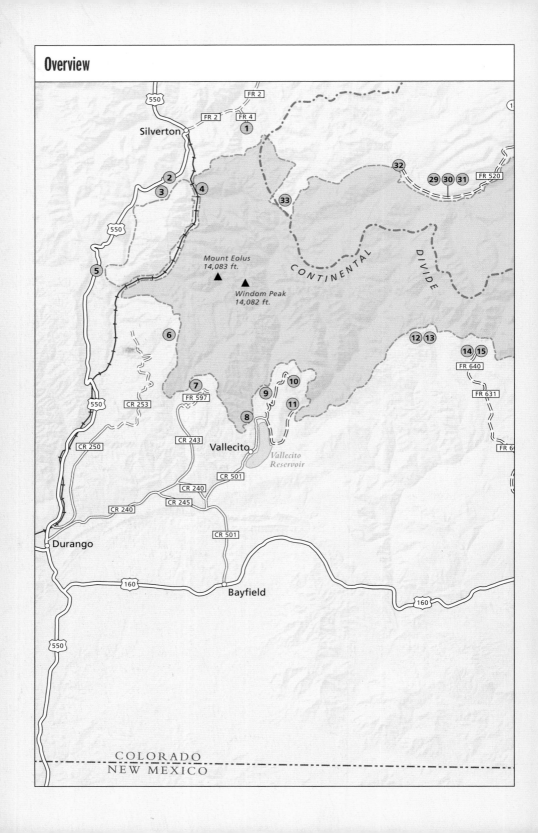

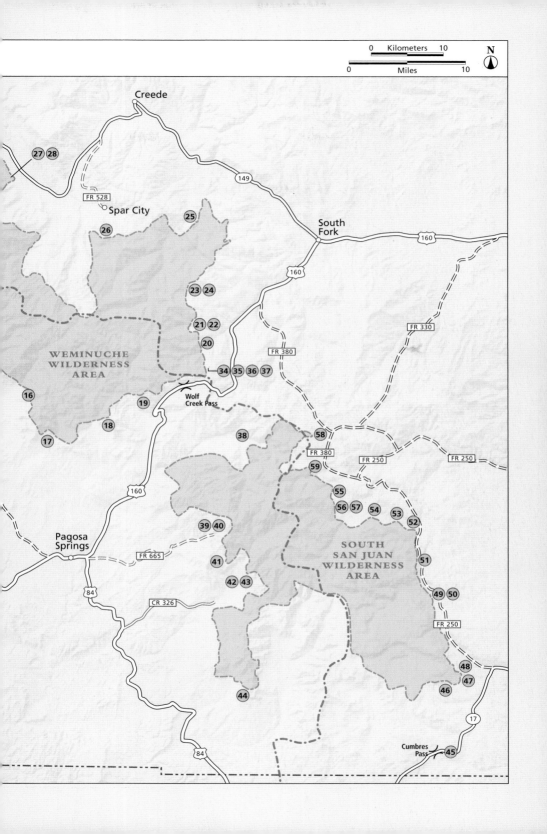

Acknowledgments

When I'm out in the wilderness, I am always thankful to God. I especially enjoy the awesome grandeur above timberline. No doubt, there's nothing like it. I thrill to wide-open places, see-forever views as well as tiny wildflowers growing above tree line, and the sound of elk bugling and American pikas chirping.

I first hiked in the Weminuche Wilderness in the summer of 1997. I was single then. I spent two summers hiking in the Weminuche, much of the time alone, but several friends—Carol Kaufman, Johnna Bambrey, and Nancy Haynes—joined me on a few hikes. During my first season in the Weminuche, I had no idea that I would come back the next time engaged to my best friend, Mike Vining. In the summer of 1998, Mike made a couple of my Weminuche hikes extra special. He completed all of the South San Juan Wilderness hikes with me when I worked on the second revision of this book after we were married. When the book came up for a third revision in 2012, Mike was right there with me, taking GPS readings, carrying some of my camera gear, and making each hike a whole lot of fun.

I'm grateful for friends Gail Harrington, Susan McNeil, and Gudrun and Beuford Durmon, who also joined me on several South San Juan hikes.

Even when I am out in the wilderness, my family travels with me, for they are forever in my heart. My parents, Donald and Beverly Ikenberry, always blessed me with their love and support. They both passed away in recent years so I constantly miss them, but they travel with me, their cremains in a little heart-shaped necklace I wear around my neck. I am especially blessed by my brother, Don, and his wife, Yolie. They are the very best of friends, loved ones I can forever count on. I'm also blessed with my husband's family, including Roger Vining, a special "dad," and the late Arlene Vining, a wonderful "mom," plus my two stepdaughters and six grandchildren.

I have many other friends to thank. Although you are too numerous to mention, you know who you are, and you are always in my thoughts and prayers.

Thanks also to Anne Klein of the Durango Area Tourism Office, who arranged for our Durango & Silverton Railroad tickets, a wonderful two-day stay at Westerly RV Park, and dinner at Linda's Local Cafe. I would like to acknowledge Imee Curiel, my contact at Globe Pequot, Melissa Baker, my map editor, and Lauren Brancato, my project editor. Thank you, Imee, Melissa, and Lauren for answering my questions promptly, for your professionalism, and for the nice personal touch as well. Last, I'm grateful to the folks at the San Juan and Rio Grande National Forests. An extra special thanks goes out to Mike Blakeman, Lisa McClure, and Amanda Walker.

Introduction

When I think of the Weminuche and South San Juan Wilderness Areas, a smile always crosses my face. Why? Because for me they are special places filled with wonderful memories. When I entered the Weminuche for the first time in 1997, I was a full-time photojournalist and traveler. I had been on the road for fourteen years, and my "home" was a fifth-wheel trailer. While working on an earlier version of this book, *Hiking Colorado's Weminuche Wilderness,* I parked my RV in the wonderful communities of Durango, Pagosa Springs, and South Fork.

It was just prior to my first summer of hiking in the Weminuche that I met my soul mate and best friend, Mike Vining. The following summer we hiked the Continental Divide Trail portion of the Weminuche together—in love, engaged, and ready to find a place where we could settle down. Mike is a collector of books and outdoor gear, and I knew my full-time traveling lifestyle would be coming to an end. After the hike Mike went back to his home in North Carolina, and I moved to South Fork for a couple of months and found the place where I want to live for the rest of my life. Mike flew out to visit and agreed with me. Happily, Mike had always planned on moving to Colorado after retiring from the US Army.

We married on January 6, 1999. A few weeks later Mike retired from the army as a sergeant major with thirty years in service, and we bought our home in South Fork in August 1999. I sold my tiny home on wheels and have never regretted that decision. It was an easy choice because Mike and I live in one of the greatest places on earth. We also live near two of the grandest wilderness areas in the country: The Weminuche Wilderness is a few miles to the west, and the South San Juan Wilderness is not far to our south.

Both wilderness areas are filled with see-forever views. They are places where waves of mountains rush to the horizon, where peaks stretch into the heavens. Coyotes yelp in wildflower-blessed meadows, snowshoe rabbits scamper down willow-lined trails, and beavers slap at sunset on silent lakes. In addition, black bears roam through lush forests, and elk herds tiptoe quietly through woods or congregate in meadows, feeding while hikers watch from a ridge above.

Tucked away in Colorado's southwest corner, the Weminuche (pronounced WHEM-a-nooch) Wilderness is the larger of the two wilderness areas with 499,771 acres. Named for a band of Ute Indians who lived, hunted, and fished in and honored the spirit of this stunning land, the area was first designated a wilderness in 1975. It's easy to find: Just get a map and look for the quaint towns of Durango, Silverton, Creede, South Fork, and Pagosa Springs. Then connect the dots of these towns. The Weminuche is smack-dab in the center, in the heart of the stunning San Juan Mountains.

I spent two wonderful summers hiking many of the trails in the Weminuche Wilderness. I chose distinct paths through diverse country. My goal was to best showcase

Yellow-bellied marmots (Marmota flaviventris) *are often seen and heard while hiking in the Weminuche and South San Juan Wilderness Areas. Their nickname is whistle pig.*

the wilderness, something I needn't have bothered to do. After hiking about 700 miles, I've come to the conclusion that the Weminuche is its own best showcase.

The South San Juan Wilderness is just as impressive. It is located to the southeast of the southeast corner of the Weminuche; only US 160 and a few miles of national forest land separate the two. The wilderness is lengthy, stretching south from Elwood Pass to near the Colorado–New Mexico border. The South San Juan Wilderness was designated as such by an act of Congress in December 1980. Thirteen years later additional acreage was added with the passage of the Colorado Wilderness Act of 1993. Today 158,790 acres make up the lovely region known as the South San Juan Wilderness.

My husband and I have spent a lot of time in the South San Juan Mountains hiking, backpacking, and backcountry skiing. During the summer I was working on this book, we hiked nearly 400 miles and climbed more than 75,000 feet. When the summer was over, we noticed something. We thought back to our hikes in both wildernesses and realized that no matter what area we were enjoying, we did the exact same thing: If we were on a high peak in the South San Juan Wilderness, then we spent time peering toward the Weminuche, and if we were in the Weminuche, we were smiling at the South San Juan. Both places are special to us, and we hope that they will be special to you. Happy hiking!

Weather

The hiking and backpacking season for the Weminuche and South San Juan Wilderness Areas is pretty much limited to June, July, August, and September. The majority of trails are open from around the first of July through mid–September. Heavy snowfall regularly blankets the San Juan Mountains, which means that you will find access restricted in June and perhaps even into July. Particularly hard winters have kept trails higher than 10,000 feet snowbound until the first week of July or even later. Although Mike and I hiked into October, we found up to 8 inches of new snow on the ground in September. Amazingly, we spent part of the Labor Day weekend in 2004 tent-bound for forty hours as a blizzard raged around us. It was both amazing and awesome!

High waters and dangerous crossings are one June obstacle; advantages to hiking early include fewer mosquitoes, fewer people, and more opportunities to see wildlife. July brings summer thunderstorms, with extended rainy periods known as the monsoon season. Mosquitoes are out in full force, and temperatures may be as high as the eighties, with lows dipping to the thirties and forties. Wildflowers are at their finest during this month, and people come out in droves to see them. River levels drop to near normal.

Cooler weather is evident by mid–August, when the daily temperatures drop and autumn (a noticeable chill) is in the air. Erratic weather plagues this month: Some years it's mild and fair; other years it's rainy and miserable. September is quiet in the wilderness. (Although you may find hunters around then.) The crowds are gone, and it's typically a month of low precipitation. You'll find frost on your tent almost every morning and maybe snow, too, but it should melt by noon. Streams are at their lowest and easiest for crossing, and aspens dress in fall shades, adding color to an already colorful land.

Colorado's weather can (and does) change in an instant, so when you hike, you should always be prepared for different environments. High peaks create their own weather. Know that while it may be warm at the trailhead, it might be freezing cold on top of a peak. Expect snow any time of the year. Most important, in the summer (thunderstorm) season, be up to your highest point by noon or 1 p.m. so you can get to lower ground by the time the thunderstorms hit. On a special note, thunderstorms can strike earlier in the day; always be aware!

The Weminuche and South San Juan Wildernesses are not easy to access in the winter. Most trailheads are not accessible because of snow, thus a wilderness trip would be a multiday affair. If winter is your season, be sure to enter the wilderness on snowshoes or backcountry skis; carry a shovel and all the other necessities, and don't forget the avalanche beacon.

Colorado is a diverse state, with three major physiographic provinces: the Great Plains, in eastern Colorado, about two-fifths of the state; the Rocky Mountains, occupying the central and west-central portions of the state; and the Colorado Plateau, making up the remaining western portion. Colorado's Rockies comprise several ranges divided by wide-open basins, or "parks," as they are sometimes called.

Though the Rocky Mountains can claim volcanic ancestry (they belong to the Pacific Belt, where 80 percent of the world's active volcanoes are found, including the energetic peaks of the Cascades, the South American Andes, and the North American Aleutians), no active volcanoes remain here. Once, however, hot spots smoldered throughout the state, with the heart of all activity in the San Juan Mountains. Today the San Juans' 10,000 square miles of peaks compose the largest single range in the greater Rocky Mountains. Boasting thirteen peaks higher than 14,000 feet and countless more rising 11,000 feet or more into the heavens, the San Juans also embrace the Continental Divide.

The Continental Divide extends 1,700 miles through the United States from Montana to New Mexico. A common link between the Weminuche and South San Juan Wilderness Areas, it is not much more than a mild rise in the deserts of New Mexico and the flatlands of southern Wyoming. But in Colorado this legendary divide stands out. Here it is easy to see and easy to experience. Stand atop the Divide during a storm, and you'll see raindrops destined for different rivers, different oceans: On the west side, raindrops end up in the Pacific Ocean; on the east side, they flow to the Atlantic Ocean via the Gulf of Mexico. From the Divide you also can view the aftermath of heavy glacial activity. Cirques, U-shaped valleys, and horn-shaped peaks, all typical glacial features, are the result of activity about 10,000 years ago.

Colorado's characteristic life zones stretch from the Upper Sonoran zone in the eastern Colorado plains to the Arctic-Alpine zone above the timberline. If you were to start your visit in the eastern half of the state, you would pass from the Upper Sonoran zone through the Transition–Upper Sonoran zone to the Canadian, Hudsonian, and eventually Arctic-Alpine life zones. Along the way you'd see everything from sand hills and cacti to ponderosa pine and juniper, plus treeless alpine tundra with sparse vegetation and abundant wildflowers.

If you were in the wilderness, especially the Weminuche, in the late 1990s, you would have seen a far different scene than today. Then the forest was green and beautiful; now much of it is dead, killed by the spruce beetle. Unfortunately, bark beetles have killed thousands of acres of Engelmann spruce in mature spruce-fir forests in the Rio Grande National Forest. According to Mike Blakeman, public information officer for the Rio Grande National Forest, it's estimated that beetles have killed trees on more than 300,000 acres. Bark beetles are endemic and usually coexist peacefully with their host trees. They usually infest trees blown down by wind, leaving the healthy trees alone. But a drought is upon the land, and now an epidemic is in our midst. But it is the nature of things. Forest ecologists believe these epidemics occur roughly every 200 years. However, it's not all bad news: Other tree species will grow; life will go on. In the meantime we need to be aware of the danger of falling trees, practice safe fire etiquette, and enjoy the new forest that will grow in its place.

New forest will be growing in the Weminuche sooner rather than later. In June 2013, fire ravaged some of the eastern section of the Weminuche Wilderness. The first of three fires started on June 5 when lightning struck the West Fork of the San Juan River about 15 miles northeast of Pagosa Springs. The same day lightning started the Windy Pass Fire, located outside the wilderness near Wolf Creek Pass. On June 19 the Papoose Fire, also lightning caused, began at the head of Little Squaw Creek in the Weminuche Wilderness, about 19 miles southwest of Creede. The two wilderness fires, West Fork and Papoose, burned a total of 108,198 acres. The Rio Grande National Forest opened most of the burned areas on August 23, 2013, stressing that burned trees may be very unstable. They ask that hikers avoid the burned forest when it is windy. Also, there is the risk of flash floods and debris flows during high-intensity rainstorms, so hikers should stay out of narrow canyons during times of possible flash flooding. Also, hikers should always carry a saw or ax when driving in the burned areas because trees may fall at any time and block the road.

The area that encompasses the Weminuche and South San Juan Wildernesses offers an equally diverse selection of animal life. Visitors to the region often see Rocky Mountain elk, especially when traveling the higher trails. Mule deer, black bears, mountain lions, and bighorn sheep, Colorado's state animal, also live here. Mountain goats are perhaps the supreme creatures of high places. The low dips in Wyoming's Continental Divide kept goats north in Idaho, Montana, Canada, and Alaska until May 24, 1948, when the Colorado Division of Wildlife released nine mountain goats in Colorado's Sawatch Range. Over the next twenty-three years, fifty-one goats were released in the state, including some in the area near the Needles in the Weminuche Wilderness.

Canadian lynx have also been reintroduced. Once found over most of Colorado, lynx were wiped out by livestock owners and trappers. The Colorado Division of Wildlife began releasing Canadian lynx back into the wild in 1999. By 2006, 218 of these animals had been released; between 2003 and 2010, at least 141 lynx kittens were born in the state.

Known for its animal life, the South San Juans are probably best recognized as the site of the last known Colorado grizzly bear—killed by a hunter in 1979. There are many rumors that grizzlies may still live in the area, which is thought by some to be the wildest place in the state. If they do exist in Colorado, grizzlies would be likely to thrive here. Moose were introduced into the area in January 1992, when thirty-one were released in the Rio Grande National Forest between Creede and Lake City. Since that time some of the moose have traveled south and now make the Weminuche Wilderness their home. Today there are approximately 300 moose in the region.

Bull moose are always exciting to see and photograph.

Smaller mammals, such as coyotes, marmots, hares, rabbits, skunks, beavers, bobcats, badgers, weasels, porcupines, and squirrels, exist here as well. Birdlife is abundant, too. Raptors include red-tailed hawks, prairie falcons, great horned owls, and many more. Other bird species are blue, sage, and sharp-tailed grouse; gray and Steller's jays; ravens; ptarmigan; and a variety of wrens, bluebirds, woodpeckers, finches, sparrows, flycatchers, swallows, kinglets, hummingbirds, and blackbirds, to name a few.

Wilderness Restrictions/Regulations

The Weminuche and South San Juan Wilderness Areas are two of many places designated wilderness by Congress as a result of the Wilderness Act of 1964. (Today there are more than one hundred million acres of wilderness nationwide, with more than three million acres gracing the state of Colorado.) When President Lyndon Johnson signed the Wilderness Act on September 3, 1964, a portion of the law read that wilderness "shall be administered for the use and enjoyment of the American people in such a manner as will leave them unimpaired for future use and enjoyment as wilderness, and so as to provide for the protection of these areas [and] the preservation of their character."

The Weminuche Wilderness received federal protection in 1975, and the South San Juan Wilderness gained protection in December 1980, with additional acreage added with passage of the Colorado Wilderness Act of 1993.

There are certain restrictions in both wilderness areas. Of course, all wilderness areas prohibit the possession and use of motorized equipment and mechanized means of transport. This includes motor vehicles, bicycles, wagons, hang gliders, carts, chain saws, and other motorized equipment. Shortcutting of switchbacks is also prohibited. Camping is not permitted within 100 feet of streams or lakes, except as posted or designated. Wash water and disposal of human waste are prohibited within 100 feet (approximately thirty-five adult steps) of any water source. Recreational livestock are prohibited from being restrained within 100 feet of lakeshores and streams or within riparian areas. (In some areas of the South San Juans, specifically Bear, Blue, Green, and Red Lakes, you must be 200 feet away to camp or keep livestock.) In addition, all livestock feed must be certified weed-free. Pets must be under voice control or physical restraint, and they must not disturb people or wildlife.

In both wilderness areas, group size is limited to fifteen people per group, with a maximum combination of people and stock not to exceed twenty-five (fifteen people and ten stock). There are also some camping restrictions in each wilderness. I outline them within the appropriate hike chapters.

In 2014 the San Juan and Rio Grande National Forests may begin requiring visitors to register prior to entering the Weminuche Wilderness. A short two-part form will be available online, at agency offices, and at major trailheads. One part of the form will be deposited into a secure box at the trailhead and the other part will be kept with the individual or group leader while in the wilderness.

Finally, wilderness visitors should always call ahead to the local ranger district, especially during dry years, to see if there are any temporary fire bans in effect.

CORSAR CARD

Before you hike in the wilderness, consider purchasing a Colorado Outdoor Recreation Search and Rescue (CORSAR) card. This card replaces what was first known as the Colorado Hiking Certificate. The money generated from card sales goes to the Colorado Search and Rescue Fund, which provides reimbursement for expenses incurred during search-and-rescue missions. The CORSAR card comes in one- and five-year versions; the costs are $3 and $12, respectively. If you have a valid Colorado hunting, fishing, or off-highway vehicle license, then you already have contributed to the Search and Rescue Fund. Obtain your CORSAR card directly from the Colorado Department of Local Affairs at www.colorado.gov/cs/Satellite/ DOLA-Main/CBON/1251592090523. You can order online or click for a statewide list of card vendors.

Preparedness and Trail Etiquette

Prepare adequately for hikes in the Weminuche and South San Juan Wilderness Areas. These preserves are located in high-elevation areas, where you can become dehydrated quickly. Always bring plenty of water on a day hike, and remember to drink it. For overnight trips, bring a water filter. All water should be treated (either filtered or boiled) before you drink it. In addition, you should bring (and use) plenty of sunscreen. Don't forget to coat your lips! And don't forget healthy snacks to keep you fueled during your hike.

In high-elevation areas you should always dress in layers, wearing fabrics that breathe. Remember to pack rain gear. The weather can change quickly in this part of the country. You may begin hiking in bright, sunny conditions only to encounter high winds, snow, and blizzard-like conditions before the day is done. Be prepared for all kinds of weather. In addition, always take along a space blanket and a first-aid kit for emergencies. Overnight backpackers should carry essential camping equipment, enough food for the length of the trip plus an extra day for emergencies, and so on. Always carry a flashlight, even on day hikes, because you never know when you may end up hiking in the dark.

Regardless of whether you hike alone or with a friend, leave a detailed itinerary with someone before you head out. List the trails you plan to hike and the date you plan to return. Include telephone numbers of family and friends in case of an emergency, and write down your license plate number, too.

Be sure to bring a map and compass, and know how to use both. A global positioning system (GPS) can be beneficial as well, but I still recommend the use of traditional navigational aids. Although Mike and I found some inaccuracies on the maps we used, they largely kept us from getting lost and confused. We paid attention to the terrain, used the maps as guides, and turned to our compass and GPS to verify travel decisions. If we became disoriented, we stayed put until we figured out our location. I recommend that everyone do the same.

I've traveled thousands of miles through the wilderness areas in Colorado and Oregon, and while doing so, I've seen evidence that we often love these places to death. There is a proper way to behave in the wilderness: It's called Leave No Trace. This preventive education program, sponsored by the US Department of Agriculture's Forest Service, is all about being responsible, using low-impact methods of camping and traveling, taking nothing, and leaving only footprints. The goal is to act as respectful in the wilderness as you would if you were visiting family or friends. Please adhere to the following regulations.

- **Self-register at the trailhead.** This may be mandatory for those entering the Weminuche Wilderness starting in 2014 and an option for those entering the South San Juan Wilderness. Free registration for those entering the Weminuche Wilderness Area will be available online, at the managing agencies, and at major trailheads. Those entering the South San Juans can self-register (also for free) at the trailhead. For more information contact the appropriate managing agency.

- **Limit the trails to primitive traffic only.** Mountain bikes, motorcycles, hang gliders, and other mechanical or motorized modes of travel are not allowed in wilderness areas. Accepted means of travel include hiking, horseback riding (although some trails are closed to horses), and packing in with your favorite animal (a horse, mule, llama, goat, or even a backpacking dog).

- **Stay on the trail.** If the path happens to be muddy, plow right through. Don't step off to the side. If you search for higher, drier ground, it only creates another trail. Be sure to hike single file. Trails several feet wide have been created because some people insist on walking side by side. (***Note:*** If you're hiking off trail, it is better to spread out to avoid creating new trails.) Folks who cut across switch-backs also harm the area. Stay on the regular route!

- **Supervise your pet.** Sam, my Samoyed who died years ago, used to join me on all of my hikes and backpacking trips. In fact, he carried his own backpack. I know that some people oppose dogs on the trails. They can be a problem at times, but I've observed leashed, quiet, and obedient pets, too. I've never seen a dog litter a trail with beer cans or candy wrappers. Keep your pet quiet, bury its waste and keep such matter away from water sources, and maintain control so it won't chase wildlife. With such care, your pet will add joy to every outing.

- **Yield to livestock.** When hiking, move off the trail if you come across horses or llamas. If you are hiking with llamas, be sure to speak to the riders. Horses and mules that are not familiar with llamas may be startled by the odor or appearance.

- **Use a camp stove for cooking.** Some people love the warmth and comfort of a mesmerizing fire, but in certain places a fire just doesn't work. Use a portable stove unless there is ample firewood and no area restrictions against building a fire. Use wood sparingly. If you're at an established camp, use an existing fire ring. If you camp where no one has camped before, dig a hole in the dirt, then build a small fire without rocks. When the fire is out, douse the ashes with water and replace the earth. Be sure all fires are completely extinguished.

- **Carry out all litter.** Do not bury trash; wild animals may dig it up. If you choose to burn your trash, remember that foil doesn't burn completely. Many wonder what to do about human waste and toilet paper. Use the "cat hole" method when nature calls. Keeping at least 200 feet from water, camps, and trails, dig down 6 inches (a lightweight garden trowel or stick works fine) and set the topsoil aside. After using this hole as a small outdoor privy, replace the dirt and topsoil, burying all matter. Stamp the soil and cover it with a few sticks or rocks if possible. You can bury toilet paper, burn it, or put it in plastic bags and pack it out with other trash. Remember, toilet paper is trash! Women should carry out soiled sanitary pads and tampons.

- **Keep cleaning agents away from natural water sources.** On extended hikes bathing becomes necessary. You can bathe directly in natural water only if you do not use soap and are not wearing any type of insect repellent. When brushing your teeth or using soap to wash personal items, stay at least 200 feet from the water. Bury your toothpaste spittle. For quick wash-up jobs, carry hand wipes or waterless hand cleaner. Buy unscented varieties; the scented stuff may attract bugs and bears.

- **Know fish and game regulations.** Although many people enter the back-country with relaxation, sightseeing, photography, or wildlife-watching on their minds, some enter with hunting and fishing as top priorities. The latter groups should check with the appropriate managing agency for up-to-date information on permits and the opening and closing dates for the season.
- **When camping overnight, be sure to hang your food.** Black bears have voracious appetites, an acute sense of smell, and a great memory. They know where they have found meals in the past. Day or night, never leave your food unattended. Never store food or scented items in a tent, and use a bear-resistant storage container or hang your food to keep it safe.
- **Leave all treasures for others to see.** This includes man-made stuff (such as Native American artifacts) as well as rocks, wildflowers, and other plant life. Don't walk away with anything! Take only pictures; leave only footprints. If you do so, you'll come back with a mountain of memories and an album of photographs. More important, you'll leave a lasting treasure for generations to come.

Trip the dog with his backpack on the Lime Mesa Trail in the Weminuche Wilderness

How to Use This Book

This book is divided into four major sections, one each to cover the Weminuche and South San Juan Wilderness Areas and the Continental Divide Trail within those areas. Each **section introduction** gives you a sweeping look at the lay of the land. After this general overview, individual chapters feature specific hikes within that region.

Each hike chapter begins with a **summary** that gives you an idea of the adventure to follow. Next you'll find **hike specs,** the nitty-gritty details of the hike: where the trailhead is located, the hike length and difficulty, the approximate hiking time, canine compatibility, the nearest town, fees and permits, maps pertinent to the hike, and trail contacts (for updates on trail conditions). **Finding the trailhead** gives you dependable directions from a nearby city or town to where you will want to park.

The Hike is the meat of the chapter. Detailed and honest, this section contains my carefully researched impression of the trail. Although it is impossible to cover everything, you can rest assured that I have not missed what's important. In **Miles and Directions** I provide GPS coordinates and mileage cues for some key points of the hike. The **Hike Information** section at the end of each hike lists local offices that you can contact for more information, local accommodations, and other things to see and do while you're in the area.

In this book I describe several types of hikes, including both day hikes and extended backpack trips. You'll find everything from out-and-back hikes (hike from the trailhead to a destination and then back to the trailhead) to semiloop hikes (begin and end at the same trailhead, hiking at least one other trail along the way); loop hikes (follow two trails that loop together and meet at the same trailhead); and shuttle hikes (begin and end the hike at two separate trailheads; you'll need a ride at the end of your trip).

Of course, you can mix and match hikes to fit personal likes and dislikes. For example, I write about the Turkey Creek and West Fork San Juan Trails individually, but it's easy to combine the two if you have access to a shuttle. If you're interested in short day hikes, you can always follow the trail description for one of the longer day hikes or extended backpack trips. Just hike out as far as you want, enjoy the area, and then head back to the trailhead.

I have given each trail a difficulty rating, something that isn't always easy to do. Physical condition, weather, and experience can all influence a hiker's opinion of the trail, and the trail itself may vary in difficulty. I've taken all that into consideration. In this book I use the terms easy, moderate, and strenuous.

An easy hike is usually on a shorter trail, with gentle grades. It may be nearly flat. Moderate hikes are longer, but usually less than 8 miles round-trip. Elevation gains on moderate routes are usually no more than 500 feet per mile. Hikes rated strenuous are usually longer than 8 miles and have steep gains and descents. These are the thigh-pounders and calf-busters. *Please note:* Some difficult trails are short, but steep and strenuous.

Most of the trails have names, and some have numbers, too. I describe all of the trails by name, but if the Forest Service has given the trail a number, then I list that in the text as well.

How to Use the Maps and Elevation Profiles

The **route map** is your primary guide to each hike. It shows all of the accessible roads and trails, points of interest, water, towns, landmarks, and geographical features relevant to the hike. It also distinguishes trails from roads and paved roads from unpaved roads. The selected route is highlighted, and directional arrows point the way.

Route maps use elevation tints, called hypsometry, to portray relief. Each tone represents a range of equal elevation, as shown in the scale key with the map. Thus the map gives you a good idea of elevation gain and loss.

Regional maps that show larger geographic areas use shaded, or shadow, relief. Shadow relief does not represent elevation; it demonstrates slope or relative steepness. This gives an almost three-dimensional perspective of the physiography of a region and will help you see where ranges and valleys are.

Elevation Profiles

Elevation profiles for certain hikes show the ascents and descents to a given destination. Elevation is labeled on the left, with mileage indicated across the top. Points of interest along the route are identified. Note that short climbs and drops do not appear because of the small scale of the profiles; information in the route maps and text should eliminate any surprises. Also note that the scales of elevation profiles may vary, so individual profiles should not be compared side by side.

Map Legend

Municipal

═⟨160⟩═	US Highway
═⟨105⟩═	State Road
═[CR 12]═	Local/County Road
═[FR 356]═	Unpaved/Forest Road
= = = :	Gravel Road
├──┼──┤	Railroad
— · · — ·	State Boundary

Trails

-------	Featured Trail
- - - - -	Trail

Water Features

⬭	Body of Water
⸗	Marsh
〰	River/Creek
⫶	Waterfall
⟋	Spring

Symbols

≍	Bridge
▪	Point of Interest/Trailhead
▲	Campground
⟓	Pass
▲	Peak/Elevation
◈	Scenic View
○	Town
⑳	Trailhead
↗	Trail Arrows

The Weminuche Wilderness

Colorado's largest wilderness offers up a staggering average elevation of 10,000 feet. No doubt one of the highest wilderness areas in the nation, even its trailheads average a mind-boggling 9,000 feet—and that's only the beginning. Hike or backpack from one of the trailheads, and you can find yourself walking a ridge at 12,000 feet or more, with 13,000- and 14,000-foot peaks surrounding you.

Looking for a 13,000-foot peak to scale? High peaks are more than plentiful here. From almost any lofty point, you'll see waves of them to the west, north, east, and south. Three of Colorado's fifty-four "fourteeners," as they are known, grace the wilderness: Mount Eolus (14,083 feet), Sunlight Peak (14,059 feet), and Windom Peak (14,082 feet). All three peaks are popular climbs. In fact, there are so many high-elevation peaks in the Weminuche that many of them are yet unnamed.

In addition to peaks, the wilderness contains eighty-one high mountain lakes, numerous streams and creeks, and the headwaters of five rivers: the Animas, Los Pinos (the Pines), the Piedra, the Rio Grande, and the San Juan. The region is jointly managed by the San Juan and Rio Grande National Forests. Thirty-one trailheads provide access to the many trails that dissect the wilderness. There are 490 miles of managed trails, countless miles of nonmanaged trails, and abundant opportunities to bushwhack wherever your heart and feet lead you. In addition to driving to the trailhead of your choice, you can also access the Chicago Basin and Elk Park region via a narrow-gauge train, which runs from Durango to Silverton and back again.

If you have time and you like high-elevation trails, you'll want to hike the Continental Divide Trail. This long-distance trail stretches more than 3,000 miles, from Antelope Wells, New Mexico, to Waterton, Alberta. The trail crosses the Continental Divide 475 times along its route. More than 80 miles of the trail pass through the Weminuche. The 468-mile Colorado Trail, which stretches from Durango to Denver, also passes through the northwest corner of the wilderness.

1 Highland Mary Lakes Loop

Abundant wildflowers, wonderful views, and high alpine tundra are yours for the asking on this delightful loop in the northwest corner of the Weminuche. A very long day hike (it'll seem even longer at high altitudes), it can also be hiked as an overnight backpack. Horses are not allowed on the Highland Mary Lakes Trail, but they can enjoy the Cunningham Gulch and Continental Divide Trails.

Start: Lower Highland Mary Lakes/Cunningham Gulch trailhead
Distance: 8.7-mile loop
Hiking time: About 5 to 8 hours or overnight backpack
Difficulty: Strenuous due to length and some steep sections
Canine compatibility: Dogs must be under control.
Nearest town: Silverton

Fees and permits: Free registration (available online, at managing agency, or major trailheads) needed for both day hikers and overnight backpackers. Contact the managing agency for current information.
Maps: USGS Howardsville and Storm King Peak; Trails Illustrated Weminuche Wilderness; DeLorme 3D TopoQuad CD-ROM; Maptech Terrain Navigator CD-ROM
Trail contact: San Juan National Forest, Columbine Ranger District, Bayfield; (970) 884-2512; www.fs.usda.gov/sanjuan

Finding the trailhead: From the junction of US 550 and CO 110 at the southwest end of Silverton, drive northeast on CO 110 (Greene Street) through Silverton. After 1 mile go right (east) on San Juan CR 2. The road is paved for the first 2 miles, then it turns to maintained gravel. After another 2.1 miles turn right (south) onto San Juan CR 4 toward Stony Pass. Reach a fork in 0.2 mile; keep right on the lower road. After an additional 1.5 miles, the road forks again; keep right (south) on CR 4, which parallels Cunningham Creek. Drive 1.9 miles to another fork; continue right for an additional 0.1 mile and a lower parking area recommended for those with stock trailers. Hikers with two-wheel drive can also park here or continue up the steep road another 0.7 mile to another fork. If you have four-wheel drive, go left (east) from the fork and across Cunningham Creek for another 0.2 mile to the upper trailhead; if you have two-wheel drive with high clearance, you can park just beyond the fork. *DeLorme: Colorado Atlas & Gazetteer:* Page 77 B5. GPS: N37 47.266' / W107 34.736'.

The Hike

From the lower trailhead, climb the very steep, rocky road (now a trail) to the south. After 0.25 mile the trail will merge onto CR 4 as it continues to the upper trailhead at 0.7 mile. **Note:** About 0.1 mile prior to the upper trailhead, notice the sign pointing the way to the Continental Divide Trail (CDT). The trail going left (north) connects with the Cunningham Gulch Trail, the return trail. Continue right (south) to the trailhead for Highland Mary Lakes Trail 606.

Mike Vining at Highland Mary Lakes

Please sign the trail register before you begin the steep hike along Cunningham Creek. You'll wind through the trees to a trail junction at 1 mile. This trail climbs 1.6 miles to the CDT via the Cunningham Gulch Trail. If you're riding a horse, you will have to ascend via the gulch because the lakes trail is off-limits to stock. Proceed south, and you'll see why as you climb through rock pathways. As you continue the loop, be sure to look for the gorgeous waterfall at 1.2 miles. At the 1.3-mile mark, enter the wilderness. Cross Cunningham Creek at 1.8 miles and continue up the maintained trail, soon hiking out in the open. After approximately 2.1 miles the trail descends slightly and crosses a creek. It then climbs, sometimes at a steep grade, and heads south. Follow some rock cairns south and up the creek. At 2.4 miles cross to the east side of the creek and reach the first of seven Highland Mary Lakes, elevation 12,100 feet.

Unmaintained trails lead to the various lakes. It's easy to get around here; the high alpine tundra is open. The official trail passes between the two biggest lakes, continuing in a southerly direction. After reaching the easternmost lake, the trail tends to

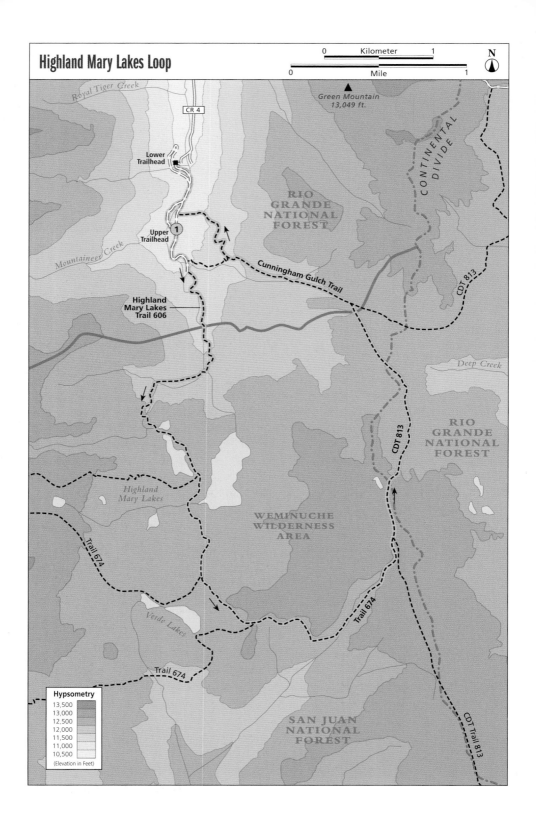

Highland Mary Lakes Loop

Kilometer
0   1
0   Mile   1

N

Royal Tiger Creek

CR 4

Green Mountain
13,049 ft.

Lower
Trailhead

RIO
GRANDE
NATIONAL
FOREST

CONTINENTAL DIVIDE

Upper
Trailhead

1

Mountaineer Creek

Cunningham Gulch Trail

CDT 813

Highland
Mary Lakes
Trail 606

Deep Creek

CDT 813

RIO
GRANDE
NATIONAL
FOREST

Highland
Mary Lakes

WEMINUCHE
WILDERNESS
AREA

Trail 674

Trail 674

Verde Lakes

Trail 674

Hypsometry

	13,500
	13,000
	12,500
	12,000
	11,500
	11,000
	10,500

(Elevation in Feet)

SAN JUAN
NATIONAL
FOREST

CDT Trail 813

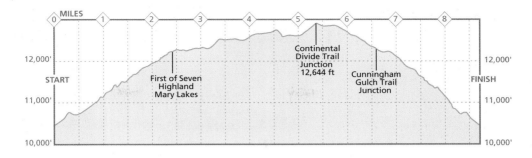

fade. Keep going south from this point, following rock cairns and post-markers south. A wonderful view of the Grenadier Range will keep you occupied as you continue.

At 3.7 miles you'll reach a saddle and post-marker. You'll see a trail marker off to the right (west). This route leads to Verde Lakes, which are visible from where you stand. Follow the trail (and post-markers) off to the left (southeast) to continue the loop with the CDT and the Cunningham Gulch Trail. From this junction hike southeast and climb for another 0.4 mile. A trail going west to Lost Lake merges with your route here. Continue east, crossing a side slope that's filled with wildflowers in midsummer. At 4.6 miles you'll drop a steep 50 feet to a drainage. Climb up the drainage gradually, crossing a creek at 5.2 miles. You'll meet unsigned Continental Divide Trail 813 at 5.3 miles. Watch for rock cairns to the south (where the CDT is en route to Hunchback Pass and eventually Mexico) and a trail heading north toward Stony Pass and Canada.

Hike to the north. You'll pass a couple of small lakes as you continue to climb. After 6.6 miles keep a sharp eye out for the place where the CDT takes off to the northeast. Signs point the way for the CDT, but there are no signs for the Cunningham Gulch Trail. Fortunately, the trail is easy to see as it heads in a northwest direction. It descends at a steep grade with some switchbacks. Exit the wilderness at 6.8 miles and reach a fork at 7.8 miles. Now you have the choice to hike one of two trails, both of which lead back to the lower and upper trailheads. If you've parked at the lower trailhead, however, where this hike begins, go right to a trail junction and trail register at 8.3 miles. You'll only hike a short distance to the right (north) before having to cross Cunningham Creek. If you've parked at the upper trailhead, from the same place hike less than 0.2 mile south to the trailhead. To continue this loop, head down the road after crossing the creek, back to the lower trailhead at 8.7 miles.

Miles and Directions

0.0   Lower Highland Mary Lakes/Cunningham Gulch trailhead.

0.7   Upper Highland Mary Lakes trailhead. GPS: N37 46.858' / W107 34.773'.

1.0   Junction with Cunningham Gulch Trail.

1.3   Wilderness boundary.

2.4   First of seven Highland Mary Lakes. GPS: N37 45.927' / W107 34.891'.

3.7   Saddle and junction with trail to Verde Lakes.

Waterfall along Cunningham Creek

5.3 Junction with Continental Divide Trail 813 (unmarked). GPS: N37 45.345' / W107 33.418'.

6.6 Unmarked junction for Cunningham Gulch Trail. GPS: N37 46.288 / W107 33.501'.

7.8 Trail junction. GPS: N37 46.798' / W107 34.436'.

8.7 Back to Lower Highland Mary Lakes/Cunningham Gulch trailhead.

Hike Information

Local information: Silverton Chamber of Commerce, Silverton; (970) 387-5654 or (800) 752-4494; www.silvertoncolorado.com.

Local events/attractions: Ride the Durango & Silverton Narrow Gauge Railroad, Durango; (970) 247-2733 or (877) 872-4607; www.durangotrain.com.

Walk around historic downtown Silverton.

Accommodations: Silverton offers a variety of private campgrounds and motels. You can camp along the road to the trailhead, but there are no established facilities.

2 Molas Trail to Elk Park

Impressive views and beautiful scenes are plentiful on this hike. Colorful wildflowers are in abundance in summer, too. A splendid day hike, the trail leads down into Animas Canyon and eventually to Elk Park. Unlike most Weminuche trails, this one descends instead of climbs, making the return leg the most difficult part of the trip. Give yourself plenty of time to hike back up the switchbacks. The trail is a terrific alternative route for those who do not wish to pay for Durango & Silverton Narrow Gauge Railroad access to the Weminuche Wilderness.

Start: Colorado Trail trailhead
Distance: 8.8 miles out and back
Hiking time: About 6 to 8 hours or overnight backpack
Difficulty: Strenuous if you hike out and back in the same day; moderate if you spend the night at the river
Canine compatibility: Dogs must be under control.
Nearest town: Silverton

Fees and permits: Free registration (available online, at managing agency, or major trailheads) needed for both day hikers and overnight backpackers. Contact the managing agency for current information.
Maps: USGS Snowdon Peak; Trails Illustrated Weminuche Wilderness; DeLorme 3D TopoQuad CD-ROM; Maptech Terrain Navigator CD-ROM
Trail contact: San Juan National Forest, Columbine Ranger District, Bayfield; (970) 884-2512; www.fs.usda.gov/sanjuan

Finding the trailhead: From the quaint town of Silverton, drive 5.2 miles south on US 550 to the trailhead, which is about 1 mile north of Molas Pass. If you're in Durango, from the junction of US 160 and US 550, drive north on US 550 for about 43 miles. Make a right (south) onto the dirt road leading to the trailhead in a hundred yards or so. A sign to the Molas Trail and Molas Lake points the way. You'll find plenty of room to park, but nothing in the way of other amenities. *DeLorme: Colorado Atlas & Gazetteer:* Page 76 C4. GPS: N37 44.855' / W107 41.286'.

The Hike

A trailhead sign points the way to the 468-mile Colorado Trail, which uses various paths (in this case Molas Trail 665) in its trek from Durango to Denver. You'll reach the trail register at 0.2 mile. After signing in, you'll hike over easy, open terrain with wonderful views southeast to the Grenadier Range, with its spiraling faces of hardened quartzite.

> The Colorado Trail stretches 468 miles from Durango to Denver. Along the way it passes through eight mountain ranges, seven national forests, six wilderness areas (including the Weminuche), and five river systems. The Colorado Trail travels through the northwest corner of the Weminuche, from Molas Pass to the Continental Divide northeast of Eldorado Lake.

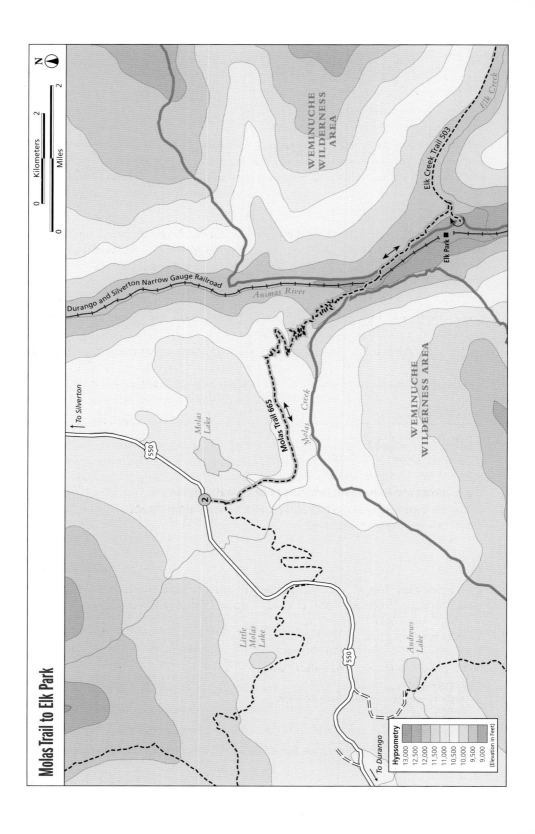

Molas Trail to Elk Park

Hypsometry

13,000
12,500
12,000
11,500
11,000
10,500
10,000
9,500
9,000

(Elevation in Feet)

To Durango

Andrews Lake

550

Little Molas Lake

2

550

To Silverton

Molas Lake

Molas Trail 665

Molas Creek

WEMINUCHE WILDERNESS AREA

Durango and Silverton Narrow Gauge Railroad

Animas River

Elk Park

Elk Creek Trail 503

WEMINUCHE WILDERNESS AREA

Elk Creek

N

0   Kilometers   2

0   Miles   2

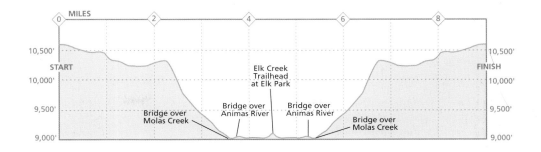

You'll drop moderately for a short distance, then continue across wide meadows, climbing a little before entering the trees at 1.2 miles. Soon afterward you'll begin dropping moderately through spruce, fir, and aspens. You'll hear Molas Creek raging off to the side and see Animas Canyon through the trees as you descend.

Thirty-five switchbacks (give or take one or two) make the 1,710-foot descent a pleasure. You'll finally get a glimpse of Molas Creek at 2.6 miles. At the 3.6-mile point, you'll cross the creek via a wooden bridge. Look for Colorado columbine, monkshood, paintbrush, and other wildflowers in this area.

Cross the Animas River via a bridge at 3.7 miles, then continue on the path. You'll cross the tracks of the Durango & Silverton Narrow Gauge Railroad after another 700 feet or so as you travel southeast to Elk Park, a railroad stop, at 4.4 miles.

Miles and Directions

0.0 Colorado Trail trailhead.

0.2 Trail register; junction with the Colorado Trail.

3.6 Bridge over Molas Creek.

3.7 Bridge over Animas River. GPS: N37 44.011' / W107 39.665'.

4.4 Elk Creek Trail junction at Elk Park. GPS: N37 43.485' / W107 39.232'.

8.8 Back to Colorado Trail trailhead.

Hike Information

Local information: Silverton Chamber of Commerce, Silverton; (970) 387-5654 or (800) 752-4494; www.silvertoncolorado.com.

Local events/attractions: Ride the Durango & Silverton Narrow Gauge Railroad, Durango; (970) 247-2733 or (877) 872-4607; www.durangotrain.com.

Walk around historic downtown Silverton.

Accommodations: Silverton offers a variety of private campgrounds and motels.

③ Crater Lake

This hike offers delightful wildflowers, a scenic lake, and gorgeous mountain views. It's a beautiful day hike or a nice overnight stay; the choice is up to you.

Start: Crater Lake trailhead at Andrews Lake
Distance: 10.4 miles out and back
Hiking time: About 6 to 8 hours or overnight backpack
Difficulty: Strenuous if you hike out and back the same day; moderate if you camp at the lake
Canine compatibility: Dogs must be under control.
Nearest town: Silverton
Fees and permits: Free registration (available online, at managing agency, or major

trailheads) needed for both day hikers and overnight backpackers. Contact the managing agency for current information.
Maps: USGS Snowdon Peak; Trails Illustrated Weminuche Wilderness; DeLorme 3D TopoQuad CD-ROM; Maptech Terrain Navigator CD-ROM
Trail contact: San Juan National Forest, Columbine Ranger District, Bayfield; (970) 884-2512; www.fs.usda.gov/sanjuan

Finding the trailhead: Drive about 8 miles south of the quaint town of Silverton on US 550, or from the junction of US 160 and US 550 in south Durango, drive north on US 550 for approximately 41 miles. If you're heading south from Silverton, turn left (south) onto the paved road leading to Andrews Lake Day Use Area, and drive about 0.7 mile until the road ends at the lake. You'll find wheelchair-accessible fishing ramps, a chemical toilet, and plenty of parking. If you'll be spending the night or you have stock animals, be sure to park in the Upper Scenic parking area. It's just up the hill from the day-use area. *DeLorme: Colorado Atlas & Gazetteer:* Page 76 C4. GPS: N37 43.685' / W107 42.659'.

The Hike

Begin by hiking up the moderate slope via the Crater Lake Trail. There's a wonderful view back to Andrews Lake and beyond. You'll level off (at least for a while) after 1.2 miles. The trail parallels a meadow and then drops some, heading through the trees, then back out into the open at 1.5 miles. Cross another meadow, then ford a creek at 1.7 miles. From here to the wilderness boundary, it's a moderate, sometimes steep, climb.

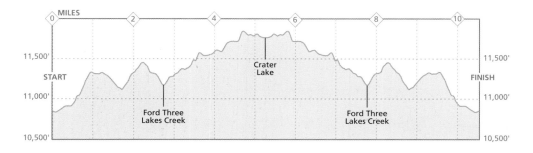

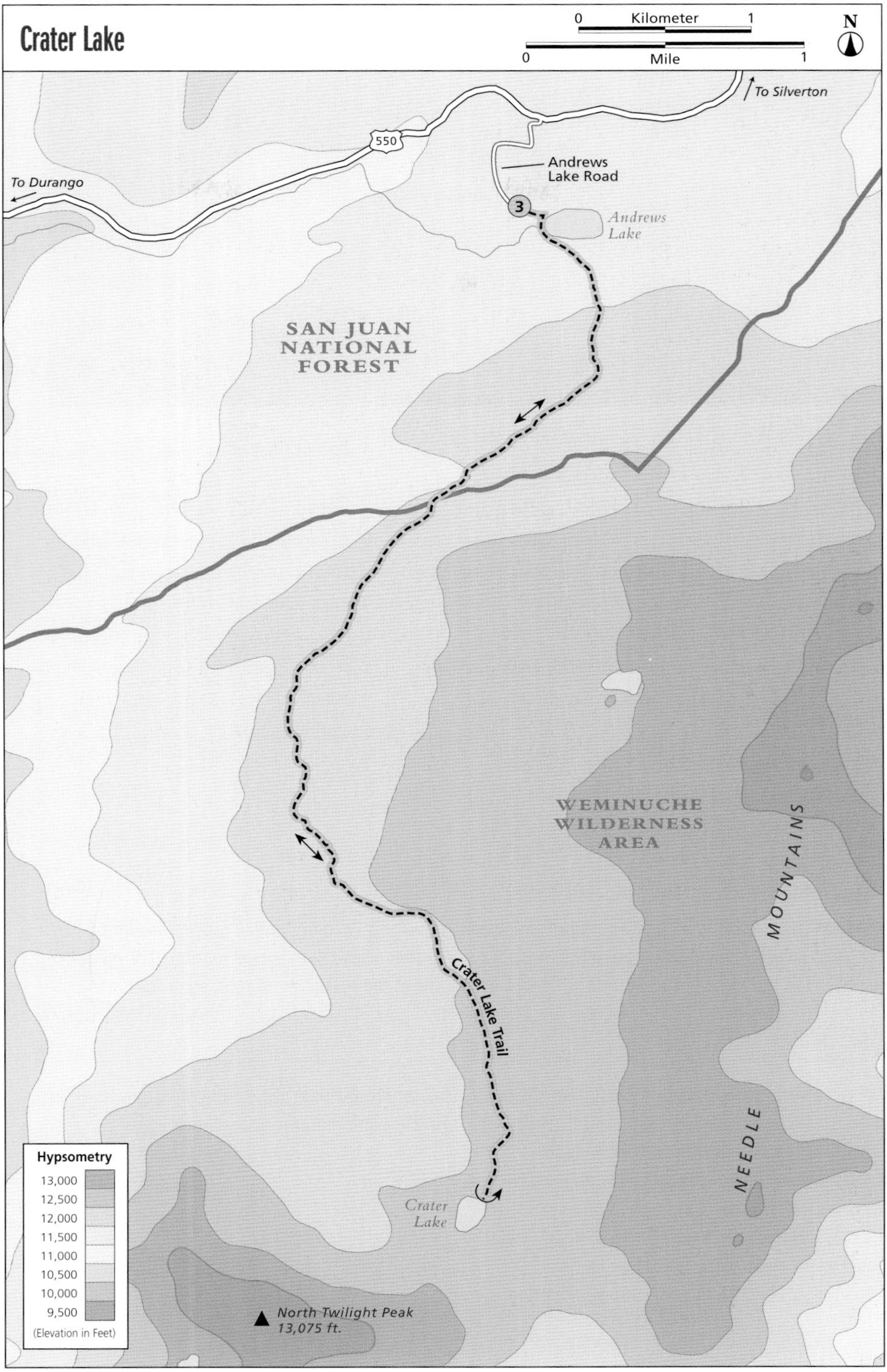

Crater Lake

	Kilometer	
0		1

	Mile	
0		1

N

To Silverton

550

Andrews
Lake Road

To Durango

3

Andrews
Lake

SAN JUAN
NATIONAL
FOREST

WEMINUCHE
WILDERNESS
AREA

Crater Lake Trail

M O U N T A I N S

N E E D L E

Hypsometry

	(Elevation in Feet)
13,000	
12,500	
12,000	
11,500	
11,000	
10,500	
10,000	
9,500	

Crater
Lake

▲ North Twilight Peak
13,075 ft.

Tall chiming bells (Mertensia ciliata) *are often seen while hiking wilderness trails.*

Enter the wilderness at the 2-mile point. The trail eases as you hike along an open slope laden with summer wildflowers. The area provides views of Hermosa Cliffs to the southwest and Engineer Mountain to the west. Descend moderately to Three Lakes Creek at 2.7 miles, one of many fords on this route. The trail stays mostly level as you cross creek after creek, alternating between trees, meadows, and open slopes. You will reach scenic Crater Lake at 5.2 miles.

Miles and Directions

0.0 Crater Lake trailhead.

2.0 Wilderness boundary.

2.7 Ford Three Lakes Creek.

5.2 Crater Lake. GPS: N37 40.511' / W107 42.795'.

10.4 Back to Crater Lake trailhead.

Option: Crater Lake is a good spot from which to climb North Twilight Peak, a jagged mountain in the West Needle Range. The peak stretches to 13,075 feet above sea level. It's about 1.2 miles farther than the lake and another 1,435 feet to the top of the mountain via the east ridge.

Hike Information

Local information: Silverton Chamber of Commerce, Silverton; (970) 387-5654 or (800) 752-4494; www.silvertoncolorado.com.

Local events/attractions: Ride the Durango & Silverton Narrow Gauge Railroad, Durango; (970) 247-2733 or (877) 872-4607; www.durangotrain.com.

Walk around historic downtown Silverton.

Accommodations: Silverton offers a variety of private campgrounds and motels.

4 Elk Park/Chicago Basin Shuttle Hike

Hike this route, and your reward will be stunning vistas, abundant animal life, colorful wildflowers, and waterfalls. This five- to six-day backpack is accessible by the Durango & Silverton Narrow Gauge Railroad, or you can reach both the Elk Park and Needleton trailheads via trails.

Start: Elk Park trailhead
Distance: 38.6-mile shuttle
Hiking time: Multiday backpack of 5 days or more
Difficulty: Strenuous due to length and elevation gain of more than 8,000 feet
Canine compatibility: Dogs must be under control.
Nearest town: Durango
Fees and permits: Free registration (available online, at managing agency, or major trailheads) needed for both day hikers and overnight backpackers. Contact the managing agency for current information.

Maps: USGS Snowdon Peak, Storm King Peak, Columbine Pass, and Mountain View Crest; Trails Illustrated Weminuche Wilderness; DeLorme 3D TopoQuad CD-ROM; Maptech Terrain Navigator CD-ROM
Trail contact: San Juan National Forest, Columbine Ranger District, Bayfield; (970) 884-2512; www.fs.usda.gov/sanjuan
Special considerations: Campfires are not allowed in the Chicago Basin and Needle Creek drainages.

Finding the trailhead: The Durango & Silverton Narrow Gauge Railroad provides transportation to both the Elk Park and Needleton trailheads. The latter is the busier of the two stops. You can purchase round-trip or one-way tickets to and from either location; call the railroad at (877) 872-4607 for more information.

If you'd rather not pay for a train ticket, you can hike to and from Elk Park via the Molas Trail (Hike 2). From Silverton drive 5.2 miles south on US 550 to the trailhead, which is about 1 mile north of Molas Pass. From the junction of US 160 and US 550 in Durango, drive north on US 550 for about 43 miles. Turn right onto the dirt road leading to the trailhead. A sign points the way to the Colorado Trail. You will reach the trail register at 0.2 mile and enter the trees at 1.2 miles. Afterward you will descend 1,710 feet via switchbacks, cross Molas Creek at 2.6 miles and then again at 3.6 miles via a wooden bridge, and cross the Animas River at 3.7 miles via a bridge. Continue on the path, crossing the railroad tracks. You will reach Elk Park at 4.4 miles. Another option is to hike down the Molas Trail, doing the entire route as described, and then hop on the train at Needleton for the short ride back to Elk Park. From there you can hike back to your vehicle at the Molas trailhead.

It's also possible to hike to and from the Needle Creek Trail junction (near Needleton) using a combination of the Purgatory Creek and Animas River Trails (Hike 5). From the junction of US 160 and US 550 in Durango, drive north on US 550 for 27.2 miles and turn right (east) at Tacoma Village. Look for the sign Purgatory Flats Trail Access 500 feet. The road is across from Durango Mountain Resort, just south of Milepost 40. (See Hike 5 for instructions.) Follow Purgatory Creek Trail 511; you will descend through trees and cross Purgatory Creek at 0.4 mile. At 1.2 miles you'll cross a small stream, then hike across Purgatory Flats. After 2 miles you'll pass through a gate and then hike along narrow canyon walls. You will reach a junction at 4 miles; keep left. At 4.1 miles you'll cross the Animas River via a bridge. Follow the trail upstream (northeast), crossing the narrow-gauge railroad tracks at 4.2 miles. Animas River Trail 675 will take you to the Needle Creek Trail junction at 9.6 miles. The train drop-off and pickup area at Needleton is another 0.8 mile to the north. *DeLorme: Colorado Atlas & Gazetteer:* Page 77 C4 (Elk Park), GPS: N37 43.485' / W107 39.232'; Page 76 C4 (Needleton), GPS: N37 38.012' / W107 41.571'.

The Hike

If you are arriving at the Elk Park trailhead on foot, hike Elk Creek Trail 503 (part of the more extensive Colorado Trail) 0.8 mile from the Animas River bridge, where you'll meet up with the spur trail on the southeast side of the tracks leading from the train drop-off point. If you arrive by train, follow the side tracks east about 100 yards to a trail that heads northeast. It's a steep climb to the main trail at 0.3 mile. At the point where both trails merge, head east and immediately enter the wilderness. There's a registration box in 100 yards or so.

The trail climbs at a moderate grade and passes a lovely waterfall in less than a mile. You can see and hear Elk Creek at various points along the way. Look for Colorado columbines, bluebells, and other wildflowers en route. The trail steepens as you continue; expect some good views and plan on crossing some small creeks, too. Around 2.8 miles look for Electric Peak and Vestal Peak, striking summits of the Grenadier Range.

You will reach some beaver ponds at 3.2 miles. If you head southeast from here, you can make a side trip up to the base of Vestal, Arrow, and Electric Peaks. There are excellent places to camp near these peaks, and it's a great place to climb.

Stick to the main route, and you'll pass through a maze of rocks, then trees, before reaching a large, flat meadow at 4.2 miles. A bevy of 13,000-foot-plus peaks surrounds the area. Look west to the West Needle Mountains, north to Arrow Mountain, southeast to Peak Two, and southwest to Electric Peak.

At the east end of the meadow, you'll reenter the trees. The trail climbs at a fairly easy pace, continuing to parallel scenic Elk Creek and crossing several smaller creeks along the way. Cross a larger creek with a log bridge and railing at 5 miles. At 5.4 miles the trail steepens, passing across an occasional open side slope painted with wildflowers in summer. Soon you will climb above the tree line.

At 6.3 miles the trail eases up somewhat, but the views remain. Turn your head to the southeast, and look for a double waterfall. You'll pass some large rockfalls (look for pikas) and fragile meadows. Cross Elk Creek at 6.7 miles; you may have to get your feet wet. You'll cross the creek again shortly thereafter. The trail is steep from this second crossing to 7.3 miles, where there's an old miner's cabin. If you need a break, this is the perfect place.

A series of two dozen or so switchbacks begins at 7.6 miles. The moderate grade and abundant wildflowers will get you to the Continental Divide (elevation 12,650

Durango & Silverton Narrow Gauge Railroad train blowing off steam while crossing a bridge

feet) and a trail junction with Continental Divide Trail (CDT) 813 at 8.4 miles. Going left (north) allows you to continue what is now both CDT 813 and the Colorado Trail. The south (right) trail is an alternate CDT that leads to Eldorado Lake, Kite Lake, and Hunchback Pass.

To continue on this hike, head north. It's a gradual downhill to a fork at 8.7 miles. Keep to the right (northeast) at this junction; the left-hand (northwest) trail heads to Stony Pass. Descend the steep right-hand trail, which parallels another trail and merges with it at the 9-mile point. You'll reach an unsigned junction at 9.7 miles: The east (straight ahead) trail continues access on the Colorado Trail; go right (southeast) to continue this hike.

You'll exit the wilderness now, continuing the steep downhill to where you cross Bear Creek at 10.1 miles. After another 0.3 mile (at 10.4 miles), the trail ends at a four-wheel-drive road; go right (west) to continue to Hunchback Pass.

You will reach a trail register and signed post pointing the way to Hunchback Pass at 10.5 miles. Turn left (south), and continue hiking the CDT. If you want to make a side trip to Kite Lake, continue up the old road for another 0.5 mile—you'll find the lake, an old miner's cabin, and a couple of mine shafts.

Back on the main route, cross several creeks as you climb a moderate-to-steep grade. There are lovely views of small tarns and big mountains from here. You'll see some old mine remains en route to Hunchback Pass (elevation 12,493 feet) and the wilderness boundary at 12.1 miles. From the pass you can gaze south toward the Guardian, the most prominent peak in view, and farther south into the Needle Mountains.

Beyond the pass the trail makes a steep descent to the 12.4-mile point and a creek crossing. The trail then levels out some, but soon descends again as it parallels the headwaters of the east fork of Vallecito Creek. In summer look for paintbrush, marsh marigolds, bluebells, hellebore, and other flowers.

Cross Vallecito Creek at 13 miles, and continue the moderate-to-steep descent. You'll reach the trees in another 0.3 mile. At 13.5 miles you'll reach an unsigned trail junction. At this point the Continental Divide Trail goes east to Nebo Pass. You'll continue south instead on Vallecito Trail 529.

For a short distance the trail parallels Nebo Creek, a lovely creek with little cascades and small pools. Cross Nebo Creek again at 14.1 miles, and soon you'll be back to paralleling Vallecito Creek.

Beyond the 14.7-mile point, the trail follows Vallecito Creek, mostly staying in the trees but venturing out into a number of lovely meadows en route. Here you'll be blessed with not only wildflowers and aspens but also wonderful views of the surrounding high peaks. Along the way you'll cross numerous small streams.

Ford Rock Creek at 16.6 miles; be prepared to get your feet wet at the crossing. As you continue, the trail grade stays mostly moderate.

At 19.3 miles you'll climb moderately, winding up through the trees. After another 0.7 mile (20 miles), you'll ford Roell Creek. There are more creek crossings before the trail heads back to Vallecito Creek and the turnoff for the bridge crossing at 22.3 miles. Make a right (west) at this turnoff for Trail 504, and hike 100 yards or so to the bridge. After crossing the bridge, you'll hike on nearly level terrain. Ford Johnson Creek at 22.7 miles.

The next section of the hike goes through pines and aspens and continues at an easy pace for a short time; then the grade steepens. After 23.4 miles you must ford Grizzly Gulch. Cross another small, unnamed creek in another 0.5 mile.

Over the next 0.2 mile, moderate, sometimes steep, switchbacks through the pines make life easier. Be sure to stop and observe Johnson Creek along the way; its thunderous waters plummet through rock canyons. The valley opens up after 25.3 miles, with good views of surrounding peaks. Moderate but sometimes steep switchbacks begin at 25.5 miles and end about a mile later. Trees grow sparse now, and wildflowers make an appearance. You'll cross a big rock slide at 26.3 miles.

You'll have to cross several small streams as you continue, including the stream flowing from Hazel Lake at 27.2 miles. The trail steepens at 27.5 miles. Old mining relics just off the trail may interest some. Others may be more absorbed in the yellow columbines, sulphur paintbrush, and sunflower-like flowers found along the way.

At 29.5 miles the trail crosses a stream from Columbine Lake. You'll reach the lake itself in another 0.2 mile. Camping is limited there because of the fragile terrain.

It's a very steep climb from the lake to Columbine Pass (elevation 12,680 feet) at 30.1 miles. From here you get fantastic views of countless high peaks ranging from 12,000 to more than 14,000 feet above sea level. You'll also see north into the Chicago Basin. To the southeast you'll spot the glacier-carved Johnson Creek drainage, bordered by McCauly Peak, Echo Mountain, Organ Mountain, Amherst Mountain, Mount Valois, and Florida Mountain.

A steep downhill drops you off the north side of the pass very quickly. Continue on Trail 504, which descends, with switchbacks eventually leading down into the trees. As you continue the steep descent, look for an old mineshaft and cabin. At 32.3 miles begin descending a few switchbacks that lead into the Chicago Basin, home of the Weminuche's three fourteeners—Mount Eolus (14,083 feet), Sunlight Peak (14,059 feet), and Windom Peak (14,082 feet). Ford Needle Creek at 32.6 miles. Now you'll descend at an easy-to-moderate grade, with some creek crossings along the way.

Enter the trees at 34.2 miles, and continue descending. Look for a lovely waterfall as you continue. There's a bridge over New York Creek at 36.1 miles. Afterward the trail eases up some and exits the wilderness at 37.8 miles. At the boundary there's a trail register (for those hiking in) and a trail junction. Go left (south) if you're hiking to the trailhead at Purgatory Creek; it's a total of 9.6 miles from here to the trailhead. If you're returning by train, go right (north) to Needleton. It's an easy walk to the bridge over the Animas River at 38.6 miles. You'll see a posted sign noting the train stop. This is a flagged stop, so be sure to wave your hands in front of your knees to get the conductor's attention. If it's raining and you need a dry place to hang out while waiting for the train, walk downriver 200 feet or so to an abandoned cabin.

FROM TRAIN TO TRAILS

The Durango & Silverton Narrow Gauge Railroad provides one of the more popular access routes to the Chicago Basin in the Weminuche Wilderness. The town of Durango was founded by the Denver & Rio Grande Railway in 1879 and formally established in 1881. The railroad was built in an amazing nine months, linking towns that today can be accessed by the railhead or by US 550. Although the railroad was built primarily to haul silver and gold ore, passengers soon realized that the scenery was well worth the trip. Passengers still ride for the views, and the railroad has been in continuous operation for more than 130 years. Vintage steam engines haul passengers along the Animas River, dropping hikers off at two trailheads—Needleton and Elk Park—along the way.

Elk Park/Chicago Basin Shuttle Hike

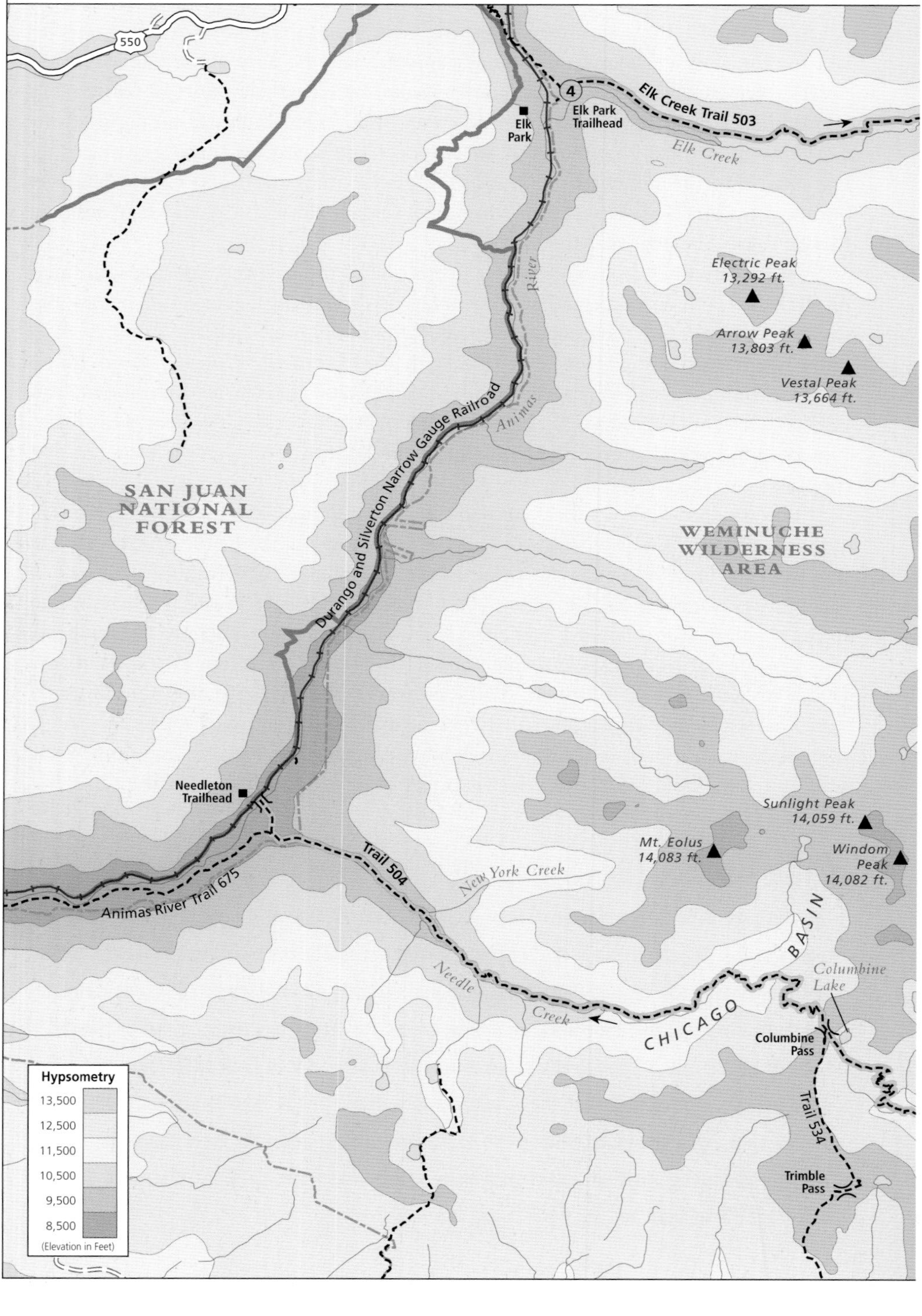

Map legend:

Hypsometry

Elevation in Feet
13,500
12,500
11,500
10,500
9,500
8,500

(Elevation in Feet)

Map labels:

- 550
- Elk Park
- 4
- Elk Park Trailhead
- Elk Creek Trail 503
- Elk Creek
- Electric Peak 13,292 ft.
- Arrow Peak 13,803 ft.
- Animas River
- Vestal Peak 13,664 ft.
- SAN JUAN NATIONAL FOREST
- Durango and Silverton Narrow Gauge Railroad
- WEMINUCHE WILDERNESS AREA
- Needleton Trailhead
- Sunlight Peak 14,059 ft.
- Mt. Eolus 14,083 ft.
- Windom Peak 14,082 ft.
- Trail 504
- New York Creek
- Animas River Trail 675
- Needle Creek
- CHICAGO BASIN
- Columbine Lake
- Columbine Pass
- Trail 534
- Trimble Pass

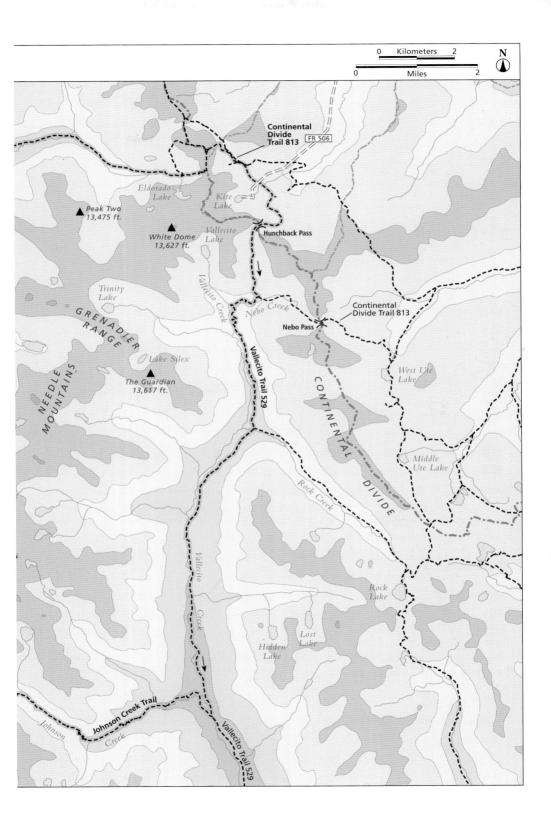

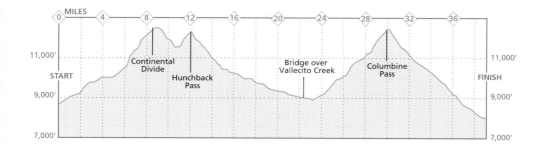

Miles and Directions

0.0   Elk Park train drop-off and pickup point.

0.3   Elk Park trailhead and wilderness boundary. GPS: N37 43.631' / W107 39.267'.

4.2   Large meadow.

7.3   Old miner's cabin. GPS: N37 43.035' / W107 32.583'.

8.4   Continental Divide.

12.1   Hunchback Pass. GPS: N37 42.284' / W107 31.206'.

16.6   Rock Creek crossing.

22.3   Bridge over Vallecito Creek. GPS: N37 35.050' / W107 31.870'.

30.1   Columbine Pass. GPS: N37 35.926' / W107 36.185'.

32.6   Ford Needle Creek.

36.1   New York Creek crossing.

37.8   Wilderness boundary and Animas River Trail junction. GPS: N37 37.405' / W107 41.716'.

38.6   Needleton train drop-off and pickup point.

Options: If you're interested in hiking to Trimble Pass via the Endlich Mesa Trail, you'll pass the trail junction 60 feet or so below Columbine Pass (see Hike 7, Options, for more information). Another great side trip will take you up to Nebo Pass from mile 13.5. It's 1.6 miles and 930 feet up to the Continental Divide at Nebo Lake and a grand east–west view.

Hike Information

Local information: Durango Area Tourism; (970) 247-3500 or (800) 525-8855; www .durango.org.

Local events/attractions: Ride the Durango & Silverton Narrow Gauge Railroad, Durango; (970) 247-2733 or (877) 872-4607; www.durango train.com.

Raft the Animas River.

Walk around historic downtown Durango.

Accommodations: Durango offers a number of private campgrounds as well as numerous motels.

5 Purgatory Creek/Animas River Trails

These trails travel through scenic canyons and provide access to the Weminuche Wilderness. You'll gain 900 feet en route and descend 1,500 feet. It's a very long day hike to the Animas River and back, or a two- to three-day backpack if you explore Animas Canyon.

Start: Purgatory Creek trailhead
Distance: 19.2 miles out and back
Hiking time: 2- to 3-day backpack
Difficulty: Moderate
Canine compatibility: Dogs must be under control.
Nearest town: Durango
Fees and permits: Free registration (available online, at managing agency, or major trailheads) needed for both day hikers and overnight backpackers. Contact the managing agency for current information.
Maps: USGS Engineer Mountain, Electra Lake, and Mountain View Crest; Trails Illustrated Weminuche Wilderness; DeLorme 3D TopoQuad CD-ROM; Maptech Terrain Navigator CD-ROM
Trail contact: San Juan National Forest, Columbine Ranger District, Bayfield; (970) 884-2512; www.fs.usda.gov/sanjuan

Finding the trailhead: From the junction of US 160 and US 550 in Durango, drive north on US 550 for 27.2 miles and turn right (east) at Tacoma Village. Look for the sign PURGATORY FLATS TRAIL ACCESS 500 FEET. The road is across from Durango Mountain Resort, just south of Milepost 40. Continue 0.1 mile to the trailhead, which is marked and on the right, and park in the large gravel area to the left just beyond. *DeLorme: Colorado Atlas & Gazetteer:* Page 76 D3. GPS: N37 37.805' / W107 48.361'.

The Hike

Walk about 100 yards from the trailhead, and you'll find the trail register. After signing in, follow Purgatory Creek Trail 511 past a mix of wild roses and perhaps cows, as the area is a historical grazing area. You'll hear and sometimes see Purgatory Creek off to the north. Descend through pines and aspens, switchbacking moderately. Cross Purgatory Creek at 0.4 mile.

At 1.2 miles you'll cross a little stream, then hike across Purgatory Flats, which is west of the Cascade River. After 2 miles you'll reach a gate. Please close it after you

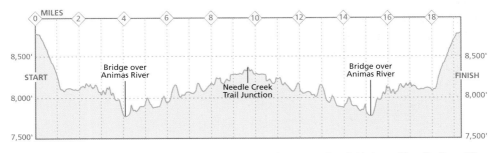

People fishing from the bridge and playing near the Animas River via the Purgatory Creek Trail

pass through. The gate prevents cattle from destroying the lush vegetation found in the canyon. You'll see bluebells and many more wildflowers as you continue.

Hike along the narrow canyon walls, ascending to about 300 feet above the creek at times. You'll reach a nice ponderosa pine overlook along the way, a place where good views of Cascade Canyon and a wonderful view toward Animas Canyon are possible.

As you hike farther along the trail, look up Cascade Canyon for a view to Engineer Mountain. The canyon widens some as the trail descends through a mix of pines and aspens. There's another ponderosa-decorated overlook at 3.6 miles, with a nice view of several peaks to the north. Switchback down now, reaching a junction at 4 miles. Keep left at this point, heading up the Animas River.

At 4.1 miles you'll cross the Animas River via a bridge and come to a sign reading CASCADE WYE. In the winter the Durango & Silverton Narrow Gauge Railroad travels

Purgatory Creek/Animas River Trails

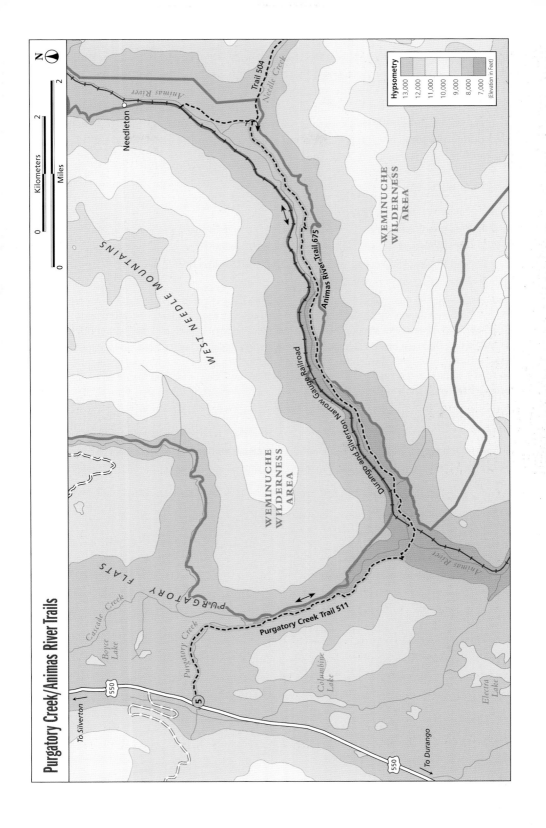

from Durango to the wye, where they turn around. The triangle-shaped track allows the train to make a three-point turn and reserve direction. Check out the wye if you would like, but then you'll want to follow the trail upstream (northeast), crossing the narrow-gauge railroad tracks at 4.2 miles. Animas River Trail 675 runs parallel to the Animas River and slowly climbs, rising 600 feet over more than 6 miles. It takes you past ponderosa pines, Colorado columbines, wild roses, and many more lovely plants. You will reach the Needle Creek Trail junction at 9.6 miles.

Miles and Directions

0.0 Purgatory Creek trailhead.

0.4 Purgatory Creek crossing.

4.1 Animas River crossing. GPS: N37 35.846' / W107 46.609'.

9.6 Needle Creek Trail junction. GPS: N37 37.405' / W107 41.716'.

19.2 Back to Purgatory Creek trailhead.

Options: Hiking this route is an alternative to using the train to get to the Chicago Basin (see Hike 4 for more information on the train). However, if you use the train for a one-way shuttle, you'll hike 9.6 miles to the Needle Creek Trail junction and then continue north another 0.8 mile to Needleton. There's a posted sign noting the train stop. This is a flagged stop, so be sure to wave your hands in front of your knees to get the conductor's attention. If it's raining and you need a dry place to hang out while waiting for the train, walk downriver 200 feet or so to an abandoned cabin.

Hike Information

Local information: Durango Area Tourism; (970) 247-3500 or (800) 525-8855; www .durango.org.

Local events/attractions: Ride the Durango & Silverton Narrow Gauge Railroad, Durango; (970) 247-2733 or (877) 872-4607; www .durangotrain.com.

Raft the Animas River.

Walk around historic downtown Durango.

Accommodations: Durango offers a number of private campgrounds as well as numerous motels.

6 Lime Mesa

Wildflowers and views of the magnificent Needle Mountains are yours on this fine day hike. In the summer, you may find sheep grazing in the area.

Start: Lime Mesa trailhead
Distance: 7.2 miles out and back
Hiking time: About 4 to 6 hours
Difficulty: Moderate due to length
Canine compatibility: Dogs must be under control.
Nearest town: Durango
Fees and permits: Free registration (available online, at managing agency, or major trailheads) needed for both day hikers and overnight backpackers. Contact the managing agency for current information.
Maps: USGS Mountain View Crest; Trails Illustrated Weminuche Wilderness; DeLorme 3D TopoQuad CD-ROM; Maptech Terrain Navigator CD-ROM
Trail contact: San Juan National Forest, Columbine Ranger District, Bayfield; (970) 884-2512; www.fs.usda.gov/sanjuan

Finding the trailhead: From the junction of US 160 and US 550 in south Durango, head north on US 550. After 2.4 miles make a right onto 32nd Street, and drive 1.3 miles to Florida Avenue (La Plata CR 250). Make a left (north), driving CR 250 for 9.5 miles to Missionary Ridge Road (La Plata CR 253). Turn right (northeast) onto CR 253, and follow this well-maintained gravel road with numerous switchbacks. It becomes FR 682 en route. Reach the junction for FR 682 and Burnt Timber Road 595 after 11.8 miles. Stay on FR 682 and reach another junction in 6.6 miles. A sign points the way to Henderson Lake via FR 081 (Henderson Lake Road). Continue past the lake and notice how the road begins to deteriorate. If you have two-wheel drive, you can continue another 2.8 miles or so before the road becomes too rough to continue. If you have four-wheel drive and high clearance, you can drive the remaining 2.4 miles to the trailhead. *DeLorme: Colorado Atlas & Gazetteer:* Page 76 D4. GPS: N37 31.842' / W107 40.823'.

The Hike

Sign the register, which you'll find at the trailhead, and then begin your hike on Lime Mesa Trail 676. You'll slowly gain altitude as you walk across Lime Mesa. You'll enter small stands of trees on occasion, but the nicest thing about this hike is that you stay mainly out in the open, where wonderful views are yours for the asking.

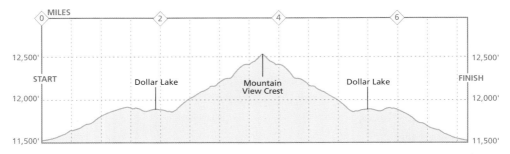

You will enter the wilderness after 0.25 mile. Hike to 0.5 mile, and you'll see a sign pointing the way east to City Reservoir. The trail is about 0.6 mile long and connects with Hike 7, the Endlich Mesa/Burnt Timber Shuttle Hike. See that chapter for more information if you are interested.

The route described here continues straight ahead. After 1.9 miles you'll reach Dollar Lake, home to marmots, pikas, and other precious critters. The lake is scenic, nearly 12,000 feet high in elevation, and a great place for a stop. Continue on, traveling past a small tarn and numerous wildflowers until you reach a saddle called Mountain View Crest at 3.6 miles. Although a faint trail continues north to Ruby, Pear, and Emerald Lakes, it is not maintained and is not recommended for hiking by the Forest Service. If you do decide to descend, however, be sure to camp at least 100 feet from the lakes. Most importantly, be sure to look north and across the Chicago Basin to Pigeon and Turret Peaks. Both are close to 14,000 feet high, and they are certainly dramatic. In addition, you'll see numerous other peaks forming the Needle Mountains. Three fourteeners—Mount Eolus, Sunlight Peak, and Windom Peak—make the Chicago Basin the most popular area in the wilderness.

Miles and Directions

0.0 Lime Mesa trailhead.

0.25 Wilderness boundary.

1.9 Dollar Lake. GPS: N37 33.313' / W107 40.364'.

HOT ROCKS

The San Juan Mountains offer much in the way of geological fascination. Along with the rest of the Colorado Rockies, they have been covered by glaciers at least three times. But they also have a long history of volcanic activity, with the first phase transpiring about thirty-five million years ago. Three classes of volcanic rocks—lava flows born of liquid magma, tuff fashioned from volcanic ash, and breccia produced from lava fragments—are present in the San Juans. Today the range includes the remains of more than a dozen volcanoes that spewed these elements and other rubble over the region during the Tertiary period. The oldest rocks in the San Juan Mountains are a middle Precambrian form called twilight gneiss. Climbers can find it on Twilight Peak, the loftiest mountain in the West Needle Range, in the northwest corner of the Weminuche Wilderness. Twilight gneiss is thought to be 1.76 billion years old—plus or minus twenty million years. Southeast of there, also in the Needle Mountains, is Mount Eolus (ay-OH-less), the namesake of one of the largest granitic bodies in the San Juan Mountains. Eolus granite is 1.46 billion years old.

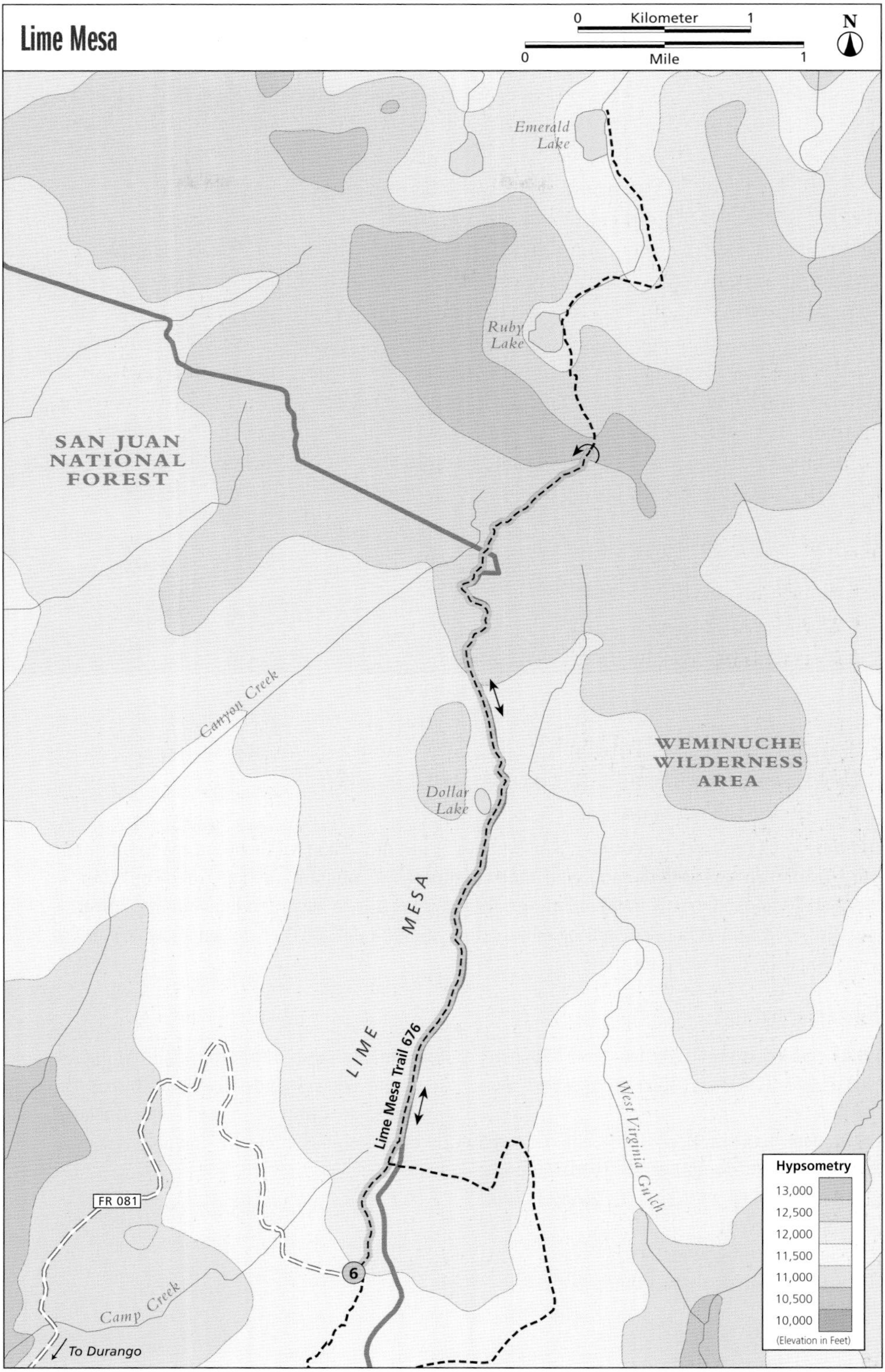

Lime Mesa

0   Kilometer   1
0   Mile   1

N

Emerald
Lake

Ruby
Lake

SAN JUAN
NATIONAL
FOREST

WEMINUCHE
WILDERNESS
AREA

Canyon Creek

Dollar
Lake

M E S A

L I M E

West Virginia Gulch

Lime Mesa Trail 676

FR 081

6

Camp Creek

To Durango

Hypsometry

	13,000
	12,500
	12,000
	11,500
	11,000
	10,500
	10,000

(Elevation in Feet)

Dollar Lake from Lime Mesa Trail

3.6 Mountain View Crest. GPS: N37 34.493' / W107 40.049'.

7.2 Back to Lime Mesa trailhead.

Options: You'll see quite a few unmaintained trails in this area. Many of them are sheep trails, but some lead to various wildflower-covered knobs and peaks. If you have the time, check out Overlook Point, the nearby peak to the northwest. It's less than 1 mile away and tops out at 12,998 feet. The country is wide open, making cross-country travel a delight. Be sure you know how to use your GPS, map, and compass.

Hike Information

Local information: Durango Area Tourism; (970) 247-3500 or (800) 525-8855; www.durango.org.

Local events/attractions: Ride the Durango & Silverton Narrow Gauge Railroad, Durango; (970) 247-2733 or (877) 872-4607; www.durangotrain.com.

Raft the Animas River.

Walk historic downtown Durango.

Accommodations: Durango offers a number of private campgrounds. There are also primitive areas to camp en route to the trailhead. Durango also has numerous motels.

7 Endlich Mesa/Burnt Timber Shuttle Hike

The route described here is an amazing hike filled with wildlife, wildflowers, grand views, and a scenic lake. It's best to do the hike in a counterclockwise direction. Do so, and you'll gain 2,550 feet and descend a total of 5,190 feet. Hike clockwise, and you'll have to gain more than 5,000 feet. You'll need a shuttle for this backpack trip because of its length. If a shuttle isn't available, or if you just feel like a day trip, you can hike the first few miles from either end.

Start: Endlich Mesa trailhead
Distance: 22.2-mile shuttle
Hiking time: 3- to 4-day backpack
Difficulty: Strenuous due to length
Canine compatibility: Dogs must be under control.
Nearest town: Durango
Fees and permits: Free registration (available online, at managing agency, or major trailheads) needed for both day hikers and overnight backpackers. Contact the managing agency for current information.

Maps: USGS Lemon Reservoir, Vallecito Reservoir, Columbine Pass, and Mountain View Crest; Trails Illustrated Weminuche Wilderness; DeLorme 3D TopoQuad CD-ROM; Maptech Terrain Navigator CD-ROM
Trail contact: San Juan National Forest, Columbine Ranger District, Bayfield; (970) 884-2512; www.fs.usda.gov/sanjuan
Special considerations: Be prepared for possible high-creek crossings, especially early in the hiking season.

Finding the trailhead: To reach the trailhead at Endlich Mesa, drive from the junction of US 160 and US 550 in south Durango, traveling north on US 550. After 0.9 mile make a right (east) onto 15th Street and travel northeast. (A sign points the way to Vallecito Reservoir.) Along the way 15th becomes Florida and eventually La Plata CR 240, all of which is paved. After 13.9 miles you will reach a fork in the road. Head left (north) onto paved La Plata CR 243; you soon will enter San Juan National Forest. After 1.7 miles the road turns to gravel. Pass Miller Creek Campground en route to the junction of FR 596 and FR 597, reached another 5.3 miles down the road. FR 597 is straight ahead (north). This long, bumpy road (passable with a high-clearance vehicle) climbs 10.7 miles to the start of this trail; it will take more than an hour to drive. The road ends at the trailhead, where facilities are nonexistent. If you want to camp at the trailhead, there are places to do so.

To drop a shuttle car off at the endpoint trailhead, back at the junction of FR 596 and FR 597, continue 0.2 mile on FR 596 to the Florida Campground. Travel through the campground and keep to the left as you continue on to Transfer Park Campground. The trailhead and campground entrance are in another 1.4 miles. There's plenty of room for parking at the trailhead, plus room to unload horses. You'll also find two hitching posts. *DeLorme: Colorado Atlas & Gazetteer:* Transfer Park trailhead, Page 86 A4; GPS: N37 27.809' / W107 40.935'. Endlich Mesa trailhead, Page 87 A5; GPS: N37 28.644' / W107 37.885'.

The Needle Mountains from Endlich Mesa

The Hike

Endlich Mesa Trail 534 begins at the northeast tip of the parking area atop Endlich Mesa. An old logging road serves as the trail, heading northeast through open woods. Rock cairns mark the way, freeing you to concentrate on the many species of summer wild-flowers. Break out of the trees at 1.1 miles, and enter the wilderness at about 1.9 miles.

The trail is a series of small roller coasters: It climbs, descends a bit, and then climbs some more, traveling across alpine tundra with see-forever views. To the west you can look at Missionary Ridge (just across the Florida drainage) and, farther west, the La Plata Mountains. Look north to see a portion of the jagged Needle Mountains and east for more of the rugged Weminuche Wilderness. Nearby a rainbow of wildflowers grows amid granite slabs and boulders, some of which are covered with colorful lichen.

You'll hike at a lofty elevation, averaging about 12,000 feet with a high of 12,288 feet, as you continue. If thunderstorms are not a threat, you can spend time just sitting and enjoying the view of 12,795-foot Sheridan Mountain to the northeast. Back on the trail you'll begin dropping into a basin, then reach a fork at 5.9 miles. Rock cairns mark both trails, but you want to head left (north), continuing to descend on the steep trail. The unmaintained trail heading straight (east) follows the contour line to another saddle and accesses a lake on the east side of the ridge.

Descend via the rerouted trail, which was created because the old trail was too steep and eroded. Stay on the trail, descending moderate switchbacks to the Florida River at 8 miles. Ford the river and then travel east between it and the waters of Missouri Gulch. The gulch soon disappears, but you'll continue to parallel the Florida River, climbing a mostly steep grade to 8.5 miles and the southwest end of City Reservoir.

Here you'll find City Reservoir Trail 542. Take it west, making sure to use the upper trail. (If you can't see a trail below you, you're not on the upper route.) The trail is nearly level as you begin, but it gets steep as you head into the trees. The trail levels off, then descends gradually to a stream crossing at 9 miles. Soon afterward look for a waterfall on the left.

At 9.5 miles the Missouri Gulch drainage widens and the grade lessens. Hike through the open forest, then cross a stream at 9.6 miles. Immediately afterward, the trail forks; head left and down into the meadow. In another 0.1 mile you'll have to ford Missouri Gulch.

Beyond the gulch head back into the trees via a moderate-to-steep trail. You'll come to another fork at 10.4 miles. Rock cairns point the way to the high trail, your route. The lower trail leads to a camping area more than a mile away, used by herders in the summer and hunters in the fall.

The high trail is sometimes very steep as you climb to the southern edge of flower- and limestone-laden West Silver Mesa at 11 miles. You'll reach 12,000 feet in elevation just beyond. Begin a gradual downhill. As you descend, watch for elk; this is prime summer habitat for these amazing creatures. You'll cross a stream at 12.5 miles, then enter an enormous meadow where there are wildflowers and nice views to the north.

After another 0.2 mile ford Virginia Gulch, then continue across the meadow and into the trees. Pass a rock outcrop at 12.8 miles, a fun place to watch for marmots and pikas. It's a moderate climb, with some steep pitches; cross more streams at 13.4 and 13.8 miles. You'll cross West Virginia Gulch at 14.5 miles. Explore this high mesa, and you'll find several tiny ponds and trees at meadow's edge.

The trail stays nearly level as you hike to a fork in the trail at 15.6 miles. A sign points west and says LIME MESA STOCK TRAIL—0.5 MILE (see Hike 6 for more information on this trail, which is officially called Lime Mesa Trail 676). The same sign points the way to TRANSFER PARK—7 MILES. To finish out the route, keep straight ahead. You are now hiking Burnt Timber Trail 667. As you continue along the ridge, moderately descending, you'll see Sheridan Mountain, Endlich Mesa, and other points to the east.

The trail heads west at 16.2 miles and turns southeast at 17.1 miles. You may see multiple paths here, as some hikers have not stayed on the main trail. The route stays fairly level across the western edge of a previously logged meadow. The wilderness has never been logged—the trail just meanders inside and outside of its western boundary.

The trail, which is sometimes an old road, provides everything from a level path to a moderate-to-very-steep descent. You'll cross several creeks en route, including North

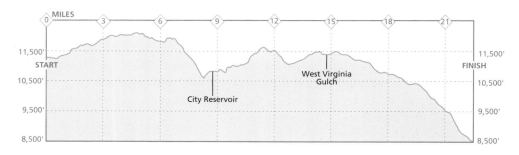

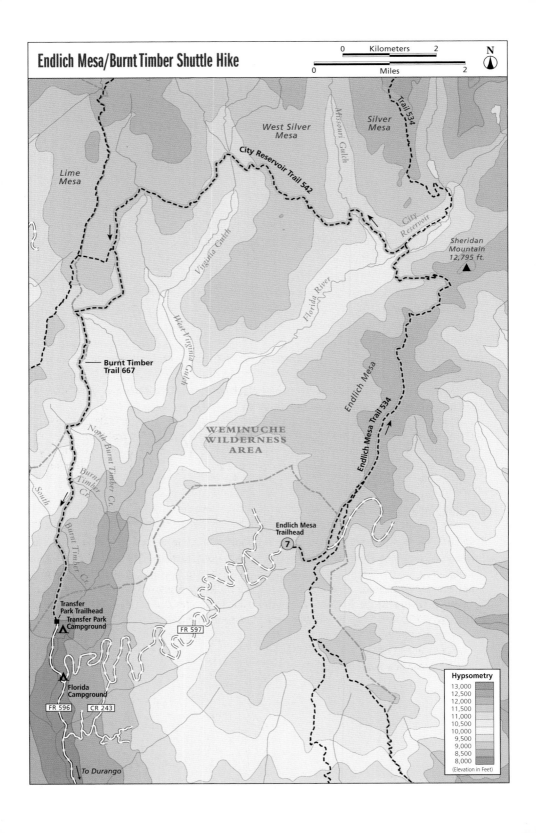

Endlich Mesa/Burnt Timber Shuttle Hike

Kilometers

Miles

N

Lime
Mesa

West Silver
Mesa

Missouri Gulch

Silver
Mesa

Trail 534

City Reservoir Trail 542

City
Reservoir

Sheridan
Mountain
12,795 ft.

Virginia Gulch

Florida River

West Virginia Gulch

Burnt Timber
Trail 667

Endlich Mesa

Endlich Mesa Trail 534

North Burnt Timber Cr.

Burnt
Timber
Cr.

WEMINUCHE
WILDERNESS
AREA

South Burnt Timber Cr.

Endlich Mesa
Trailhead

7

Transfer
Park Trailhead
Transfer Park
Campground

FR 597

Florida
Campground

FR 596   CR 243

To Durango

Hypsometry

	13,000
	12,500
	12,000
	11,500
	11,000
	10,500
	10,000
	9,500
	9,000
	8,500
	8,000

(Elevation in Feet)

Burnt Timber, Burnt Timber, and South Burnt Timber. Notice the lovely groves of aspen that pop up about this time. The trail grade eases at times, allowing you to enjoy the aspens, the variety of wildflowers, and the numerous other plants and trees, including scrub oak and ponderosa pine in the lower realms. You'll exit the wilderness at 21.8 miles. The Transfer Park trailhead is a short distance ahead, at 22.2 miles.

Miles and Directions

0.0 Endlich Mesa trailhead.

1.9 Wilderness boundary.

5.9 Fork; bear left (north).

8.0 Ford Florida River.

8.5 City Reservoir. GPS: N37 32.36' / W107 36.03'.

9.7 Ford Missouri Gulch.

14.5 West Virginia Gulch. GPS: N37 32.976' / W107 39.883'.

15.6 Junction of Burnt Timber Trail and Lime Mesa Stock Trail.

21.8 Wilderness boundary.

22.2 Transfer Park trailhead.

Options: If you do nothing else while you camp near City Reservoir, be sure to explore the Florida River drainage. Its quiet pools, raging waterfalls, tumbling cascades, amazing slabs of granite, and abundant wildflowers—columbine, hellebore, bistort, bluebells, paintbrush, and elephants head, to name a few—combine to make this a stunning place.

The Endlich Mesa Trail does not end at City Reservoir. You can continue on to the upper end of City Reservoir at 0.6 mile, then climb a steep grade to Lake Marie at 1.4 miles. From there continue up a very steep ridge to the west, then marvel at the alpine tundra of Silver Mesa. Here tiny ponds mirror granite slabs and boulders that are decorated with lichen and phlox. You will reach Trimble Pass at 4.5 miles and approximately 12,840 feet.

Hike Information

Local information: Durango Area Tourism; (970) 247-3500 or (800) 525-8855; www .durango.org.

Local events/attractions: Ride the Durango & Silverton Narrow Gauge Railroad, Durango; (970) 247-2733 or (877) 872-4607; www .durangotrain.com.

Raft the Animas River.

Walk historic downtown Durango.

Accommodations: Durango offers a number of private campgrounds. The closest campgrounds to the shuttle hike are the Florida and Transfer Park Campgrounds, national forest fee areas with water and outhouses. Durango also has numerous motels.

8 Lake Eileen Trail

Wildflowers and nice views make this day hike a wonderful outing. And if you're fortunate, you may see some ducks in the lake as well.

Start: Lake Eileen trailhead

Distance: 4.2 miles out and back

Hiking time: About 2 to 3 hours

Difficulty: Moderate to strenuous

Canine compatibility: Dogs must be under control.

Nearest town: Bayfield

Fees and permits: Free registration (available online, at managing agency, or major trailheads) needed for both day hikers and overnight backpackers. Contact the managing agency for current information.

Maps: USGS Vallecito Reservoir; Trails Illustrated Weminuche Wilderness; DeLorme 3D TopoQuad CD-ROM; Maptech Terrain Navigator CD-ROM; National Geographic Topo! Version 4.6.0

Trail contact: San Juan National Forest, Columbine Ranger District, Bayfield; (970) 884-2512; www.fs.usda.gov/sanjuan

Finding the trailhead: About 18 miles east of Durango via US 160, you'll find the small town of Bayfield. From there head north on paved La Plata CR 501 (Vallecito Lake Road). After 8.8 miles you'll reach a junction with La Plata CR 240, another possible route if you're coming from Durango. Keep straight (north) on CR 501. After an additional 9.6 miles, you'll see the trailhead on the left. The trailhead is marked with a wilderness sign and a trail register. There is room for several cars to park on the right. *DeLorme: Colorado Atlas & Gazetteer:* Page 87 A5. GPS: N37 26.566' / W107 33.473'.

Witch's hat (Hygrocybe conica)

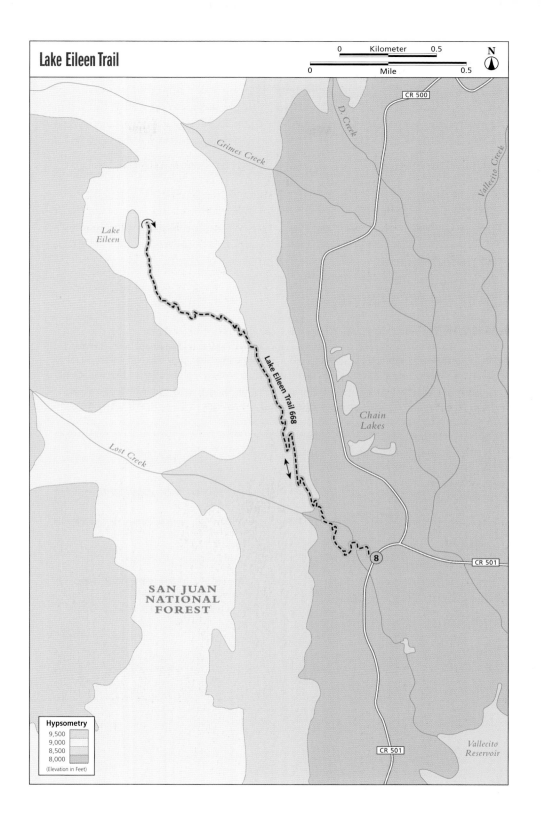

Lake Eileen Trail

0 Kilometer 0.5

0 Mile 0.5

N

CR 500

D. Creek

Grimes Creek

Vallecito Creek

Lake Eileen

Lake Eileen Trail 668

Lost Creek

Chain Lakes

SAN JUAN NATIONAL FOREST

8

CR 501

CR 501

Vallecito Reservoir

Hypsometry

9,500
9,000
8,500
8,000

(Elevation in Feet)

The Hike

Lake Eileen Trail 668 begins as a moderate climb up a side slope, but watch out for some steeper sections. You'll no doubt notice that the slope was previously burned in the Missionary Ridge Fire of 2002. You enter the wilderness almost immediately, and as you gain more than 1,000 feet in elevation via switchbacks, notice the view. You'll see down to the Chain Lakes, and off in the distance, to the north, you'll see more of the Weminuche Wilderness. The trail levels off at about 1.8 miles and continues to the east side of Lake Eileen at 2.1 miles. See old beaver cuttings, and notice how the lake is filling in with grasses: One day it will be a meadow.

Miles and Directions

0.0   Lake Eileen trailhead.

2.1   Lake Eileen. GPS: N37 27.523' / W107 34.266'.

4.2   Back to Lake Eileen trailhead.

Hike Information

Local information: Bayfield Colorado Area Chamber of Commerce, Bayfield; (970) 884-7372; www.bayfieldchamber.org. Durango Area Tourism, Durango; (970) 247-3500 or (800) 525-8855; www.durango.org.

Local events/attractions: Ride the Durango & Silverton Narrow Gauge Railroad, Durango; (970) 247-2733 or (877) 872-4607; www.durangotrain.com.

Raft the Animas River.

Walk historic downtown Durango.

Accommodations: Bayfield and nearby Durango offer a number of private and public campgrounds. Durango also has numerous motels.

9 Vallecito Creek Trail

Wildflowers and a lovely creek with tiny pools and waterfalls make this hike extra special. If you're in want of a stunning day hike, try the first few miles. If not, the entire out-and-back hike makes a nice backpack trip.

Start: Vallecito Creek trailhead
Distance: 39 miles out and back
Hiking time: 4- to 6-day backpack
Difficulty: Strenuous due to length; easy if you cover only the first few miles as a day hike
Canine compatibility: Dogs must be under control.
Nearest town: Bayfield
Fees and permits: Free registration (available online, at managing agency, or major trailheads) needed for both day hikers and overnight backpackers. Contact the managing agency for current information.

Maps: USGS Vallecito Reservoir, Columbine Pass, and Storm King Peak; Trails Illustrated Weminuche Wilderness; DeLorme 3D TopoQuad CD-ROM; Maptech Terrain Navigator CD-ROM
Trail contact: San Juan National Forest, Columbine Ranger District, Bayfield; (970) 884-2512; www.fs.usda.gov/sanjuan
Special considerations: The third bridge up from the trailhead was swept away by an avalanche in the winter of 2004–5. Though the trail was cleared, there are no plans to replace the bridge: Hikers will have to ford the creek. Vallecito Creek is challenging to ford, and is especially dangerous during high water.

Finding the trailhead: About 18 miles east of Durango via US 160, you'll find the small town of Bayfield. From there head north on paved La Plata CR 501 (Vallecito Lake Road). After 8.8 miles you'll reach a junction with La Plata CR 240, another possible route if you're coming from Durango. Keep straight (north) on CR 501. After an additional 9.7 miles, you'll come to another fork. Bear left (north) here onto paved La Plata CR 500 to reach the Vallecito Campground and trailhead parking in 2.8 miles. There's a picnic area and outhouse at the trailhead, plus water and plenty of room for both automobile and horse trailer parking. *DeLorme: Colorado Atlas & Gazetteer:* Page 87 A5. GPS: N37 28,490' / W107 32.902'.

The Hike

Vallecito Creek Trail 529 begins in a ponderosa pine forest interspersed with aspens and conifers amid the steep granite walls of a narrow, impressive canyon. The trail skirts the western edge of the Vallecito Campground, reaching the north end in 0.6 mile. Soon afterward you will cross Fall Creek via a bridge. The trail then climbs gradually, entering the wilderness after 0.7 mile. The route splits for 0.5 mile or so: Horseback riders bear left, and hikers continue straight ahead. At the 1.1-mile mark you'll head away from the steep canyon walls, climbing the ridge between the Vallecito Creek drainage to the east and the Weasel Skin and Fall Creek drainages to the west. Around 1.3 miles you'll come out onto a semiopen slope of granite and various trees.

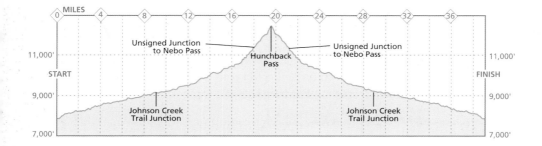

The trail climbs gradually, gently descending now and then as you parallel the creek. You'll start out high above the water, then descend and hike next to it. Along the way there are wildflowers. Look for fireweed, daisies, blue columbines, wild geraniums, and a whole lot more.

The trail splits again at 1.7 miles, this time for only 0.1 mile: Hikers head right, horses bear left. In a short distance you'll see up the drainage to the pointed crown of Irving Peak. Switchback down, and meet the river up close and personal at 2 miles.

After 3.3 miles you'll have to ford Taylor Creek. Later in the season it's possible to hop rocks, but before that you may have to get your feet wet. Just after crossing you'll find a place to camp in an aspen grove. This area gets a lot of use, so please continue on if you can.

You'll cross Vallecito Creek at this point. Fortunately, a bridge makes for an easy crossing. Proceed up the trail, fording First Creek at 3.7 miles. The easy-to-moderate climb continues across a slope, then heads back along Vallecito Creek in a mile or so. There's a grove of aspens on a bench above the river at 5.1 miles.

Ford Second Creek at 5.6 miles. You'll cross another bridge soon after and travel along the west side of the creek, passing by some campsites that are close to the water. You'll see a huge variety of wildflowers here come summer. On an open slope you may spot wild roses, some sort of orange lily, columbines, geraniums, violets, wild chives, daisies, bluebells, and wild strawberries.

The trail crosses a side creek at 6.9 miles. Farther along, a bridge used to cross Vallecito Creek at 7.1 miles, but it was swept away by an avalanche in the winter of 2004–5. You now have to ford the creek. From here there's an even better view of Irving Peak to the north.

As you continue you'll hike through meadows and aspen groves, with a few pine stands thrown in as well. The trail continues at an easy-to-moderate grade, crossing several small streams en route. At 9.3 miles you'll see a bridge across Vallecito Creek. This leads to the Johnson Creek Trail and Columbine Pass (see Hike 4 for more information).

Colorado's state flower is the lovely Colorado columbine. Easy to spot, the flower has five white funnel-shaped petals surrounded by five blue-to-lavender sepals. Yellow stamens protrude from the middle of each flower.

Vallecito Creek

After 11.6 miles you'll ford Roell Creek, and at 15 miles you'll ford Rock Creek; be prepared to get your feet wet at this crossing. Wonderful views continue as you hike through an array of wildflower-filled meadows. Ford Vallecito Creek at 17.8 miles. Look for waterfalls, cascades, and pools just before and in this area. The trail begins to steepen as you proceed, paralleling Nebo Creek for a short distance.

After 18.1 miles you'll reach an unsigned trail junction on the right (east). This is the Continental Divide Trail (CDT), which heads over Nebo Pass and eventually south to Mexico. Stay straight here; you will now be hiking the northbound CDT, which ultimately leads to Canada. The trail first goes to Hunchback Pass, your destination if you so desire.

Cross a small creek at 18.6 miles, and continue the steep (sometimes very steep!) ascent to Hunchback Pass at 19.5 miles. Wildflowers and plant life are abundant here in summer, with paintbrush, marsh marigolds, bluebells, hellebore, and other flowering plants.

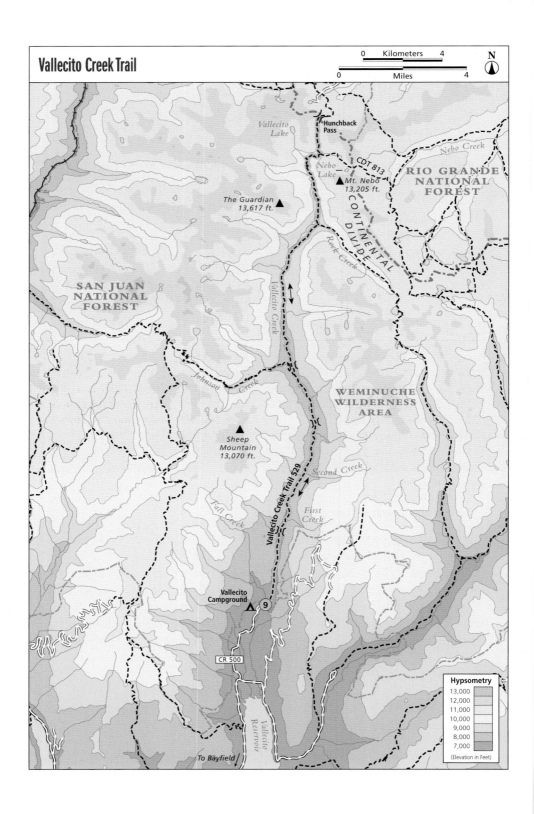

Vallecito Creek Trail

Vallecito
Lake

Hunchback
Pass

Nebo Creek

Nebo
Lake

CDT 813

Mt. Nebo
13,205 ft.

RIO GRANDE
NATIONAL
FOREST

The Guardian
13,617 ft.

C O N T I N E N T A L

D I V I D E

Rock Creek

SAN JUAN
NATIONAL
FOREST

Vallecito Creek

Johnson   Creek

WEMINUCHE
WILDERNESS
AREA

Sheep
Mountain
13,070 ft.

Vallecito Creek Trail 529

Second Creek

Fall Creek

First
Creek

Vallecito
Campground

9

CR 500

Vallecito
Reservoir

To Bayfield

Hypsometry

	13,000
	12,000
	11,000
	10,000
	9,000
	8,000
	7,000

(Elevation in Feet)

Miles and Directions

0.0 Vallecito Campground and trailhead.

0.7 Wilderness boundary.

3.3 Ford Taylor Creek; bridge across Vallecito Creek.

5.6 Ford Second Creek.

7.1 Ford Vallecito Creek.

9.3 Bridge over Vallecito Creek; access to Johnson Creek. GPS: N37 35.050' / W107 31.870'.

15.0 Ford Rock Creek.

18.1 Unsigned junction to Nebo Pass.

19.5 Hunchback Pass. GPS: N37 42.284' / W107 31.206'.

39.0 Back to Vallecito Campground and trailhead.

Option: From the junction at mile 18.1, you can make the sometimes-steep climb to Nebo Pass, where you'll find quaint Nebo Lake. There's a grand view west to the Trinity Peaks and Storm King Peak, plus a spectacular view east to the Rio Grande Pyramid and the Window. If you take this option, you'll have to hike an additional 1.6 miles and ascend 930 feet to the pass.

Hike Information

Local information: Bayfield Colorado Area Chamber of Commerce, Bayfield; (970) 884-7372; www.bayfieldchamber.org. Durango Area Tourism, Durango; (970) 247-3500 or (800) 525-8855; www.durango.org.

Local events/attractions: Ride the Durango & Silverton Narrow Gauge Railroad, Durango; (970) 247-2733 or (877) 872-4607; www.durangotrain.com.

Raft the Animas River.

Walk historic downtown Durango.

Accommodations: Bayfield and nearby Durango offer a number of private and public campgrounds. The trailhead is at Vallecito Campground, a national forest campground. It's a fee area with drinking water and outhouses. Durango also has numerous motels.

10 Cave Basin Trail

Wildflowers and fantastic views make this long day hike a real treat.

Start: Cave Basin trailhead
Distance: 10.4 miles out and back
Hiking time: About 5 to 7 hours
Difficulty: Strenuous due to length and elevation gain
Canine compatibility: Dogs must be under control.
Nearest town: Bayfield
Fees and permits: Free registration (available online, at managing agency, or major trailheads) needed for both day hikers and overnight backpackers. Contact the managing agency for current information.
Maps: USGS Vallecito Reservoir and Emerald Lake; Trails Illustrated Weminuche Wilderness; DeLorme 3D TopoQuad CD-ROM; Maptech Terrain Navigator CD-ROM; National Geographic Topo! Version 4.6.0
Trail contact: San Juan National Forest, Columbine Ranger District, Bayfield; (970) 884-2512; www.fs.usda.gov/sanjuan

Finding the trailhead: About 18 miles east of Durango via US 160, you'll find the small town of Bayfield. From there head north on paved La Plata CR 501 (Vallecito Lake Road). After 8.8 miles you'll reach a junction with La Plata CR 240, another possible route if you're coming from Durango. Keep straight (north) on CR 501. After an additional 9.7 miles, you'll come to the junction of CR 501 and La Plata CR 500. Stay right (east) on CR 501 and drive 1 mile to Middle Mountain Road. Turn left (east and then the road heads north) onto Middle Mountain, a gravel road in fairly good condition. Drive another 10 miles to the Cave Basin trailhead on the left (east) side of the road. The trailhead is marked with a wilderness sign and a trail register. There is room for several cars to park on the right, but no room to camp. *DeLorme: Colorado Atlas & Gazetteer:* Page 87 A5. GPS: N37 29.806' / W107 30.253'.

The Hike

Cave Basin Trail 530 climbs at a moderate-to-steep grade through an open meadow for about a mile then enters into the trees. The forest is lush, and if it's a warm day, you will welcome the shade.

Enter the wilderness at 1.3 miles. Continue climbing and descending and sometimes contouring on relatively flat ground through both meadows and trees to 2.7 miles. You'll cross one more meadow, then notice the trees disappear as you exit tree line. The trail can now be difficult to follow as you bushwhack through thigh-high willows and hike past lonely tarns. Look for sinkholes in the limestone deposits as you continue. If you're lucky, you'll see where streams disappear into the ground. Also, in July there are many alpine wildflowers, including Arctic gentian, to see and photograph. Wonderful views of the Weminuche can be had year-round.

Hike to 5.2 miles and the end of the trail, where there are good views of Dollar Lake to the east. You'll see portions of Emerald Lake as well.

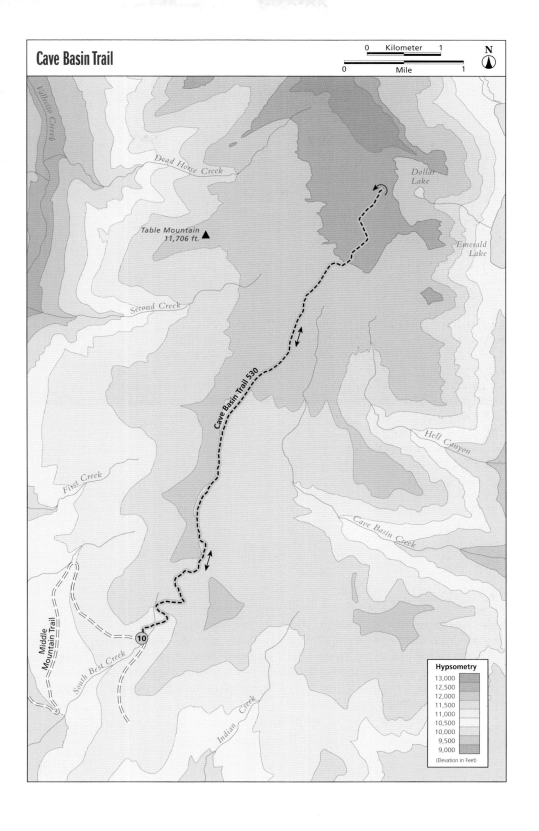

Cave Basin Trail

0   Kilometer   1

0   Mile   1

N

Vallecito Creek

Dead Horse Creek

Dollar Lake

Table Mountain
11,706 ft.

Emerald Lake

Second Creek

Cave Basin Trail 530

Hell Canyon

First Creek

Cave Basin Creek

Middle Mountain Trail

10

South Best Creek

Indian Creek

Hypsometry

| 13,000 |
| 12,500 |
| 12,000 |
| 11,500 |
| 11,000 |
| 10,500 |
| 10,000 |
| 9,500 |
| 9,000 |

(Elevation in Feet)

View of Dollar Lake (in front) and Emerald Lake (in back) from the end of the Cave Basin Trail
MIKE VINING

Miles and Directions

0.0 Cave Basin trailhead.

1.3 Wilderness boundary.

5.2 End of trail and overlook. GPS: N37 33.185' / W107 28.049'.

10.4 Back to Cave Basin trailhead.

Hike Information

Local information: Bayfield Colorado Area Chamber of Commerce, Bayfield; (970) 884-7372; www.bayfieldchamber.org. Durango Area Tourism, Durango; (970) 247-3500 or (800) 525-8855; www.durango.org.

Local events/attractions: Ride the Durango & Silverton Narrow Gauge Railroad, Durango; (970) 247-2733 or (877) 872-4607; www.durangotrain.com.

Raft the Animas River.

Walk historic downtown Durango.

Accommodations: Bayfield and nearby Durango offer a number of private and public campgrounds. Durango also has numerous motels.

11 Pine River/Flint Creek Semiloop

Hike this semiloop, known also as a lollipop, and you'll enjoy scenic lakes, wildflowers, and wildlife. If all you want is a day hike, just travel along Pine River as far as you wish to go. If you want to do the hike described here, which is much recommended, then head into the high country for a few days and more than 5,000 feet of vertical gain.

Start: Pine River trailhead
Distance: 41.6-mile semiloop
Hiking time: 5- to 6-day backpack
Difficulty: Strenuous due to length; easy if you cover only the first few miles as a day hike
Canine compatibility: Dogs must be under control.
Nearest town: Bayfield
Fees and permits: Free registration (available online, at managing agency, or major trailheads) needed for both day hikers and overnight backpackers. Contact the managing agency for current information.
Maps: USGS Vallecito Reservoir, Granite Peak, Emerald Lake, and Granite Lake; Trails Illustrated Weminuche Wilderness; DeLorme 3D

TopoQuad CD-ROM; Maptech Terrain Navigator CD-ROM
Trail contact: San Juan National Forest, Columbine Ranger District, Bayfield; (970) 884-2512; www.fs.usda.gov/sanjuan
Special considerations: Portions of the trail are not maintained. High-river crossings are possible, especially early in the hiking season. Camping and campfires are restricted in certain areas. There is no camping within 0.5 mile north of Emerald Lake, a day-use area only. No camping or campfires within 0.25 mile of Emerald and Little Emerald Lakes except in designated campsites. Saddle/pack stock are not allowed within 200 feet of any of the above-mentioned lakes.

Finding the trailhead: Go about 18 miles east of Durango via US 160, and you'll reach the small town of Bayfield. From there head north on paved La Plata CR 501 (Vallecito Lake Road). After 8.8 miles you'll reach a junction with La Plata CR 240, another possible route if you're coming from Durango. Keep straight (north) on CR 501 for another 4.4 miles; a sign points the way to Vallecito-area campgrounds. (You can also follow signs left and around the west side of Vallecito Reservoir if you want to bypass a short section of bumpy road and drive 12.2 miles.)

The shortest access is via CR 501A, which almost immediately changes to FR 603. Turn right (east) onto FR 603, which is paved as it crosses the dam but turns to maintained gravel beyond. You'll pass three Forest Service campgrounds—Graham Creek, North Canyon, and Pine Point—as you travel around the east end of Vallecito Reservoir. Drop down a short, steep section to a privately owned resort and cross a bridge over Los Pinos (called the Pine River by locals) after 4.6 miles. Make a left (west), and go 0.3 mile, entering another resort where there are cabins. Keep to the right (east) as you travel through the resort, crossing a cattle guard and merging with FR 602 in 0.1 mile as you continue. Turn right (east), and drive another 3.6 miles to the Pine River Campground. Head through the campground to reach the trailhead in another 0.1 mile. You'll find plenty of parking, hitching posts, and an outhouse. *DeLorme: Colorado Atlas & Gazetteer:* Page 87 A5. GPS: N37 26.855' / W107 30.292'.

The Hike

Enter through a private gate (please close it behind you) adjacent to Granite Peaks Ranch. This is private property, but hikers are allowed if they stay on the trail (no camping). Aspens, ponderosa pines, and a variety of conifers will keep you company as you gradually ascend along Pine River Trail 523. You'll see the Pine River, also known as Los Pinos, off to the east as you begin. Later trees and ranch sounds block the view and river sounds.

At 1.2 miles you'll cross Indian Creek. About 0.2 mile beyond this crossing, you'll pass through another gate; be sure to close it. The trail reaches a point near the river at 2.5 miles. It enters the San Juan National Forest in another 0.2 mile, then crosses into the wilderness.

Cross a huge rock outcrop at 3.2 miles; be sure to look for pika and marmots. As you continue, you'll pass some meadows. Although you will be heading away from the river at times, it is visible on occasion. Cross the bridge over Lake Creek at 6.2 miles. Soon after you will reach the junction for Emerald Lake Trail 528. You'll have to cross a creek as you continue up the steep trail. Fortunately, the trail eases up a bit at the 8.6-mile mark. As you continue, cross a meadow, pass a mecca of aspens and false hellebore, and witness an array of wildflowers.

Ford a creek at 8.9 miles, then hike gradually through dense woods alongside Lake Creek. Later the hike resumes its steep ascent, switchbacking up through dense woods. You'll emerge from the thick trees at 10 miles to find young aspens and spruce sharing the landscape with various wildflowers. You return to the trees at 10.4 miles. Over the next 0.4 mile, you'll see places to camp on the left. The next available stopping point is the north end of Emerald Lake, a long haul from here if you are tired.

Beyond these campsites you'll see Little Emerald Lake off to the left as you descend gradually. At 11 miles Emerald Lake appears. It's a beautiful place, one you'll want to spend time exploring. As the trail skirts the east edge of the lake, it climbs and drops 10 to 20 feet in turn, sometimes at a steep grade. This roller coaster continues past a number of small streams and a lovely wildflower-filled meadow to the north end of the lake, 12.5 miles from the trailhead.

Past the lake there are more creek crossings, including a ford of Lake Creek (high until late summer). If it's been a wet year, you'll have a muddy trail to hike as you

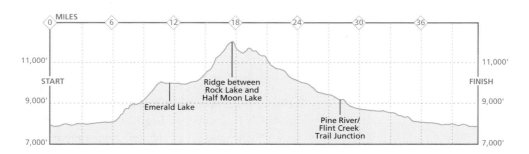

continue up the Lake Creek drainage. Still, there are numerous willows, the occasional moose, and an assortment of wildflowers to keep you amused.

You'll make a gradual climb now as you head north, but the break doesn't last for long. Notice the waterfall on the left at 13.8 miles. In just 0.5 mile more, you'll have to ford Lake Creek. The creek can be high until late summer.

A steep climb begins just before the ford, and from here the trail continually ascends, heading in and out of the trees. Along the way you'll pass assorted waterfalls, and you'll have to ford Lake Creek once again. Moon Lake, with its lovely view of Mount Oso (elevation 13,684 feet), is at mile 15.9.

An unmaintained trail (shown on some maps) leads up and over the north ridge to Rock Lake. It's easy to follow, with rock cairns to point the way. However, horses are not recommended on this route because it is too steep and rocky. From Moon Lake ford the outflow, and round the north shore. The slope here offers an abundance of wildflowers. After snowmelt you may see marsh marigolds, primroses, and glacier lilies. You'll reach the other end of the lake and the inflow creek as you hike north. Don't cross this stream; instead, head up the steep drainage. After climbing for 0.5 mile, you'll enter a rock field and cross stream; notice the mini–hanging gardens. In another 0.2 mile, at 16.8 miles, you'll reach Half Moon Lake. This is a great place to look for ptarmigan. Half Moon is a beautiful little lake and well worth a visit.

The trail continues upward on the west side of the lake, climbing at a steep grade. At 17.3 miles you'll reach the head of a stream that flows into Half Moon Lake. Cross it, and continue following the rock cairns to the top of the ridge, at 12,390 feet above sea level. From here look northwest to Peters Peak and northeast to the Rio Grande Pyramid and the Window.

This hike is best done after any snow has had a chance to melt off the north-facing slope. You'll head down from the ridge on a steep trail that could be slippery when wet or icy. At 17.7 miles you'll come to a massive rock outcrop. There's a tiny lake on the right soon afterward. Surprisingly, it can have ice floating on it in mid-August. Cross the lake outflow, and continue down the steep trail through willows, flowers, and other dense vegetation. You'll soon reach Rock Lake at 18.1 miles.

The trail forks at 18.5 miles. The Rock Creek Trail takes off to the northwest. Head right instead to continue this loop via Flint Creek Trail 527. You'll begin climbing at 18.9 miles, where moderate-to-steep switchbacks lead to the high tundra and nearly level terrain. There's a lovely tarn just after you level off, and as you descend gradually, you'll see other pools. You'll come to a gentle ridge at 19.4 miles. If you step off the trail a bit, you'll have a view down to Flint Lakes.

Next you'll descend moderately into the trees. The area around Flint Lakes is for day use only, so you'll have to camp elsewhere. You'll reach a junction at 20.6 miles. The left (north) trail goes to Ute Lake; this trail also accesses the Pine River via La Osa. Keep straight to reach Flint Creek and the remainder of this loop.

The trail gradually descends to the 20.8-mile point, then begins a steep drop into the Flint Creek drainage. Later it eases off, descending moderately and sometimes

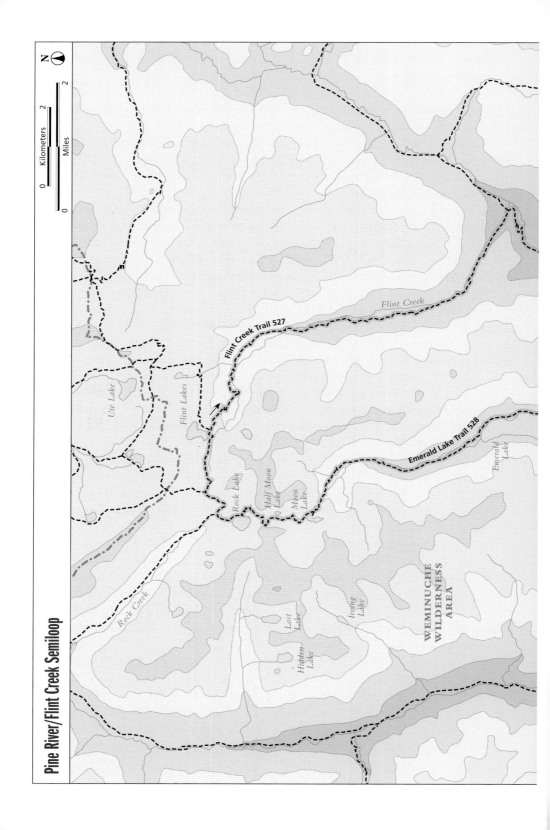

Pine River/Flint Creek Semiloop

Flint Creek Trail 527

Flint Creek

Emerald Lake Trail 528

Ute Lake

Flint Lakes

Rock Creek

Rock Lake

Half Moon Lake

Moon Lake

Emerald Lake

Lost Lake

Hidden Lake

Irving Lake

WEMINUCHE WILDERNESS AREA

N

0   Kilometers   2

0   Miles   2

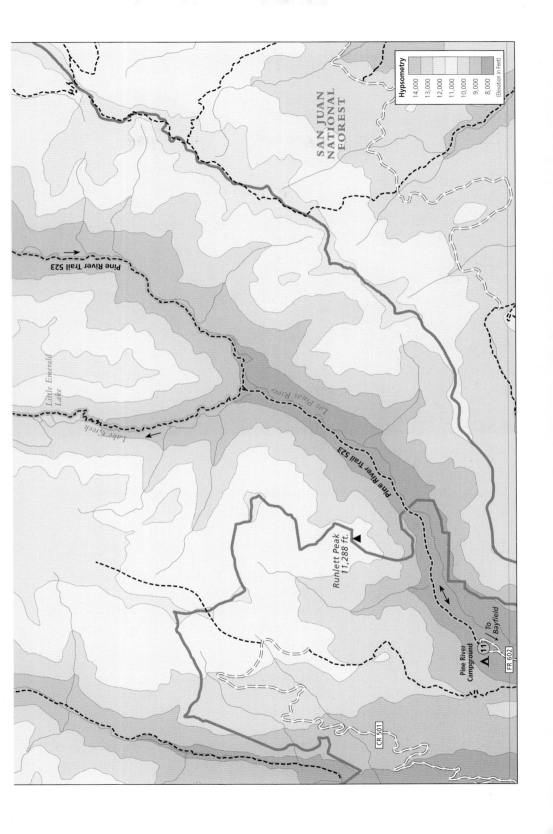

After a storm—tarn near Flint Lake

even ascending in and out of the trees and through a number of meadows. You'll cross many creeks en route.

Ford Flint Creek at 23.8 miles. Just before the ford you'll see the remains of a huge mudslide that occurred in 1995. Fortunately, the trail was repaired and rerouted in 1996.

Around 26.5 miles the trail parallels Flint Creek, its waters cascading through the narrow canyon. You'll come to the junction of the Pine River Trail at 28.5 miles. From the junction head right (south) to continue this loop, and descend moderately. (Going left, or north, leads to the Continental Divide Trail.) Like many of the trails in this region, this one is deeply rutted in places.

You'll soon descend into the textbook-like, glacier-carved Pine River realm, where there are abundant aspens and wildflowers. The route fords a creek at 29.9 miles. Notice the tremendous waterfall off to the east as you continue down the trail. Falls Creek offers a double waterfall at about 31.5 miles.

You'll pass through an area rich in willows, then ford aptly named Willow Creek at 32 miles. From here continue the gradual descent through this lovely valley. You'll

North American porcupines are large rodents usually found in coniferous and mixed forested areas. Cute, but not so cuddly, the word *porcupine* means "spiny pig." Porcupines are slow-moving and nearsighted. If you are fortunate, you may see one while hiking wilderness trails.

North American porcupine (Erethizon dorsatum)

make several creek crossings before meeting the trail that leads to Emerald Lake at 35.3 miles. Continue straight and back to the trailhead at 41.6 miles.

Miles and Directions

0.0 Pine Creek trailhead.

2.7 Wilderness boundary.

6.2 Lake Creek crossing. GPS: N37 29.919' / W107 26.055'.

11.0 Emerald Lake.

15.9 Moon Lake. GPS: N37 35.999' / W107 28.326'.

18.1 Rock Lake.

20.6 Junction with trail to Ute Lake. GPS: N37 37.354' / W107 26.957'.

28.5 Pine River Trail junction. GPS: N37 33.544' / W107 23.074'.

41.6 Back to Pine Creek trailhead.

Option: From the junction of the Pine River and Flint Lake Trails, which is 13.1 miles from the trailhead, you can continue up the Pine River Trail for another 11.2 miles to the Continental Divide at Weminuche Pass. Do so, and you might see moose or beavers; you're sure to see expansive meadows and beautiful scenes.

Hike Information

Local information: Bayfield Colorado Area Chamber of Commerce, Bayfield; (970) 884-7372; www.bayfieldchamber.org. Durango Area Tourism, Durango; (970) 247-3500 or (800) 525-8855; www.durango.org.

Local events/attractions: Ride the Durango & Silverton Narrow Gauge Railroad, Durango; (970) 247-2733 or (877) 872-4607; www.durangotrain.com.

Raft the Animas River.

Walk historic downtown Durango.

Accommodations: Bayfield and nearby Durango offer a number of private and public campgrounds. Pine River Campground, a national forest site, is located at the trailhead. You won't have to pay a fee, but note that water is not available. Durango also has numerous motels.

12 Divide Lakes

Expect to see wildflowers on this hike in midsummer; you may see animal life throughout the hiking season. The first 2-plus miles make a nice day hike; otherwise, it's a two-day backpack. Trips to the Granite Lake Trail and East Fork Weminuche Trail (see Options) are also possible with the following trip information.

Start: Poison Park trailhead
Distance: 18 miles out and back
Hiking time: 2- to 3-day backpack
Difficulty: Strenuous due to length; moderate if you hike only the first 2 miles as a day trip
Canine compatibility: Dogs must be under control.
Nearest town: Pagosa Springs
Fees and permits: Free registration (available online, at managing agency, or major trailheads) needed for both day hikers and overnight backpackers. Contact the managing agency for current information.
Maps: USGS Granite Lake; Trails Illustrated Weminuche Wilderness; DeLorme 3D TopoQuad CD-ROM; Maptech Terrain Navigator CD-ROM
Trail contact: San Juan National Forest, Pagosa Ranger District, Pagosa Springs; (970) 264-2268; www.fs.usda.gov/sanjuan
Special considerations: High-creek crossings are possible, especially early in the season. Expect heavy trail use during hunting season.

Finding the trailhead: From downtown Pagosa Springs, head west on US 160 for approximately 3 miles and make a right (north) turn onto Piedra Road, which becomes Archuleta CR 600 immediately upon turning. After 6.2 miles the pavement ends and the road becomes a well-maintained gravel road named FR 631. Stay on gravel FR 631, passing Bridge Campground en route, to the junction of Williams Creek Road (FR 640) at 15.6 miles. Make a right (northwest) onto FR 640, passing both Williams Creek and Teal Campgrounds. You'll reach another fork in 3.5 miles. Here FR 640 goes right to the Williams Creek trailhead; the Poison Park trailhead is to the left via Poison Park Road (FR 644). Stay left (northwest) on FR 644. Drive another 3 miles to the trailhead at road's end; amenities include plenty of parking (including for horse trailers), hitching posts, a vault toilet, trail register, and wilderness map. Camping at the trailhead is prohibited. *DeLorme: Colorado Atlas & Gazetteer:* Page 77 D7. GPS: N37 32.042' / W107 15.133'.

The Hike

Begin hiking Weminuche Creek Trail 592. You'll cross a large meadow of false hellebore and stunning summer wildflowers, including Colorado's state flower (the columbine) and wild irises. Aspens and pines create a lush canopy. The trail remains fairly level for the first 0.8 mile, then descends moderately along the slope. Long, lazy switchbacks make the grade much easier. Along the way there's a stream crossing or two. You'll descend about 400 feet in 1.6 miles, then level off before descending a second time.

At 2.1 miles you'll come to a ranch fence that protects private property; please do not go beyond this fence. Instead, keep to the right, crossing the drainage ditch, and enter the trees. Ford Hossick Creek at 2.4 miles (the crossing can be rough in early summer) to enter the wilderness.

Next you'll continue into a meadow. Ascend through the open area, watching for wildlife. Look for mountain bluebirds, robins, and turkey vultures. Leave the meadow and continue through the trees, crossing Milk Creek at 3.1 miles.

The trail climbs at a steep grade for nearly a mile, then levels off some. At 4.3 miles you'll hike straight up, going across a semiopen slope with pines, aspens, and lots of ferns. You'll reach level ground again at 4.6 miles, hiking through a mixed grove of young and mature aspens. This is Elk Park, a garden of grasses and wildflowers. You may see wildlife here, including elk. Bald Mountain is visible to the southwest.

As you hike along, the trail skirts the meadow and enters the woods now and then for nearly a mile. You'll have to make several small stream crossings as you go. Look for Granite Peak, which is to the northwest. You'll cross another stream at 5.8 miles. As you hike you'll occasionally see yellow signs that say CENTER STOCK DRIVEWAY. At one time this route was used for moving sheep into the high country.

At 6.3 miles you'll enter deep woods. Descend gradually, crossing another stream before reaching the East Fork Weminuche Creek at 7 miles. The remains of an old bridge wait at the crossing. Here you'll have to decide whether to ford the creek (which can be raging until mid-July) or cross on one of several logs. Whatever you decide, use caution.

There's a big meadow on the north side of the East Fork, but horses are not allowed to graze in this meadow. You'll see the East Fork Weminuche Trail (see Options) heading off to the right as you enter the meadow. Continue straight, entering the trees and walking to another expansive meadow at 7.3 miles. Cross it and climb to the junction of the Weminuche Creek and Divide Trails at 7.8 miles. Take the left fork to Divide Lakes via Divide Trail 539.

At 8.2 miles you'll cross a meadow. There are two more creeks to ford before you reach the lakes, one at 8.3 miles. Next you'll switchback up a moderate slope to 8.8 miles. Continue to the north end of the biggest of the Divide Lakes, 9 miles from where you started. If you spend the night, be sure to sit around the lake and watch for beavers. Please note that the smaller lakes are too swampy for camping and too difficult to reach.

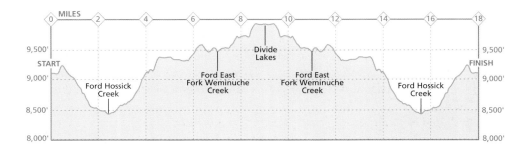

Divide Lakes; Granite Lake

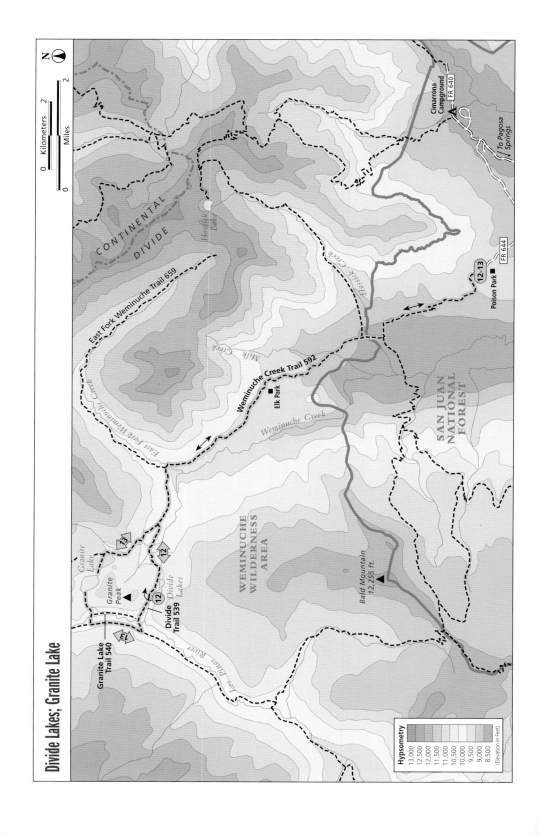

Miles and Directions

0.0 Poison Park trailhead.

2.1 Junction with ranch fence.

2.4 Ford Hossick Creek; wilderness boundary. GPS: N37 33.437' / W107 16.143'.

4.6 Elk Park.

7.0 Ford East Fork Weminuche Creek. GPS: N37 35.864' / W107 18.322'.

7.8 Granite Lake junction on the right.

9.0 North end of Divide Lakes. GPS: N37 35.855' / W107 20.530'.

18.0 Back to Poison Park trailhead.

Options: This hike is especially lovely from the trailhead to the meadow just north of Hossick Creek. It's a great day hike, with moderate switchbacks leading you down to the meadow and then back up to the trailhead. If you're camped at Divide Lakes, you also may want to travel to Granite Lake (see Hike 13 for more information). In addition, from the trail to Divide Lakes, you can access East Fork Weminuche Trail 659 after you ford East Fork Weminuche Creek. You'll have to cross many streams en route to Grouse Rincon Creek, a couple of miles up from the junction.

Hike Information

Local information: Pagosa Springs Chamber of Commerce, Pagosa Springs; (970) 264-2360 or (800) 252-2204; www.pagosachamber.com.
Local events/attractions: The Pagosa Hot Springs, reputed to be the world's hottest mineral springs, are known for their healing qualities. Contact the Springs Resort at (800) 225-0934, www.pagosahotsprings.com; Healing Waters Resort & Spa at (800) 832-5523, www.pshotsprings.com; or Overlook Mineral Springs Spa at (970) 264-4040, www.overlook hotsprings.com, for more information.

Chimney Rock National Monument (designated a national monument by President Barack Obama in September 2012) is open mid-May through the end of September. Call (970) 883-5359 or go to www.chimneyrockco.org.
Accommodations: Pagosa Springs has a number of private campgrounds and motels. You must pass Bridge, Williams Creek, and Teal Campgrounds, all national forest facilities, en route to the trailhead. Cimarrona Campground is the closest campground to the trailhead. It's 0.4 mile northwest of the junction of FR 640 and FR 644, off FR 640. All are fee areas with water and vault toilets.

13 Granite Lake

This day hike or overnight backpack begins at Divide Lakes. Trails lead to both the west and east sides of Granite Lake, but they do not connect, so they are described separately below. The west-side approach involves a 2-mile one-way hike with a gain of 410 feet and a loss of 110 feet. Approach from the east side, and you'll hike 2.9 miles one-way, gaining 620 feet and losing 320 feet en route. You'll see wildflowers and wildlife on this excursion from the Divide Lakes.

See map page 68
Start: North end of Divide Lakes
Distance: 4 miles out and back (west side); 5.8 miles out and back (east side)
Hiking time: About 2 to 3 hours for each hike; 5 to 6 hours if you do both of them. Can also be done as an overnight backpack trip from Divide Lakes.
Difficulty: Moderate
Canine compatibility: Dogs must be under control.
Nearest town: Pagosa Springs
Fees and permits: Free registration (available online, at managing agency, or major trailheads) needed for both day hikers and overnight backpackers. Contact the managing agency for current information.
Maps: USGS Granite Lake; Trails Illustrated Weminuche Wilderness; DeLorme 3D TopoQuad CD-ROM; Maptech Terrain Navigator CD-ROM
Trail contact: San Juan National Forest, Pagosa Ranger District, Pagosa Springs; (970) 264-2268; www.fs.usda.gov/sanjuan
Special considerations: High-creek crossings are possible, especially early in the season. Expect heavy trail use during hunting season. The trail can be slippery and has some steep spots, so horses are not recommended.

Finding the trailhead: These hikes begin at the north side of the largest of the Divide Lakes. It is a 9-mile hike from the Poison Park trailhead to the lakes (Hike 12). To reach the trailhead from downtown Pagosa Springs, head west on US 160 for approximately 3 miles and make a right (north) turn onto Piedra Road, which becomes Archuleta CR 600 immediately upon turning. After 6.2 miles the pavement ends and the road becomes a well-maintained gravel road named FR 631. Stay on gravel FR 631, passing Bridge Campground en route, to the junction of Williams Creek Road (FR 640) at 15.6 miles. Make a right (northwest) onto FR 640, passing both Williams Creek and Teal Campgrounds. You'll reach another fork in 3.5 miles. Here FR 640 goes right to the Williams Creek trailhead; the Poison Park trailhead is to the left via Poison Park Road (FR 644). Stay left (northwest) on FR 644. Drive another 3 miles to the trailhead at road's end; amenities include plenty of parking (including for horse trailers), hitching posts, a vault toilet, trail register, and wilderness map. Camping at the trailhead is prohibited. *DeLorme: Colorado Atlas & Gazetteer:* Page 77 D7. GPS: N37 32.042' / W107 15.133'.

To reach the lakes, take Weminuche Creek Trail 592. It remains fairly level for the first 0.8 mile, then descends moderately. Long, lazy switchbacks make the grade easier. There's a stream crossing or two. You'll descend about 400 feet in 1.6 miles, then level off and descend a second time. At 2.1 miles you'll come to a ranch fence that protects private property; keep to the right, crossing the drainage ditch, and enter the trees. Ford Hossick Creek at 2.4 miles (the crossing can be rough in early summer) to enter the wilderness. You'll go through a meadow and then back into the trees, crossing Milk Creek at 3.1 miles. The trail climbs at a steep grade for nearly a mile. At 4.3 miles you'll ascend sharply, reaching level ground and Elk Park at 4.6 miles. Continue hiking; you will cross several small streams, including one at 5.8 miles. At 6.3 miles you'll enter deep woods and then descend gradually, crossing another stream before reaching the East Fork Weminuche Creek at 7 miles. Ford it cautiously. Continue straight; enter the trees and walk to another meadow at 7.3 miles. Cross it and climb to the junction of the Granite and Divide Trails at 7.8 miles. Take the left fork to Divide Lakes via Divide Trail 539. You'll cross a meadow at 8.2 miles and ford two more creeks before you reach the lakes, one at 8.3 miles. Then you'll switchback up a moderate slope to 8.8 miles. Continue to the north end of the biggest of the Divide Lakes. (**Note:** The smaller lakes are too swampy for camping and too difficult to reach.)

The Hike

Both trails begin from the north side of the largest of the Divide Lakes. To hike to the western side of Granite Lake, descend Divide Trail 539 to a junction at 0.6 mile.

You'll pass the other lakes en route, but you won't see them unless you climb the ridge separating the trail from the lakes. Please note that the trail passes high above the lakes, making them difficult to reach.

At the junction you'll find Trail 540, which leads to Granite Lake. (Be aware that the entire trail is not shown on some maps.) Go right. At this point you are 0.1 mile east of the Pine River, also called Los Pinos in these parts. From the junction look for 12,323-foot Flag Mountain to the south/southwest. As you continue up the valley, notice the willows. This is a good place to look for moose. You also may see snowshoe hares and other interesting creatures.

The trail stays mostly level for the first mile, then a sign points the way up (it really is up) to Granite Lake. The trail is steep with some slippery spots, so traveling it with horses is not recommended. You'll climb to 10,300 feet above sea level at the 2-mile point. The trail levels off as you near the lake.

Fishing at Divide Lakes

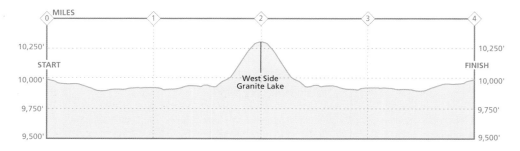

To hike from the Divide Lakes to the east side of Granite Lake, travel east on Divide Trail 539. Ford a creek. You'll reach the junction to Granite Lake at 1.2 miles. Head left on Weminuche Creek Trail 592, hiking up a moderate slope that can be steep at times. Cross a meadow, and at 1.6 miles begin hiking up a very steep slope. The trail is badly rutted in sections, but lovely wildflowers provide a welcome distraction in summer. These include paintbrush, wild strawberries, bluebells, a number of yellow composites, and many more.

After 1.8 miles the trail eases, climbing gradually along Weminuche Creek, which is to the left. At 2 miles you'll ford the creek; notice the waterfall upstream. There's a fork immediately after this crossing. Both nonsystem trails (the Forest Service does not maintain them) lead to the same place. Where they meet (about 100 yards away), you'll see another fork. One trail goes straight uphill. Take the other (left) trail, a cross-country route with nice views. You'll climb at a very steep grade, crossing the mostly open slope to a ridgetop at 2.5 miles.

At 2.6 miles the two trails meet in a meadow. At 10,410 feet above sea level, this is the high point of this trail. Keep left (west), and at 2.8 miles descend one of several steep, rutted trails leading to Granite Lake at 2.9 miles.

The wilderness areas are home to numerous varieties of paintbrush, including narrowleaf, northern, rosy, scarlet, and western yellow. Rosy paintbrush varies in color from rose pink to purple, red, or yellow. Look closely, and you may find a combination of colors.

Rosy paintbrush
(Castilleja rhexifolia)

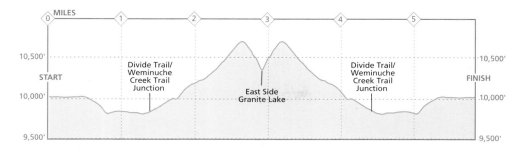

Miles and Directions (west side)

0.0 North side of Divide Lakes. GPS: N37 35.855' / W107 20.530'.

0.6 Junction with Trail 540.

1.0 Steep climb begins.

2.0 Granite Lake (west side). GPS: N37 36.838' / W107 20.397'.

4.0 Back to north side of Divide Lakes.

Miles and Directions (east side)

0.0 North side of Divide Lakes. GPS: N37 35.855' / W107 20.530'.

1.2 Junction with Weminuche Creek Trail 592.

2.0 Weminuche Creek crossing.

2.5 Ridgetop.

2.9 Granite Lake (east side). GPS: N37 36.712' / W107 20.104'.

5.8 Back to north side of Divide Lakes.

Options: You can camp at the Divide Lakes and then either day hike to Granite Lake or pack up your belongings and camp there for a night as well.

Hike Information

Local information: Pagosa Springs Chamber of Commerce, Pagosa Springs; (970) 264-2360 or (800) 252-2204; www.pagosachamber.com.
Local events/attractions: The Pagosa Hot Springs, reputed to be the world's hottest mineral springs, are known for their healing qualities. Contact the Springs Resort at (800) 225-0934, www.pagosahotsprings.com; Healing Waters Resort & Spa at (800) 832-5523, www.pshotsprings.com; or Overlook Mineral Springs Spa at (970) 264-4040, www.overlook hotsprings.com, for more information.

Chimney Rock National Monument (designated a national monument by President Barack Obama in September 2012) is open mid-May through the end of September. Call (970) 883-5359 or go to www.chimneyrockco.org.
Accommodations: Pagosa Springs has a number of private campgrounds and motels. You must pass Bridge, Williams Creek, and Teal Campgrounds, all national forest facilities, en route to the trailhead. Cimarrona Campground is the closest campground to the trailhead. It's 0.4 mile northwest of the junction of FR 640 and FR 644, off FR 640. All are fee areas with water and vault toilets.

14 Williams Creek to the Continental Divide

A wonderful multiday hike to above tree line, with the possibility of seeing wildlife along the way. It's a great way to gain entry into the Weminuche and then connect with one of many other trails in the area.

Start: Williams Creek trailhead

Distance: 20.6 miles out and back

Hiking time: 2- to 3-day backpack

Difficulty: Strenuous due to length and elevation gain of more than 3,000 feet

Canine compatibility: Dogs must be under control.

Nearest town: Pagosa Springs

Fees and permits: Free registration (available online, at managing agency, or major trailheads) needed for both day hikers and overnight backpackers. Contact the managing agency for current information.

Maps: USGS Cimarrona Peak and Little Squaw Creek; Trails Illustrated Weminuche Wilderness; DeLorme 3D TopoQuad CD-ROM; Maptech Terrain Navigator CD-ROM

Trail contact: San Juan National Forest, Pagosa Ranger District, Pagosa Springs; (970) 264-2268; www.fs.usda.gov/sanjuan

Special considerations: High-creek crossings are possible, especially early in the season.

Finding the trailhead: From downtown Pagosa Springs, head west on US 160 for approximately 3 miles and make a right (north) turn onto Piedra Road, which becomes Archuleta CR 600 immediately upon turning. After 6.2 miles the pavement ends and the road becomes a well-maintained gravel road named FR 631. Stay on gravel FR 631, passing Bridge Campground en route, to the junction of Williams Creek Road (FR 640) at 15.6 miles. Make a right (northwest) onto FR 640, passing Williams Creek, Teal, and Cimarrona Campgrounds en route to road's end and the trailhead at 4.8 miles. You'll find Palisades Campground, an equestrian-only campground, near the trailhead. People sans horses will have to stay at Cimarrona, which is only 1 mile back. Trailhead amenities include plenty of room for parking (including horse trailers), water, a trail register, wilderness map, and vault toilet. *DeLorme: Colorado Atlas & Gazetteer:* Page 77 D7. GPS: N37 32.481' / W107 11.875'.

The Hike

After signing in at the trail register, gradually climb along Williams Creek Trail 587, entering the wilderness after 0.2 mile. You'll soon climb moderately—sometimes very steeply—to reach a nice view of Williams Creek and its unique rock formations.

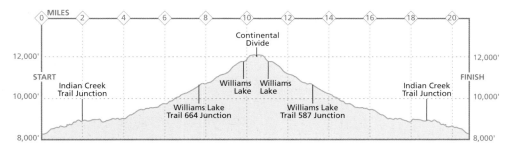

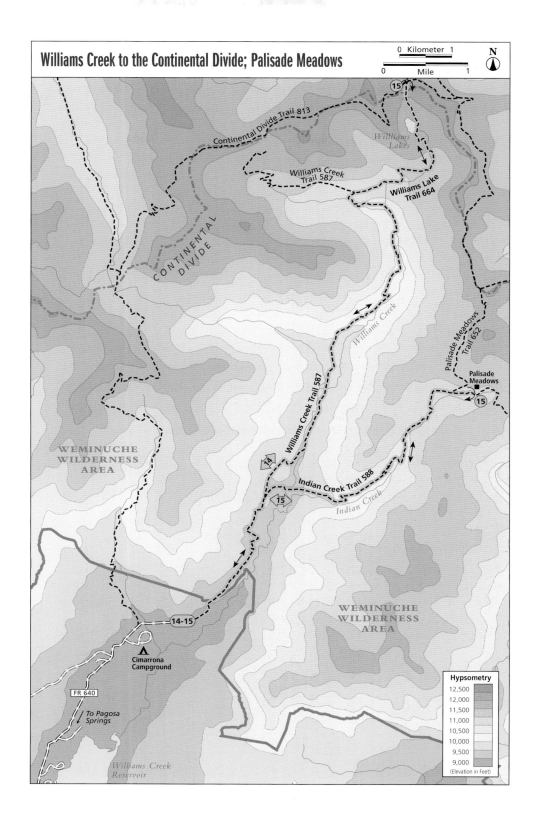

Williams Creek to the Continental Divide; Palisade Meadows

0 Kilometer 1

0 Mile 1

N

Continental Divide Trail 813

Williams Lakes

Williams Creek Trail 587

Williams Lake Trail 664

CONTINENTAL DIVIDE

Williams Creek

Palisade Meadows Trail 652

Palisade Meadows

15

Williams Creek Trail 587

WEMINUCHE WILDERNESS AREA

14

Indian Creek Trail 588

15

Indian Creek

15

WEMINUCHE WILDERNESS AREA

14-15

Cimarrona Campground

FR 640

To Pagosa Springs

Williams Creek Reservoir

Hypsometry

| 12,500 |
| 12,000 |
| 11,500 |
| 11,000 |
| 10,500 |
| 10,000 |
| 9,500 |
| 9,000 |

(Elevation in Feet)

Switchbacking even higher above the creek, you'll come to a stream crossing after 1.2 miles.

Continue on, crossing another stream at 1.4 miles. You'll reach the Indian Creek Trail 588 junction at the 2-mile point. If you'd like to hike to Palisade Meadows, turn here (see Hike 15 for more information). Otherwise, continue straight ahead through a meadow, then head into the trees for a short distance. You'll cross several small streams en route and enter a big meadow at 2.3 miles. Circle around to the north end, where you'll enter the trees again and climb a ridge, topping off at 2.7 miles. Now descend along Williams Creek. You'll eventually ford it at 3 miles.

Look for a spur trail off to the left (west) at 3.5 miles; it leads to a bench along Williams Creek. At 3.7 miles the trail enters a meadow and soon afterward fords Williams Creek. This crossing may be a bit easier than your last one, though there are no guarantees.

You'll cross more meadows and streams as you proceed to the Continental Divide. Aspens decorate the area, especially in fall when their vibrant colors brighten up the place. At the 5.3-mile point, a spur trail leads near the creek. The main route

American pikas live on talus slopes at high elevation. While hiking in the high country, listen for their high-pitched squeaks. The small, hamster-size mammals make hay from flowers and grasses by curing them in the sun and storing them under rocks. Pikas do not hibernate in the winter; instead, they travel under the snow in tunnels that connect their "hay barns." Pikas have tiny ears and feet and no tail, thus they preserve body heat.

American pika (Ochotona princeps)

switchbacks upward. Soon after look for some interesting rock formations, with lichen blanketing the rocks and pikas scampering about them. You'll cross a meadowy side slope as you continue across several small streams.

After 5.8 miles you'll hike near Williams Creek again. Ford the creek at 6.5 miles, then cross it once more at 7 miles. You'll come to a junction with Williams Lake Trail 664 at 7.6 miles. Williams Creek Trail 587 continues up the West Fork (left) and leads to the Continental Divide, but you should keep to the right and take Trail 664. You'll ascend a steep grade, dropping a mere 30 feet to cross a stream at 8.1 miles. You'll then climb some more. The trail eases as you follow the contour line to cross two more streams at 8.7 miles.

The trail continues, deeply rutted in places, as you make the very steep climb to several small lakes. The largest of the Williams Lakes is at 9.6 miles. Continue to Continental Divide Trail 813 at 12,010 feet by ascending another 0.7 mile to the top at 10.3 miles.

Miles and Directions

0.0 Williams Creek trailhead.

0.2 Wilderness boundary.

2.0 Indian Creek Trail junction. GPS: N37 34.046' / W107 10.958'.

3.7 Ford Williams Creek.

7.6 Williams Lake Trail junction. GPS: N37 37.079' / W107 9.955'.

9.6 Largest of Williams Lakes. GPS: N37 37.762' / W107 9.162'.

10.3 Continental Divide Trail. GPS: N37 38.247' / W107 9.361'.

20.6 Back to Williams Creek trailhead.

Hike Information

Local information: Pagosa Springs Chamber of Commerce, Pagosa Springs; (970) 264-2360 or (800) 252-2204; www.pagosachamber.com.
Local events/attractions: The Pagosa Hot Springs, reputed to be the world's hottest mineral springs, are known for their healing qualities. Contact the Springs Resort at (800) 225-0934, www.pagosahotsprings.com; Healing Waters Resort & Spa at (800) 832-5523, www.pshotsprings.com; or Overlook Mineral Springs Spa at (970) 264-4040, www.overlook hotsprings.com, for more information.

Chimney Rock National Monument (designated a national monument by President Barack Obama in September 2012) is open mid-May through the end of September. Call (970) 883-5359 or go to www.chimneyrockco.org.
Accommodations: Pagosa Springs has a number of private campgrounds and motels. You must pass Bridge, Williams Creek, Teal, and Cimarrona Campgrounds, all national forest facilities, en route to the trailhead. All are fee areas with water and vault toilets.

15 Palisade Meadows

Hikers will enjoy wildflowers and wildlife on this path along both Williams and Indian Creeks. The trip makes for a long day hike or a two-day backpack, and it provides access to other parts of the wilderness.

See map page 75
Start: Williams Creek trailhead
Distance: 11.6 miles out and back
Hiking time: About 4 to 8 hours
Difficulty: Strenuous due to length and elevation gain of more than 2,000 feet
Canine compatibility: Dogs must be under control.
Nearest town: Pagosa Springs
Fees and permits: Free registration (available online, at managing agency, or major trailheads) needed for both day hikers and

overnight backpackers. Contact the managing agency for current information.
Maps: USGS Cimarrona Peak and Palomino Mountain; Trails Illustrated Weminuche Wilderness; DeLorme 3D TopoQuad CD-ROM; Maptech Terrain Navigator CD-ROM
Trail contact: San Juan National Forest, Pagosa Ranger District, Pagosa Springs; (970) 264-2268; www.fs.usda.gov/sanjuan
Special considerations: Some high-creek crossings are possible, especially early in the season.

Finding the trailhead: From downtown Pagosa Springs, head west on US 160 for approximately 3 miles and make a right (north) turn onto Piedra Road, which becomes Archuleta CR 600 immediately upon turning. After 6.2 miles the pavement ends and the road becomes a well-maintained gravel road named FR 631. Stay on gravel FR 631, passing Bridge Campground en route, to the junction of Williams Creek Road (FR 640) at 15.6 miles. Make a right (northwest) onto FR 640, passing Williams Creek, Teal, and Cimarrona Campgrounds en route to road's end and the trailhead at 4.8 miles. You'll find Palisades Campground, an equestrian-only campground, near the trailhead. People sans horses will have to stay at Cimarrona, which is only 1 mile back. Trailhead amenities include plenty of room for parking (including horse trailers), water, a trail register, wilderness map, and vault toilet. *DeLorme: Colorado Atlas & Gazetteer:* Page 77 D7. GPS: N37 32.481' / W107 11.875'.

The Hike

After signing in at the trailhead register, hike Williams Creek Trail 587 at a gradual grade. You'll enter the Weminuche Wilderness after 0.2 mile. Next you'll climb—sometimes at a very steep grade—to a nice view of Williams Creek and its unique

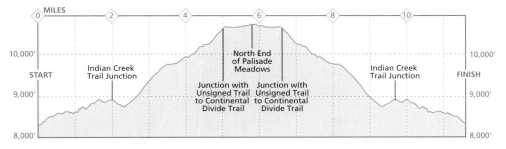

rock formations. After 1.1 miles you'll start to switchback even higher above the creek. You'll cross one stream at 1.2 miles and another at 1.4 miles. You'll reach the Indian Creek Trail 588 junction at 2 miles. (You can continue up Williams Creek as a side trip if you wish; see Hike 14 for more information.)

Turn right (east) onto the Indian Creek Trail. You'll descend here, eventually dropping about 90 feet to a stream. Hikers obviously camp at this crossing, but please don't. In the wilderness you need to camp at least 100 feet from the water. Continuing on, you'll ford Williams Creek at 2.3 miles. By summer's end you may be able to do so with your shoes and socks on, keeping your feet dry.

The trail climbs after the Williams Creek crossing, sometimes at a steep grade. Switchbacks help make the grade more bearable. After 4.3 miles you'll ford Indian Creek, and then you'll do it again at 4.7 miles. The trail gets very steep as you head up to an open slope beyond the ford.

Hike along Indian Creek to reach an unsigned trail junction at the 5-mile mark. From this point the Indian Creek Trail continues to the right (east), linking up to the Continental Divide Trail. You can see the bald dome of an unnamed 12,153-foot peak to the north.

Take Palisade Meadows Trail 651, which continues north through Palisade Meadows and eventually connects with the Continental Divide Trail, too. Continue across Palisade Meadows to mile 5.8 and the end of this hike.

Miles and Directions

0.0 Williams Creek trailhead.
0.2 Wilderness boundary.
2.0 Indian Creek Trail junction. GPS: N37 34.046' / W107 10.958'.
2.3 Ford Williams Creek.
5.0 Unsigned junction to the Continental Divide Trail.
5.8 Palisade Meadows. GPS: N37 34.966' / W107 8.631'.
11.6 Back to Williams Creek trailhead.

Hike Information

Local information: Pagosa Springs Chamber of Commerce, Pagosa Springs; (970) 264-2360 or (800) 252-2204; www.pagosachamber.com.
Local events/attractions: The Pagosa Hot Springs, reputed to be the world's hottest mineral springs, are known for their healing qualities. Contact the Springs Resort at (800) 225-0934, www.pagosahotsprings.com; Healing Waters Resort & Spa at (800) 832-5523, www.pshotsprings.com; or Overlook Mineral Springs Spa at (970) 264-4040, www.overlookhotsprings.com, for more information.

Chimney Rock National Monument (designated a national monument by President Barack Obama in September 2012) is open mid-May through the end of September. Call (970) 883-5359 or go to www.chimneyrockco.org.
Accommodations: Pagosa Springs has a number of private campgrounds and motels. You must pass Bridge, Williams Creek, Teal, and Cimarrona Campgrounds, all national forest facilities, en route to the trailhead. All are fee areas with water and vault toilets.

16 Piedra Falls

This short day hike to pretty Piedra Falls is a wonderful walk for children.

Start: Piedra Falls trailhead
Distance: 1.2 miles out and back
Hiking time: About 1 hour
Difficulty: Easy
Canine compatibility: Dogs must be under control.
Nearest town: Pagosa Springs
Fees and permits: Free registration (available online, at managing agency, or major trailheads) needed for both day hikers and overnight backpackers. Contact the managing agency for current information.

Maps: USGS Pagosa Peak; Trails Illustrated Weminuche Wilderness; DeLorme 3D Topo-Quad CD-ROM; Maptech Terrain Navigator CD-ROM
Trail contact: San Juan National Forest, Pagosa Ranger District, Pagosa Springs; (970) 264-2268; www.fs.usda.gov/sanjuan
Special considerations: Use extreme caution, and please don't climb the slippery rocks near the falls; a young girl fell and drowned here in the summer of 1998.

Finding the trailhead: From Hot Springs Boulevard and US 160 in downtown Pagosa Springs, head west on US 160. After 2.8 miles make a right (north) onto Piedra Road, which immediately becomes Archuleta CR 600. After 6.2 miles the pavement ends and the good gravel road is now called FR 631. Drive another 11.4 miles to reach a fork with FR 636, aka Middle Fork Road. Go right (northeast) on gravel FR 636. A sign points the way to Piedra Falls. Continue 1.8 miles to another junction. FR 636 continues north at this point, but you'll want to stay on Toner Road (FR 637), which winds around to the east. At the junction another sign points the way to Piedra Falls. Travel the maintained road for 7.5 miles to the trailhead. You'll find plenty of space to park and lots of space for a primitive camp along the East Fork Piedra River. There are no other amenities. *DeLorme: Colorado Atlas & Gazetteer:* Page 88 A1. GPS: N37 28.741' / W107 6.099'.

The Hike

From the marked trailhead, follow Piedra Falls Trail 671 along the East Fork Piedra River for 0.2 mile. A sign points the way at a trail intersection. You'll head into the trees (conifers and aspens) until the 0.5-mile point. After leaving the shelter of the trees, you'll reach the multitiered falls at 0.6 mile.

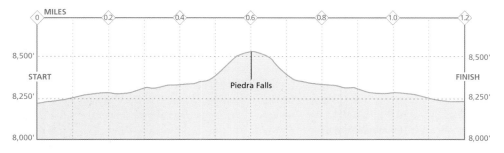

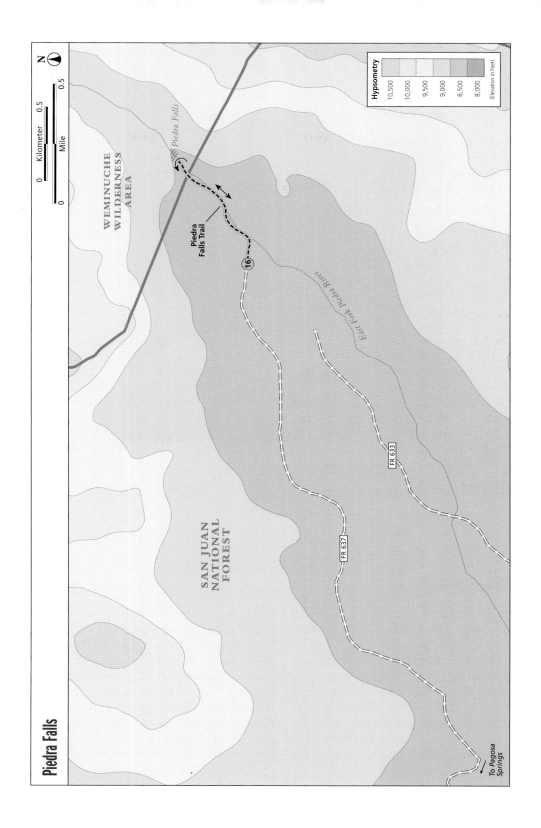

Piedra Falls

Piedra Falls

Miles and Directions

0.0   Piedra Falls trailhead.
0.6   Piedra Falls. GPS: N37 28.993' / W107 5.729'.
1.2   Back to Piedra Falls trailhead.

Hike Information

Local information: Pagosa Springs Chamber of Commerce, Pagosa Springs; (970) 264-2360 or (800) 252-2204; www.pagosachamber.com.
Local events/attractions: The Pagosa Hot Springs, reputed to be the world's hottest mineral springs, are known for their healing qualities. Contact the Springs Resort at (800) 225-0934, www.pagosahotsprings.com; Healing Waters Resort & Spa at (800) 832-5523, www.pshotsprings.com; or Overlook Mineral Springs Spa at (970) 264-4040, www.overlook hotsprings.com, for more information.

Chimney Rock National Monument (designated a national monument by President Barack Obama in September 2012) is open mid-May through the end of September. Call (970) 883-5359 or go to www.chimneyrockco.org.
Accommodations: Pagosa Springs has a number of private campgrounds and motels. There's room for a primitive camp near the trailhead.

17 Fourmile Lake Loop

You'll find wildflowers, wildlife, a scenic lake, and waterfalls on this loop. The loop is done in clockwise fashion, traveling up the Anderson Trail and down the Fourmile Creek Trail.

Start: Fourmile Creek trailhead
Distance: 12.4-mile loop
Hiking time: About 6 to 8 hours for a long day hike, or 2-day backpack
Difficulty: Strenuous due to length and elevation gain of more than 2,000 feet
Canine compatibility: Dogs must be under control.
Nearest town: Pagosa Springs
Fees and permits: Free registration (available online, at managing agency, or major trailheads) needed for both day hikers and overnight backpackers. Contact the managing agency for current information.
Maps: USGS Pagosa Peak; Trails Illustrated Weminuche Wilderness; DeLorme 3D TopoQuad CD-ROM; Maptech Terrain Navigator CD-ROM
Trail contact: San Juan National Forest, Pagosa Ranger District, Pagosa Springs; (970) 264-2268; www.fs.usda.gov/sanjuan
Special considerations: High-creek crossings are possible, especially early in the season. Horses are not recommended on the trail above Fourmile Falls.

Finding the trailhead: To reach the Fourmile Creek trailhead, travel west on US 160 from the junction of Hot Springs Boulevard and US 160 in downtown Pagosa Springs. After 0.2 mile make a right (north) onto Lewis Street. The paved road forks immediately; keep straight (north) on North Fifth Street. Travel another 0.4 mile to the junction of Fifth and Juanita Streets. Keep straight (north) here, driving on paved Fourmile Road (Archuleta CR 400). The road not only turns to well-maintained gravel en route, but it also becomes FR 645, a narrow lane with turnouts. You'll reach the end of the road and the trailhead after another 12.7 miles. Trail amenities include hitching posts, a vault toilet, and a parking area for those with horse trailers. The upper parking lot is for cars and includes a vault toilet. There's a trail register and wilderness map as well. Camping isn't allowed at either trailhead. *DeLorme: Colorado Atlas & Gazetteer:* Page 88 A1. GPS: N37 24.561' / W107 03.166'.

The Hike

At the trailhead you'll find Anderson Trail 579 on the left and Fourmile Trail 569 straight ahead. You can do the loop in either direction (or forget the loop altogether

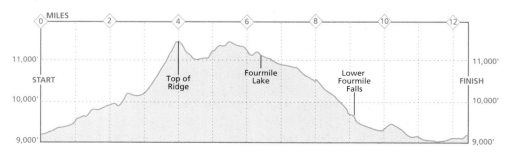

and walk directly to Fourmile Falls, a popular destination). However, the Forest Service recommended that I climb the Anderson Trail and descend via the Fourmile Trail because of the steepness and deteriorating condition of the latter.

Head up the Anderson Trail, looking for wildlife such as elk and deer and wildflowers such as bluebells, larkspur, wild roses, spirea, paintbrush, primrose, and marsh marigolds. You'll cross several streams as you climb the gradual-to-moderate slope. After about 0.4 mile there's a view to the south. You'll switchback up to a wilderness sign at 0.9 mile, and a short time later travel through an area where aspens are predominant. It's a grand place come fall. Down the trail, pines and spruces take top prize.

You'll cross an open slope farther ahead, then it's back into the trees and more switchbacks as you continue up and up. Along the way you'll see Pagosa Peak and hike across an open slope, a nice place to view the aftereffects of avalanches. The switchbacks continue, sending you back into the trees at 3.7 miles and to the top of a ridge at 4 miles. Next you'll descend through trees before entering a lovely meadow at 4.9 miles.

The trail climbs to 5.4 miles and then descends again, crossing a beautiful, wildflower-blessed stream at 6.2 miles. Continue to the 6.4-mile point, where you'll find Fourmile Lake. Set among enormous granite boulders, with wildflowers all around, the lake is a wonderful place to explore.

The Anderson Trail continues beyond the lake, descending at an easy-to-moderate grade. It steepens for a bit before the Fourmile Trail junction at 7.5 miles. If you head

Found along streams, American dippers bob up and down. Watch for them as they stand on rocks, dive under the water, swim, and walk on the bottom of swift streams while searching for insects and small fish.

American dipper (Cinclus mexicanus)

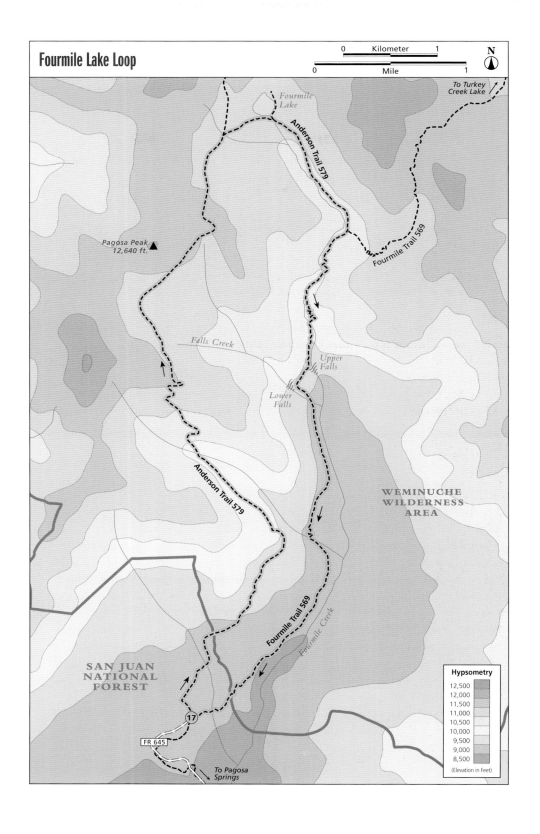

Fourmile Lake Loop

0 — Kilometer — 1

0 — Mile — 1

N

To Turkey Creek Lake

Fourmile Lake

Anderson Trail 579

Fourmile Trail 569

Pagosa Peak
12,640 ft.

Falls Creek

Upper Falls

Lower Falls

Anderson Trail 579

WEMINUCHE WILDERNESS AREA

Fourmile Trail 569

Fourmile Creek

SAN JUAN NATIONAL FOREST

17

FR 645

To Pagosa Springs

Hypsometry

12,500
12,000
11,500
11,000
10,500
10,000
9,500
9,000
8,500

(Elevation in Feet)

Lower Fourmile Falls in the fall

east, you'll reach Turkey Creek Lake (see Hike 18 for more information). The loop described here continues south. You will now be hiking the Fourmile Trail.

Streams rush throughout the area early in the season, with the ground quite boggy at times. Prepare to get wet! At 8 miles you'll cross Fourmile Creek. Look for American dippers in this and other streams. These fascinating birds walk and swim underwater, searching for insect larvae and fish eggs. You'll hike near the creek and then away from it, sometimes descending via a steep, rocky trail.

Notice the waterfall at 8.1 miles. In another 0.1 mile you'll cross Fourmile Creek once again. You'll be able to see another falls back up the creek as you cross again at 8.5 miles. There's a wonderful cascade on the left at 8.9 miles, and as you continue dropping steeply, you'll see a double falls on the left. This is known locally as the Upper Falls.

You'll come to the Lower Falls on the right at 9.2 miles. This is the most impressive of the falls along this trail, tumbling about 300 feet from cliffs to the rocks below. As you head around the loop, you'll cross Falls Creek, which flows from the falls.

LOVELY LEAVES

Fall is a magical time of year. It's also a colorful time, as Colorado's aspens, cottonwoods, willows, and other deciduous trees and plants change to varying shades of gold, red, and orange. Weather affects the fall colors so that no two autumns are the same. If there is excessive summer rainfall, it can reduce anthocyanin levels in the leaves, and dull colors may result. Conversely, a severe drought can speed up color change. The result? Leaves may fall from trees prematurely. For the best fall colors, hope for bright, sunny days and cool nights. Dry weather is also important. If all three conditions exist, you may end up with a rich, colorful autumn.

Fortunately, the trail eases as you hike south. Look to the east for a good view of the ragged crests of Eagle Mountain. You'll have to cross several more creeks, enter a meadow, and then hike back into the trees as you descend. Exit the wilderness around 11.8 miles, and return to the trailhead at 12.4 miles.

Miles and Directions

0.0 Fourmile Creek trailhead.
0.9 Wilderness boundary.
4.0 Top of ridge. GPS: N37 26.526' / W107 3.340'.
4.9 Meadow.
6.4 Fourmile Lake. GPS: N37 28.105' / W10 2.735'.
7.5 Fourmile Trail junction.
9.2 Lower Fourmile Falls. GPS: N37 26.513' / W107 2.467'.
11.8 Wilderness boundary.
12.4 Back to Fourmile Creek trailhead.

Hike Information

Local information: Pagosa Springs Chamber of Commerce, Pagosa Springs; (970) 264-2360 or (800) 252-2204; www.pagosachamber.com.
Local events/attractions: The Pagosa Hot Springs, reputed to be the world's hottest mineral springs, are known for their healing qualities. Contact the Springs Resort at (800) 225-0934, www.pagosahotsprings.com; Healing Waters Resort & Spa at (800) 832-5523, www.pshotsprings.com; or Overlook Mineral Springs Spa at (970) 264-4040, www.overlook hotsprings.com, for more information.

Chimney Rock National Monument (designated a national monument by President Barack Obama in September 2012) is open mid-May through the end of September. Call (970) 883-5359 or go to www.chimneyrockco.org.
Accommodations: Pagosa Springs offers a number of private campgrounds and motels.

18 Turkey Creek Trail

Wildlife and a scenic creek await you on the Turkey Creek Trail. Day hike the first few miles, or make it a four- to five-day backpack on the entire trail, the longest in this part of the wilderness.

Start: Turkey Creek trailhead
Distance: 40.6 miles out and back
Hiking time: 4- to 5-day backpack
Difficulty: Strenuous due to length and elevation gain of more than 4,600 feet; easy if you cover only the first few miles as a day hike
Canine compatibility: Dogs must be under control.
Nearest town: Pagosa Springs
Fees and permits: Free registration (available online, at managing agency, or major trailheads) needed for both day hikers and overnight backpackers. Contact the managing agency for current information.
Maps: USGS Saddle Mountain, Pagosa Peak, and Palomino Mountain; Trails Illustrated Weminuche Wilderness; DeLorme 3D TopoQuad CD-ROM; Maptech Terrain Navigator CD-ROM
Trail contact: San Juan National Forest, Pagosa Ranger District, Pagosa Springs; (970) 264-2268; www.fs.usda.gov/sanjuan
Special considerations: High-creek crossings are possible, especially early in the season.

Finding the trailhead: Reach the Turkey Creek trailhead by heading east from Pagosa Springs for 6.6 miles or southwest from South Fork for 34.8 miles via US 160. Go north onto signed Jackson Mountain Road (FR 037), a dirt road. Drive 4.5 miles to the end of the road and trailhead. *DeLorme: Colorado Atlas & Gazetteer:* Page 88 B2. GPS: N37 22.627' / W106 58.005'.

The Hike

After signing in at the trail register, begin the gradual descent via Turkey Creek Trail 580 to a gate at 0.6 mile. After passing through this gate, be sure to close it. Soon after you'll begin climbing an easy-to-moderate grade. After 0.8 mile you'll have to cross an irrigation canal via a wooden plank bridge.

Be sure to enjoy the spruce and pine forest as you continue. At 2.8 miles you'll cross a stream and hike across a lush meadow with a view of Saddle Mountain, 12,033 feet above sea level. You'll cross more streams en route to the wilderness boundary at 5.2 miles. In another 0.1 mile you'll have to ford Turkey Creek. Expect to get your feet wet here at almost any time of the year.

At 5.7 miles you'll cross yet another creek, then begin a steep climb (moderate on occasion), crossing several more streams along the way. At 8.1 miles the trail flattens out somewhat; it fords Turkey Creek at 8.3 miles.

You'll climb at a moderate grade across a semiopen slope until the 8.7-mile point, where the trail flattens and parallels a meadow. Ford Turkey Creek again at 8.9 miles. The trail crosses another stream at 9.2 miles and begins a steep climb. There's a nice waterfall on Turkey Creek after 9.3 miles.

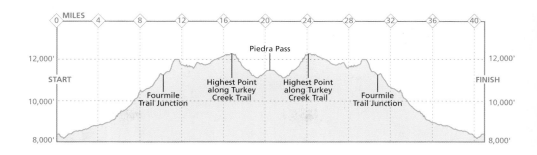

You must cross several more streams en route to a junction at 10.1 miles. From here you will hike toward the Continental Divide at Piedra Pass by continuing right (northeast) on the Turkey Creek Trail. (If you want to reach Turkey Creek Lake via Fourmile Trail, go left; it's only 0.2 mile and a steep, 100-foot descent away.)

You'll climb a steep grade to the 11.2-mile mark, where you'll circle the first of several scenic basins. Look for wildflowers in early summer. Now it's a moderate 0.1-mile climb to the top of a ridge. From the ridgetop there's a grand view of South River Peak, Red Mountain, Sawtooth Mountain, and a whole lot more. Descend on a moderate slope, entering the middle basin where there's a little lake.

You'll reach a creek and a wooden post-marker at 11.7 miles. Soon afterward you'll hike into the trees and then across a side slope. After 12.4 miles the trail enters another basin, reaching the lowest part of the basin at 12.6 miles. Cross Rainbow Creek at 12.9 miles, then climb moderately to 13.4 miles and the top of the ridge. From here the route follows the elevation contour line, where there's an easy-to-moderate ascent past the steep walls of the massive rock formation known as the Puerto Blanco ("white door" in Spanish).

At 14.1 miles you'll cross another creek. Follow the wooden post-markers as you continue. If they're difficult to see, just aim for the ridge to the northeast. You will pass a scenic bench before you reach the top of another ridge after 15.1 miles. Nice views continue from this point on.

Continue hiking across the high, open plateau to 16.5 miles and the highest point along the Turkey Creek Trail. After enjoying the view, descend some steep switchbacks to 17.4 miles and a creek crossing. It's a moderate descent to where you'll cross a stream, paralleling a vast meadow along the East Fork Piedra River.

Wooden post-markers may be scarce as you enter the meadow at 18.5 miles. Walk to the north/northwest, aiming for the trees. You will cross the East Fork Piedra along the way. The Turkey Creek Trail is in the trees at 18.9 miles, along with a definite spur trail heading northwest up a drainage to Palomino Mountain. Stay in the trees, aiming northeast and up the East Fork Piedra drainage.

You'll cross a creek after 19.1 miles. You are now hiking through the meadow again, paralleling the East Fork Piedra River. Cross another stream or two en route to the junction with Continental Divide Trail (CDT) 813 at 20.1 miles. Signs point the way back to the East Fork Piedra River, Turkey Creek Lake, and the Turkey Lake

Turkey Creek Trail; West Fork San Juan Trail

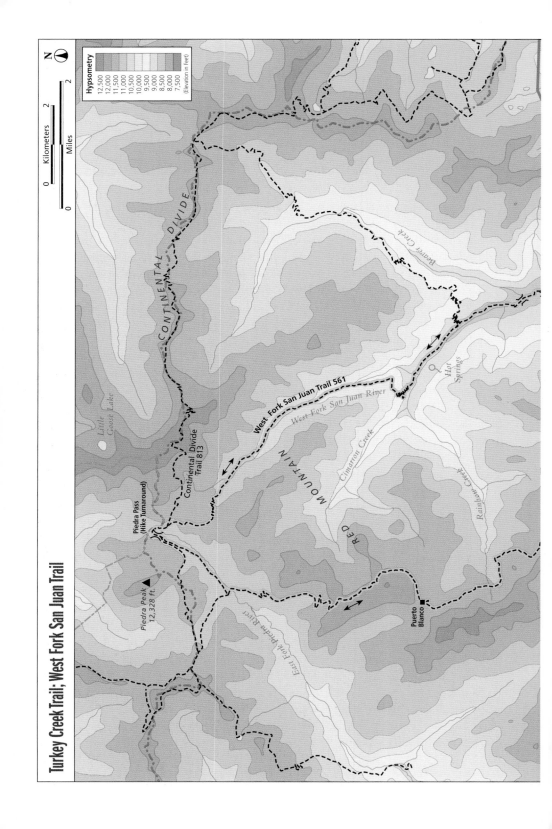

Hypsometry

12,500
12,000
11,500
11,000
10,500
10,000
9,500
9,000
8,500
8,000
7,500

(Elevation in Feet)

N

Kilometers
0   2

Miles
0   2

CONTINENTAL   DIVIDE

Little
Goose Lake

Piedra Pass
(Hike Turnaround)

Piedra Peak
12,328 ft.

Continental Divide
Trail 813

West Fork San Juan Trail 561

West Fork San Juan River

RED

MOUNTAIN

Cimarron Creek

Rainbow Creek

Bear Creek

Hot
Springs

Puerto
Blanco

East Fork Piedra River

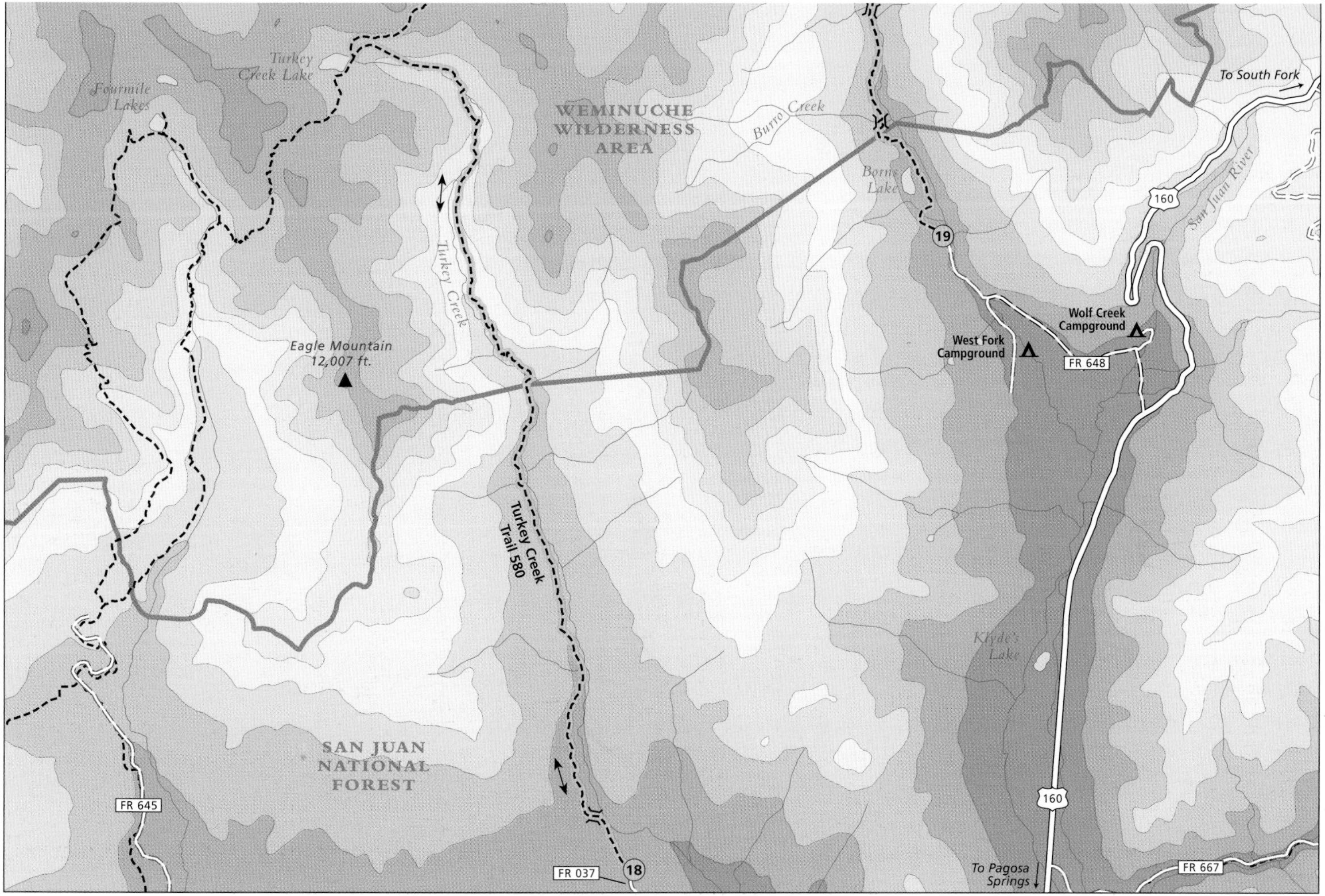

To South Fork

San Juan River

160

FR 667

Wolf Creek
Campground

FR 648

West Fork
Campground

160

Ryder's Lake

To Pagosa
Springs

19

Bonc
Lake

Burro Creek

WEMINUCHE
WILDERNESS
AREA

18

FR 037

Turkey Creek
Trail 580

Turkey Creek

Eagle Mountain
12,007 ft.

SAN JUAN
NATIONAL
FOREST

Turkey
Creek Lake

Fourmile
Lake

FR 645

Trail. A CDT sign points the way west. Continue on to Piedra Pass at 20.3 miles. Just beyond is the junction with West Fork San Juan Trail 561, which leads to the West Fork trailhead (see Option).

Miles and Directions

0.0   Turkey Creek trailhead.

5.2   Wilderness boundary.

8.3   Ford Turkey Creek.

10.1   Fourmile Trail junction. GPS: N37 28.701' / W107 0.887'.

12.9   Rainbow Creek crossing.

16.5   Highest point along Turkey Creek Trail.

18.5   Meadow along East Fork Piedra River.

20.1   Continental Divide Trail. GPS: N37 34.205' / W107 0.206'.

20.3   Piedra Pass. GPS: N37 34.251' / W107 0.053'.

40.6   Back to Turkey Creek trailhead.

Option: Turkey Creek Trail can be combined with Hike 19 (West Fork San Juan Trail) for a shuttle hike known locally as the Rainbow Trail. The combined route is 32.3 miles long.

Hike Information

Local information: Pagosa Springs Chamber of Commerce, Pagosa Springs; (970) 264-2360 or (800) 252-2204; www.pagosachamber.com.

Local events/attractions: The Pagosa Hot Springs, reputed to be the world's hottest mineral springs, are known for their healing qualities. Contact the Springs Resort at (800) 225-0934, www.pagosahotsprings.com; Healing Waters Resort & Spa at (800) 832-5523, www.pshotsprings.com; or Overlook Mineral Springs Spa at (970) 264-4040, www.overlook hotsprings.com, for more information.

Chimney Rock National Monument (designated a national monument by President Barack Obama in September 2012) is open mid-May through the end of September. Call (970) 883-5359 or go to www.chimneyrockco.org.

Accommodations: Pagosa Springs offers a number of private campgrounds and motels.

19 West Fork San Juan Trail

Hike the West Fork Trail, and you'll find a scenic river, hot springs, wildlife, and wild-flowers. It's a nice day hike if you concentrate on the first few miles of the trail, or you can make it a multiday backpack to Piedra Pass.

See map pages 90-91
Start: West Fork trailhead
Distance: 24 miles out and back
Hiking time: 2- to 3-day backpack
Difficulty: Strenuous due to length and elevation gain of more than 3,600 feet; moderate if you cover only the first few miles as a day hike
Canine compatibility: Dogs must be under control.
Nearest town: Pagosa Springs
Fees and permits: Free registration (available online, at managing agency, or major trailheads) needed for both day hikers and overnight backpackers. Contact the managing agency for current information.

Maps: USGS Saddle Mountain and South River Peak; Trails Illustrated Weminuche Wilderness; DeLorme 3D TopoQuad CD-ROM; Maptech Terrain Navigator CD-ROM
Trail contact: San Juan National Forest, Pagosa Ranger District, Pagosa Springs; (970) 264-2268; www.fs.usda.gov/sanjuan
Special considerations: There is no overnight stock use near the hot springs. Camping is allowed only in designated sites; campfires are not permitted. High-creek crossings are possible, especially early in the season. The West Fork Fire ravaged much of the area in June 2013, so use caution when hiking through the burn area.

Finding the trailhead: Reach the West Fork trailhead by heading east from Pagosa Springs for 13.6 miles on US 160, or southwest from South Fork for 27.8 miles via the same road. Turn north onto signed West Fork Road (FR 648), a dirt road. As you travel along, you'll enter the San Juan National Forest and pass the West Fork Campground at 1.6 miles. Cross a bridge over the West Fork San Juan River after another 0.6 mile. Keep right and continue to the signed trailhead, a mere 0.8 mile past the bridge. *DeLorme: Colorado Atlas & Gazetteer:* Page 88 A2. GPS: N37 27.468', W106 55.165'.

The Hike

There's a vault toilet and a registration box at the trailhead for West Fork Trail 561. From there climb up the dirt road at a moderate grade, gaining 150 feet en route to the Borns Lake Ranch entrance at 0.3 mile. You'll walk past three cabins, crossing an unnamed creek just before reaching the third cabin at 0.4 mile. Here the road forks (a sign marks the trail) to the right and continues past a small lake not visible from the trail.

Views of the river are possible off and on beginning around the 1-mile mark. About the same time you will find new joy in walking a trail instead of an old road. At 1.2 miles you'll enter the national forest. All of the PRIVATE PROPERTY–KEEP OUT signs will now disappear.

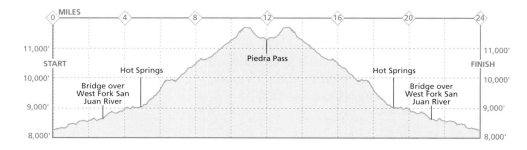

You'll mostly climb as you travel through the previously burned area. Although much of the trail is of a moderate grade, expect some short, steep sections. These may be easier to bear if you concentrate on the columbine, bluebells, wild strawberries, ferns, vine maples, and many other varieties of plants and flowers along the trail. Head away from the ridge overlooking the river and into a false hellebore–blessed meadow at 1.4 miles.

You'll enter the wilderness at 1.6 miles and cross a bridge over Burro Creek soon afterward. There is another false hellebore–laden meadow—and more views of nearby peaks—around the 2-mile mark. As you head back into the trees, expect to cross some small creeks. The trail then switchbacks down about 30 feet to the West Fork San Juan River at 2.7 miles. At 2.9 miles you cross the river via a wonderful wooden bridge.

Proceed through the trees to a bridge over Beaver Creek at 3.1 miles. A new portion of the trail goes north from this point, climbing at a moderate grade and then gradually ascending to the Beaver Creek Trail junction, at 4.4 miles. Take this route. You will continue to climb gradually and cross more streams en route to a heavily used camp area at 5 miles, on a bluff above the hot springs. Hikers must camp in designated campsites. Campfires are not permitted.

The springs are several spur trails away. Rock barriers usually keep the cold river water from mixing with the hot sulphur water. If you visit on a high-river day, however, the cooler river will mix with the hot springs, making a dip in the pool less than delightful.

Continue up the trail. You'll pass an open meadow, gradually climbing to 5.6 miles and the West Fork San Juan River. Ford it (the crossing may be difficult in early summer). You are now close to where Rainbow and Cimarrona Creeks unite with the river. Climb steep switchbacks to 6.4 miles and a nice place for a break. After you've rested, drop over the ridge and proceed high above the West Fork San Juan River. You'll hike through the trees, crossing a stream now and then. Although the ascent is mostly moderate, you will encounter some steep sections.

Drop to the West Fork San Juan River at 8.1 miles, and ford it again. You'll cross an occasional meadow but hike mostly in the trees. Some are marked with red tags.

Climb a moderate slope to another river crossing. This point, 9.5 miles from where you started, is near the headwaters of the West Fork San Juan River. The crossing should be fairly easy. The trail then continues in the trees and later goes across a semiopen slope to a ridge at 11,620 feet above sea level. From the 10.8-mile point, the trail winds around the slope, offering views of the East Fork Piedra River drainage. Continue across the slope and into the trees. You'll emerge in time to meet the Continental Divide Trail at Piedra Pass at 12 miles.

Miles and Directions

0.0 West Fork San Juan River trailhead.

2.9 Bridge over West Fork San Juan River.

5.0 Hot springs. GPS: N37 30.526' / W106 56.832'.

5.6 Ford West Fork San Juan River (first time).

8.1 Ford West Fork San Juan River (second time).

10.8 High point on ridge.

12.0 Piedra Pass. GPS: N37 34.251' / W107 0.053'.

24.0 Back to West Fork San Juan River trailhead.

Option: You can combine this trip with Hike 18 (Turkey Creek Trail) for a long shuttle hike known locally as the Rainbow Trail. The combined route is 32.3 miles long.

Hike Information

Local information: Pagosa Springs Chamber of Commerce, Pagosa Springs; (970) 264-2360 or (800) 252-2204; www.pagosachamber.com.

Local events/attractions: The Pagosa Hot Springs, reputed to be the world's hottest mineral springs, are known for their healing qualities. Contact the Springs Resort at (800) 225-0934, www.pagosahotsprings.com; Healing Waters Resort & Spa at (800) 832-5523, www.pshotsprings.com; or Overlook Mineral Springs Spa at (970) 264-4040, www.overlook hotsprings.com, for more information.

Chimney Rock National Monument (designated a national monument by President Barack Obama in September 2012) is open mid-May through the end of September. Call (970) 883-5359 or go to www.chimneyrockco.org.

Accommodations: Pagosa Springs and South Fork have a number of private campgrounds and motels. In addition, you'll pass one national forest campground—West Fork—en route to the trailhead. It is a fee area with water and vault toilets.

20 South Fork/Archuleta Lake Semiloop

Hike this semiloop, and you'll find scenic lakes and solitude. Note, however, that the South Fork Trail is *very* difficult to follow. There are many downed trees, and often the trail just disappears: Carry and know how to use a map and compass and/or GPS. The first 3 miles or so make this a wonderful day hike.

Start: Archuleta trailhead
Distance: 18.3-mile semiloop
Hiking time: 2- to 3-day backpack
Difficulty: Strenuous due to length and elevation gain of nearly 3,000 feet; moderate if you cover only the first 3 miles as a day hike
Canine compatibility: Dogs must be under control.
Nearest town: South Fork
Fees and permits: Free registration (available online, at managing agency, or major trailheads) needed for both day hikers and overnight backpackers. Contact the managing agency for current information.

Maps: USGS Mount Hope and South River Peak; Trails Illustrated Weminuche Wilderness; DeLorme 3D TopoQuad CD-ROM; Maptech Terrain Navigator CD-ROM
Trail contact: Rio Grande National Forest, Divide Ranger District, Creede; (719) 658-2556; www.fs.usda.gov/riogrande
Special considerations: You may not camp—or picket, hobble, tether, or graze pack or riding stock—within 200 feet of Archuleta Lake. Campfires are also prohibited. High-creek crossings are possible, especially early in the season.

Finding the trailhead: To reach the trailhead at Big Meadows Reservoir, drive southwest from the junction of US 160 and CO 149 in South Fork, taking US 160 for 11.7 miles. Turn right (southwest) onto Big Meadow Reservoir Road (FR 410), a well-maintained gravel road that's paved for the first 0.4 mile. After 1.4 miles there's a fork: Big Meadows Campground is to the left (south); Archuleta Trail and the reservoir—a state wildlife area and popular fishing locale—are to the right (west). Stay right and go 0.2 mile to another fork in the road. The trailhead and boat ramp are 0.1 mile to the left (west); FR 430 is to the right (north). At the trailhead you'll find plenty of room to park. There's a vault toilet for your convenience. *DeLorme: Colorado Atlas & Gazetteer:* Page 78 D3. GPS: N37 32.503' / W106 48.164'.

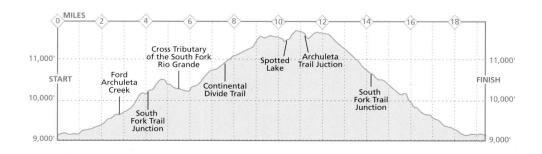

The South Fork Rio Grande with fireweed in the foreground

The Hike

Archuleta Trail 839 provides access for backpackers and day hikers intent on seeing a potpourri of cascades, falls, and swirling pools along the South Fork Rio Grande. For a shorter trip you can hike in 3 miles and out again, gaining only 520 feet in elevation.

The trail skirts the northwest edge of Big Meadows Reservoir. Along the way look for wildflowers such as scarlet gilia, elephant head, penstemon, bluebells, and wild roses. You'll cross a bridge at 0.4 mile; at 0.8 mile you'll reach the end of the reservoir. Continue to the Loop Trail junction at 1.1 miles. The main trail proceeds straight ahead (southwest) here, climbing along the scenic river. At 1.2 miles you'll enter the wilderness.

At the 2.8-mile mark, ford Archuleta Creek. This can be tricky early in the season, so use caution. Proceed up the moderate-to-steep slope, which has some switchbacks. You'll cross Archuleta Creek again at 3.2 miles.

You'll come to a junction at 4.1 miles with South Fork Trail 750 on the left. If you've shared the trail with other hikers up to this point, you should now have the route all to yourself. The South Fork Trail is little traveled and offers plenty of solitude. Sometimes it can be difficult to follow as well. You'll ford Archuleta Creek just after taking the trail, then begin to climb via steep switchbacks to the ridgetop separating the South Fork from the Archuleta drainages.

Eventually descend, sometimes at a steep grade, to 4.8 miles where the trail is fairly level. It remains at the same contour line as you cross several streams through this boggy area. After another 0.7 mile you'll cross a tributary of the South Fork Rio Grande. This also can be a tough crossing, so use caution. Upon reaching the 5.8-mile point, you will begin traveling along the South Fork Rio Grande. It can be a raging river, a thrill to just sit and watch.

Soon after you leave the river, you'll cross a meadow. Watch for blazed trees, or you might lose your way. Post-markers indicate the trail. Please note that early in the season and after rainstorms, the last 2 miles of the South Fork Trail can be slick and boggy. Numerous streams flow in the area, and you'll have to cross several creeks. The trail continues through alternating meadows and trees. You'll enter one last meadow (look for post-markers) and cross another stream at 7.2 miles before entering the trees.

At 7.6 miles you'll reach Continental Divide Trail 813. Make a right (north) here, climbing a moderate-to-steep slope into the trees. Along the way you can look south for a good view of the South San Juan Mountains. You'll reach a ridgetop at 8.4 miles. Hike along the open rock face. The grade is nearly level as you cross several small streams. At the 9.6-mile point in this hike, the trail climbs more moderately. You'll reach the top of yet another ridge at 9.9 miles; from here you can see north across the wilderness to the gray mass known as Mount Hope.

Continue north across a vast talus slope. At 10.2 miles you'll begin to switchback down to Spotted Lake, another 0.2 mile away. You're near the Continental Divide here, so expect strong winds and fierce storms. The lake is beautiful, however, and worthy of a visit.

Watch for elk as you hike on to Archuleta Lake, climbing another 150 feet or so. After this rise the trail remains nearly level to the Archuleta Trail 839 junction at 11.2 miles. Turn right (east) here to take Trail 839. Your route skirts the southern end of Archuleta Lake.

Beyond the lake it's a steep descent to Archuleta Creek at 11.9 miles. Cross the creek, then enter a meadow where the trail descends gradually. There are nice views of the South San Juans as you look ahead. This enormous meadow graces the side slope for the next mile or so and makes the moderate-to-steep descent more bearable. Look for wildflowers along the way and marmots that go bounding down the trails, their heels kicking up a stampede of dust.

You'll cross streams and descend several switchbacks as you continue your descent. Cross a semiopen slope at 13.8 miles. After that it's back into the trees. From the 14.1-mile point it's a short, steep descent to the South Fork Trail at 14.2 miles. At the trail junction head back the way you came in. You'll reach the trailhead after hiking a total of 18.3 miles.

South Fork/Archuleta Lake Semiloop

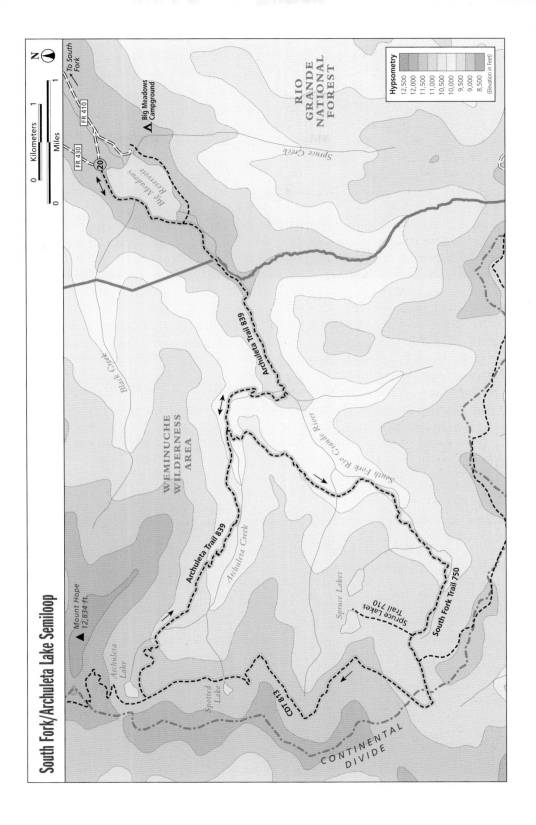

Northern pocket gopher (Thomomys talpoides)

Miles and Directions

0.0 Archuleta trailhead at Big Meadows Reservoir.

2.8 Ford Archuleta Creek.

4.1 South Fork Trail junction. GPS: N37 31.635' / W106 50.410'.

5.5 Cross tributary of the South Fork Rio Grande.

7.6 Continental Divide Trail; head north. N37 30.245' / W106 52.482'

10.4 Spotted Lake. GPS: N37 31.598' / W106 52.633'.

11.2 Archuleta Trail junction.

14.2 South Fork Trail junction.

18.3 Back to Archuleta trailhead.

Option: If you want to see the Spruce Lakes, take a short side trip from the meadow at mile 7.3. Spruce Lakes Trail 710 begins on its eastern side. I could not find the trail junction, but if you follow the edge of the meadow northeast a short way, you'll eventually see blazed trees. Once you find the blazes, it's a cinch to reach your destination. You'll climb about 200 feet and descend about 100 feet during the 0.5-mile hike to the lakes, which are surrounded by boggy areas.

Hike Information

Local information: South Fork Chamber of Commerce, South Fork; (719) 873-5556; www.southforkcolorado.org.

Local events/attractions: Attend the Little Britches Rodeo (June), Logger Days Festival (July), Rhythms of the Rio Music Festival (August), or Chili Cookoff (October).

Raft or fish the Rio Grande.

Accommodations: South Fork has a number of private campgrounds and motels. One national forest campground—Big Meadows—is located near the trailhead. It's a fee area with drinking water and vault toilets.

21 Hope Creek Trail

This is a nice hike along a creek; there are also meadows with wildflowers, and a chance of seeing wildlife. As you hike up high, there are good views of Mount Hope, Sawtooth Mountain, and the Continental Divide. The trail makes for a long day hike or overnight backpack.

Start: Hope Creek trailhead
Distance: 11.6 miles out and back
Hiking time: About 5 to 7 hours or overnight backpack
Difficulty: Moderate due to elevation gain of 2,400 feet
Canine compatibility: Dogs must be under control.
Nearest town: South Fork
Fees and permits: Free registration (available online, at managing agency, or major trailheads) needed for both day hikers and overnight backpackers. Contact the managing agency for current information.
Maps: USGS Mount Hope; Trails Illustrated Weminuche Wilderness; DeLorme 3D Topo-Quad CD-ROM; Maptech Terrain Navigator CD-ROM
Trail contact: Rio Grande National Forest, Divide Ranger District, Creede; (719) 658-2556; www.fs.usda.gov/riogrande
Special considerations: The West Fork Fire ravaged much of the area in June 2013, so use caution when hiking through the burn area.

Finding the trailhead: To reach the trailhead at Hope Creek, drive southwest from the junction of US 160 and CO 149 in South Fork, following US 160 for 11.7 miles. Turn right (southwest) onto Big Meadow Reservoir Road (FR 410), a well-maintained gravel road that's paved for the first 0.4 mile. After 1.4 miles you'll come to a fork. Big Meadows Campground is to the left (south), and Hope Creek (a sign says Shaw Lake via Forest Road 430) is to the right (west). Keep right (north) at the next fork in 0.2 mile, driving FR 430 another 1.2 miles to the Hope Creek trailhead. There is little room to park at the actual trailhead, but you can drive up the road a short distance and find a few more spaces. *DeLorme: Colorado Atlas & Gazetteer:* Page 78 D3. GPS: N37 33.252' / W106 48.161'.

The Hike

Sign in at the trail register, then begin hiking Hope Creek Trail 838. You'll travel through burned timber with nice views of Hope Creek. The trail grade is mostly easy for the first few miles. You'll cross a stream at 0.6 mile and enter a meadow at 1 mile.

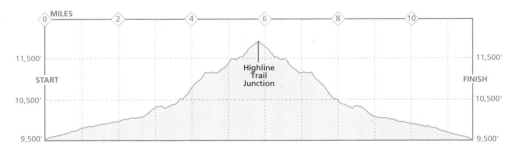

Hope Creek Trail; Kitty Creek Trail; Hunters Lake Loop; Highline Trail

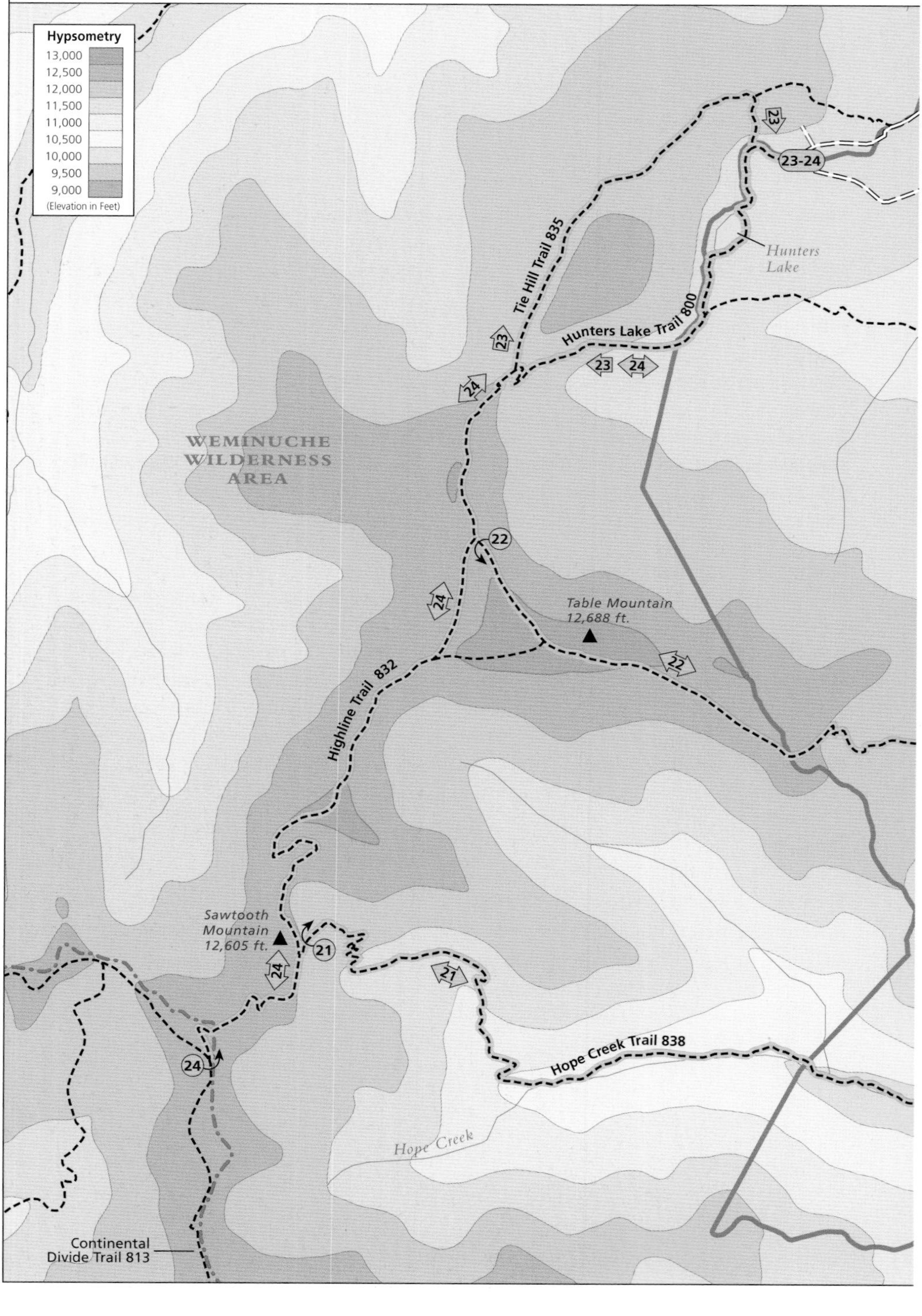

Hypsometry

13,000	
12,500	
12,000	
11,500	
11,000	
10,500	
10,000	
9,500	
9,000	

(Elevation in Feet)

Tie Hill Trail 835

Hunters Lake Trail 800

Hunters Lake

23

23-24

23 24

23

24

22

WEMINUCHE WILDERNESS AREA

24

Table Mountain
12,688 ft.

22

Highline Trail 832

Sawtooth Mountain
12,605 ft.

21

24

21

24

Hope Creek Trail 838

Hope Creek

Continental Divide Trail 813

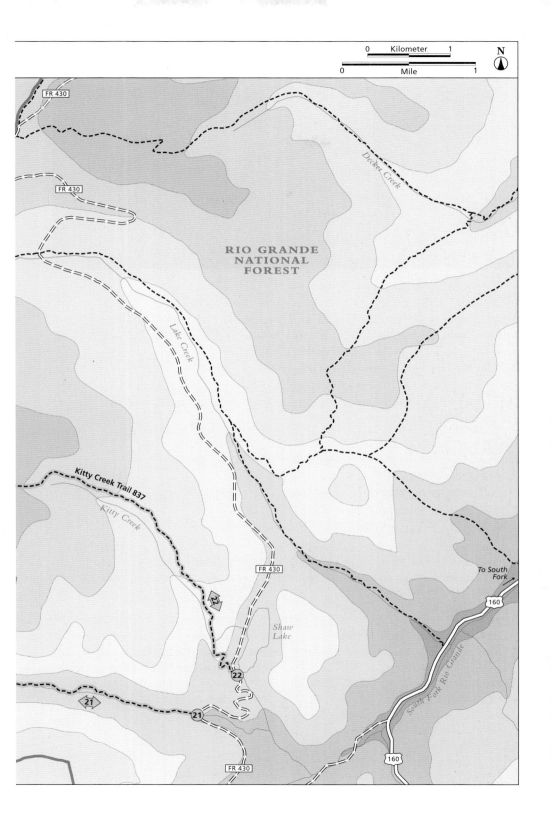

Fly amanita mushrooms (Amanita muscaria)

At 1.3 miles you'll enter the wilderness. There are more stream and meadow crossings as you proceed. When the trail gets a little steeper, an occasional switchback (like the one at mile 3.7) helps ease the way.

At 4.2 miles you'll cross a large meadow with good views to the south and west. At 4.9 miles the trail enters a scenic basin semi-surrounded by mountains. You'll reach the tree line at 5.6 miles and the junction with Highline Trail 832 (often called the Highland Trail) at 5.8 miles.

Miles and Directions

- **0.0** Hope Creek trailhead.
- **1.3** Wilderness boundary.
- **5.8** Highline Trail junction. GPS: N37 33.925' / W106 52.473'.
- **11.6** Back to Hope Creek trailhead.

Option: You can combine this trail with Hike 22 (Kitty Creek Trail) and a 2.6-mile portion of Hike 24 (Highline Trail) for a long loop of 14.8 miles. This option includes walking a gravel road for 1.1 miles between the two trailheads. If you add the loop, the trip becomes a multiday backpack.

Hike Information

Local information: South Fork Chamber of Commerce, South Fork; (719) 873-5556; www.southforkcolorado.org.

Local events/attractions: Attend the Little Britches Rodeo (June), Logger Days Festival (July), Rhythms of the Rio Music Festival (August), or Chili Cookoff (October).

Raft or fish the Rio Grande.

Accommodations: South Fork has a number of private campgrounds and motels. One national forest campground—Big Meadows—is located en route to the trailhead. It's a fee area with drinking water and vault toilets.

22 Kitty Creek Trail

You'll see great views once you emerge from the trees near Table Mountain. There's an opportunity to observe abundant animal life as well. Because camping sites are limited, it is best to plan this trip as a long day hike.

See map pages 102-103
Start: Kitty Creek trailhead
Distance: 10.6 miles out and back
Hiking time: About 5 to 7 hours
Difficulty: Strenuous due to length, some steep grades, and elevation gain of more than 2,700 feet
Canine compatibility: Dogs must be under control.
Nearest town: South Fork
Fees and permits: Free registration (available online, at managing agency, or major trailheads) needed for both day hikers and overnight backpackers. Contact the managing agency for current information.
Maps: USGS Mount Hope; Trails Illustrated Weminuche Wilderness; DeLorme 3D TopoQuad CD-ROM; Maptech Terrain Navigator CD-ROM
Trail contact: Rio Grande National Forest, Divide Ranger District, Creede; (719) 658-2556; www.fs.usda.gov/riogrande
Special considerations: The West Fork Fire ravaged much of the area in June 2013, so use caution when hiking through the burn area.

Finding the trailhead: To reach the trailhead at Kitty Creek, drive southwest from the junction of US 160 and CO 149 in South Fork, going 11.7 miles on US 160. Turn right (southwest) onto Big Meadow Reservoir Road (FR 410), a well-maintained gravel road that is paved for the first 0.4 mile. After 1.4 miles there's a fork: Big Meadows Campground (fee area) is to the left (south); the Kitty Creek Trail (the sign says SHAW LAKE VIA FOREST ROAD 430) is to the right (west). Keep right (north) at the next fork in 0.2 mile, driving FR 430 another 2.3 miles to the Kitty Creek trailhead at Shaw Lake. There is little parking space at the trailhead, so park at the lake, where there is plenty of room and a vault toilet. The trailhead is just across the road. *DeLorme: Colorado Atlas & Gazetteer:* Page 78 D3. GPS: N37 33.573' / W106 47.922'.

The Hike

Sign in at the trail register. Kitty Creek Trail 837 begins in an area ravaged by fire in June 2013. Expect to cross many a fallen tree along this trail. The path is steep in places. Follow switchbacks up to the ridge on which you'll stay for the first half of your hike. You'll cross Kitty Creek after 0.6 mile; this is the only time you'll see it.

Be forewarned that you are hiking through a logged area that was more recently burned. (The trail may be difficult to find, so I provide GPS readings for two road crossings in the Miles and Directions section.) The trail eases up just before an old logging road, which you'll encounter at 1.1 miles. Keep straight, crossing the road and entering the woods once again. The trail alternates between a fairly flat grade and a steep one. You'll reach another old logging road at 2.2

Red anemone (Anemone multifida globosa)

miles. Cross it and continue, hiking about 100 feet west on the road before picking up the trail and hiking to the northwest.

At 2.5 miles you'll cross a creek; head southwest through the boggy areas. Look for elk and grouse as you continue. At 3.3 miles you'll emerge from the trees. Follow the post-markers and/or rock cairns up the slope to the west, which is very steep in sections. You'll pass stunted trees and tiny alpine wildflowers.

At 3.4 miles the trail enters the wilderness. Notice the faint trail heading southwest. Post-markers continue to mark your way, making life a whole lot easier. After another 0.3 mile you'll see post-markers to the northwest. Look back to see the Sangre de Cristo Mountains across the broad San Luis Valley; south to see the South San Juan Mountains; and southwest to see Mount Hope, Sawtooth Mountain, and the Continental Divide.

The trail eases, making for an easy-to-moderate climb with wonderful views to 5.3 miles and Highline (also known as Highland) Trail 832. A sign points the way to the Continental Divide Trail, which you can take if you want to connect with the Hope Creek Trail (see Option). At this point you are very close to the top of 12,688-foot Table Mountain, so you may want to stand on top and enjoy the view.

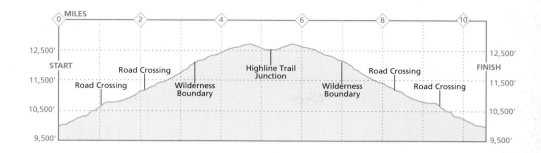

Miles and Directions

0.0 Kitty Creek trailhead.

1.1 Road crossing. GPS: N37 34.250' / W106 48.338'.

2.2 Road crossing. GPS: N37 34.783' / W106 49.141'.

5.3 Highline Trail junction. GPS: N37 35.495' / W106 51.725'.

10.6 Back to Kitty Creek trailhead.

Option: Combine this trail with the Hope Creek Trail (Hike 21) and a 2.6-mile portion of the Highline Trail (Hike 24) for a long loop of 14.8 miles. This option includes walking a gravel road for 1.1 miles between the two trailheads.

Hike Information

Local information: South Fork Chamber of Commerce, South Fork; (719) 873-5556; www.southforkcolorado.org.

Local events/attractions: Attend the Little Britches Rodeo (June), Logger Days Festival (July), Rhythms of the Rio Music Festival (August), or Chili Cookoff (October).

Raft or fish the Rio Grande.

Accommodations: South Fork has a number of private campgrounds and motels. One national forest campground—Big Meadows—is located en route to the trailhead. It's a fee area with drinking water and vault toilets.

23 Hunters Lake Loop

On this loop wildflowers (and perhaps wildlife, too) are yours for the asking. The route is a combination of two trails: the Hunters Lake Trail and a portion of the Tie Hill Trail (Hike 24).

See map pages 102-103
Start: Hunters Lake trailhead
Distance: 4.1-mile loop
Hiking time: About 2 to 3 hours
Difficulty: Moderate due to length and elevation gain of 728 feet
Canine compatibility: Dogs must be under control.
Nearest town: South Fork

Fees and permits: Free registration (available online, at managing agency, or major trailheads) needed for both day hikers and overnight backpackers. Contact the managing agency for current information.
Maps: USGS Mount Hope; Trails Illustrated Weminuche Wilderness; Topo! Colorado CD-ROM
Trail contact: Rio Grande National Forest, Divide Ranger District, Creede; (719) 658-2556; www.fs.usda.gov/riogrande

Finding the trailhead: To reach the trailhead near Hunters Lake, drive southwest from the junction of US 160 and CO 149 in South Fork. Take US 160 for 11.7 miles, then take a right (southwest) onto Big Meadow Reservoir Road (FR 410), a well-maintained gravel road that is paved for the first 0.4 mile. After 1.4 miles you'll come to a fork. Big Meadows Campground is to the left (south), and Hunters Lake (the sign says Shaw Lake via Forest Road 430) is to the right (west). Keep right (north) at the next fork in 0.2 mile. From there drive FR 430 another 9.6 miles to the Hunters Lake turnoff. Turn left (west) here. In 0.1 mile you'll reach the trailhead, where there is plenty of parking and nice, big horse-unloading ramps. *DeLorme: Colorado Atlas & Gazetteer:* Page 78 D3. GPS: N37 36.935' / W106 50.366'.

The Hike

From the trailhead Hunters Lake Trail 800 goes southwest through the trees and past a meadow on your left. You'll cross a stream at 0.2 mile; about this time you'll pass your return trail, marked by a rock cairn. It may be difficult to follow the trail from here, so I suggest hiking in a clockwise direction. Continue on the main trail

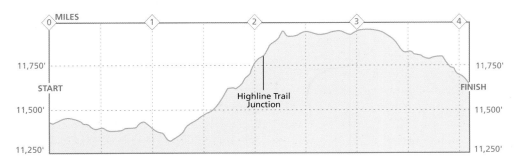

Highline Trail sign

and reach the north end of Hunters Lake at 0.5 mile; the south end of the lake is 0.3 mile farther.

Watch for tree blazes and rock cairns as you head south. Be sure to stop and fill out the trail register. You'll eventually cross an open slope with brilliant wildflowers, including Colorado columbine. As you enter the wilderness at 1.2 miles, you'll see an unsigned trail junction. This left-hand path is the Lake Creek Trail, which eventually descends to US 160.

Your route continues to the right across a semiopen slope decorated with spruces and other trees. You'll head into the trees at 1.5 miles and climb moderately. At 2 miles you'll begin to switchback up to the Highline Trail 832 (often called the Highland Trail) and Tie Hill Trail 835 junction at 2.1 miles. Make a right (north) onto the Tie Hill Trail to continue this loop. (If you'd rather hike the more scenic portion of the Highline Trail, see Hike 24 for details.)

The trail stays nearly level through the trees and enters a meadow as you hike northeast. Posts and rock cairns mark your way. You'll exit this meadow and enter a smaller one before descending a moderate grade that turns easy. A trail junction at 3.7 miles is marked only with two posts, one on each side of the trail. If you look to

Mike Vining checking GPS at Highline Trail junction

the right, you'll see another post. Hike down to it; from that point the path is easy to follow and marked with tree blazes.

You'll reach the Hunters Lake Trail at 3.9 miles. (If you're doing the loop in reverse, look for the rock cairn on the north side of the main trail. At one time a post marked the spot, but it is no longer in place.) Turn left (east) onto the Hunters Lake Trail, and head back to the trailhead at 4.1 miles.

Miles and Directions

0.0   Hunters Lake trailhead.

1.2   Wilderness boundary. GPS: N37 36.291' / W106 50.747'.

2.1   Highline and Tie Hill trail junction. GPS: N37 36.158' / W106 51.553'.

3.7   Unsigned trail junction. GPS: N37 37.170' / W106 50.530'.

3.9   Back to Hunters Lake Trail.

4.1   Back to Hunters Lake trailhead.

Hike Information

Local information: South Fork Chamber of Commerce, South Fork; (719) 873-5556; www.southforkcolorado.org.

Local events/attractions: Attend the Little Britches Rodeo (June), Logger Days Festival (July), Rhythms of the Rio Music Festival (August), or Chili Cookoff (October).

Raft or fish the Rio Grande.

Accommodations: South Fork has a number of private campgrounds and motels. One national forest campground—Big Meadows—is located en route to the trailhead. It's a fee area with drinking water and vault toilets. There are also places for primitive camping available along the drive to the trailhead.

24 Highline Trail

Hike the Highline Trail, which is often called the Highland Trail, and you'll see wildflowers and grand views. There's a good chance of seeing wildlife as well. Day hike to the top of the Stairsteps, or do a longer hike to the Continental Divide Trail. Make it an overnight backpack if you'd prefer.

See map pages 102-103
Start: Hunters Lake trailhead
Distance: 13.4 miles out and back (5 miles out and back if you hike to the top of the Stairsteps)
Hiking time: About 6 to 8 hours
Difficulty: Strenuous due to length and elevation gain of nearly 2,000 feet
Canine compatibility: Dogs must be under control.
Nearest town: South Fork

Fees and permits: Free registration (available online, at managing agency, or major trailheads) needed for both day hikers and overnight backpackers. Contact the managing agency for current information.
Maps: USGS Mount Hope and South River Peak; Trails Illustrated Weminuche Wilderness; DeLorme 3D TopoQuad CD-ROM; Maptech Terrain Navigator CD-ROM
Trail contact: Rio Grande National Forest, Divide Ranger District, Creede; (719) 658-2556; www.fs.usda.gov/riogrande

Finding the trailhead: To reach the trailhead near Hunters Lake, drive southwest from the junction of US 160 and CO 149 in South Fork, following US 160 for 11.7 miles. Make a right (southwest) onto Big Meadow Reservoir Road (FR 410), a well-maintained gravel road that's paved for the first 0.4 mile. After 1.4 miles there's a fork: Big Meadows Campground is to the left (south), and Hunters Lake (a sign says Shaw Lake via Forest Road 430) is to the right (west). Go right. Keep right (north) at the next fork in 0.2 mile, driving FR 430 another 9.6 miles to the Hunters Lake turnoff. Turn left (west), and you'll reach the trailhead in 0.1 mile. There is plenty of parking plus nice, big horse-unloading ramps. *DeLorme: Colorado Atlas & Gazetteer:* Page 78 D3. GPS: N37 36.935' / W106 50.366'.

The Hike

Hunters Lake Trail 800 begins through the trees and goes past a meadow on your left. You'll cross a stream at 0.2 mile and reach the north end of Hunters Lake at 0.5 mile. The lake's south end is about 1.0 mile from where you began.

Watch for tree blazes and rock cairns as you head south, eventually crossing an open slope sporting a rainbow of summer wildflowers. Enter the Weminuche Wilderness at the 1.2-mile point; you'll see a trail junction. This is the unsigned Lake Creek Trail. It eventually descends to US 160. Keep going straight ahead to continue this hike.

You'll head across a semiopen slope of spruce trees. Hike into the trees and climb moderately. At 2 miles you'll start to switchback up to the junction of Highline Trail 832 (also called Highland Trail) and Tie Hill Trail 835, located at the 2.1-mile point.

At the trail junction go left (south), and hike for 0.1 mile, continuing through the trees to the beginning of what is known as the Stairsteps. These volcanic rocks are a joy to hike up and play host to an assortment of lichens. A wide array of wildflowers—including columbines, asters, and phlox—add to the magic of the place. You'll climb about 400 feet in a little more than half a mile, so expect the trail to be steep. (Not surprisingly, the trail is not recommended for horse travel.) Remember, once you're on top, the terrain levels off. At that point you'll have nothing to do but enjoy the see-forever views.

You'll reach one of the highest points along the trail at about 2.7 miles. From there you can look down into the nearby meadow for elk, which are abundant. Follow rock cairns across the nearly level plateau to reach another trail junction at 3.2 miles. You could head southeast from here to Table Mountain and the Kitty Creek Trail (see Options), but you'll probably want to stay high on the Highline Trail, traveling south toward the Continental Divide.

Continue following rock cairns to a point near Sawtooth Mountain. If you don't mind descending and ascending another 400 feet or so, switchback down to the junction of the Hope Creek Trail at 5.8 miles. From there it's another 0.9 mile to 6.7 miles and a junction with the Continental Divide Trail.

Miles and Directions

0.0 Hunters Lake trailhead.

1.2 Wilderness boundary. GPS: N37 36.291' / W106 50.747'.

2.1 Highline and Tie Hill trail junction. GPS: N37 36.158' / W106 51.553'.

3.2 Kitty Creek Trail junction.

5.8 Hope Creek Trail junction. GPS: N37 33.925' / W106 52.473'.

6.7 Continental Divide Trail junction.

13.4 Back to Hunters Lake trailhead.

Options: The Highline Trail is a wonderful way to connect with the Continental Divide Trail (see Hikes 34 and 35 for more information). You can also combine part of this trail with the Hope Creek Trail (Hike 21) and Kitty Creek Trail (Hike 22). If you choose this option, you'll hike a 2.6-mile portion of the Highline Trail, which will link the other two trails. The loop is 14.8 miles long and includes a 1.1-mile walk on a gravel road between the two trailheads.

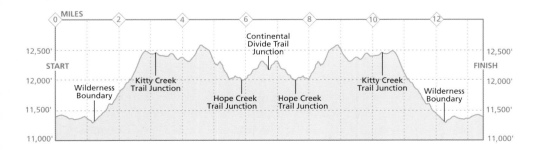

Rosy paintbrush and the view from the Highline Trail

Hike Information

Local information: South Fork Chamber of Commerce, South Fork; (719) 873-5556; www.southforkcolorado.org.

Local events/attractions: Attend the Little Britches Rodeo (June), Logger Days Festival (July), Rhythms of the Rio Music Festival (August), or Chili Cookoff (October).

Raft or fish the Rio Grande.

Accommodations: South Fork has a number of private campgrounds and motels. One national forest campground—Big Meadows—is located en route to the trailhead. It's a fee area with drinking water and vault toilets. There are also places for primitive camping available along the drive to the trailhead.

25 Fisher Mountain

Once you get near the top of the mountain, wonderful views are yours for the asking. There are also wildflowers and animal life on this lovely day hike.

Start: North Lime Creek trailhead
Distance: 8.2 miles out and back
Hiking time: About 4 to 6 hours
Difficulty: Strenuous due to length and elevation gain of more than 2,000 feet
Canine compatibility: Dogs must be under control.
Nearest town: Creede
Fees and permits: Free registration (available online, at managing agency, or major trailheads) needed for both day hikers and overnight backpackers. Contact the managing agency for current information.
Maps: USGS Spar City; Trails Illustrated Weminuche Wilderness; DeLorme 3D TopoQuad CD-ROM; Maptech Terrain Navigator CD-ROM
Trail contact: Rio Grande National Forest, Divide Ranger District, Creede; (719) 658-2556; www.fs.usda.gov/riogrande

Finding the trailhead: From Creede drive southwest on CO 149 for 6.2 miles. Turn left (south) onto Middle Creek Road (also known as FR 523). Marshall Park Campground is just across the Rio Grande at the turn. Continue on; after another 3.9 miles you'll reach a fork. Keep left (southeast) on Lime Creek Road (FR 528). Go another 2.5 miles to the junction of FR 526, FR 527, and FR 528; keep to the right (southwest) as they all begin to merge. (A road to Spar City continues straight, or east.) Drive another 0.2 mile to reach another junction. Keep left on FR 528, then drive another 5.9 miles to the North Lime Creek trailhead on the right (south) side of the road. You can access two trails—Roaring Creek and Fisher Mountain—from this point. The Roaring Creek Trail takes off from the trailhead and leads the long way around to sites such as Goose Lake and the Continental Divide Trail. The Fisher Mountain Trail hike begins a short distance up FR 440. *DeLorme: Colorado Atlas & Gazetteer:* Page 78 C2. GPS: N37 41.796' / W106 54.830'.

The Hike

To reach Fisher Mountain hike up FR 440, a four-wheel-drive road, for 0.1 mile. You'll see a trail taking off to the right (south) and a sign pointing the way to the Fisher Mountain Trail. Follow this sign. You'll climb a moderate-to-strenuous grade

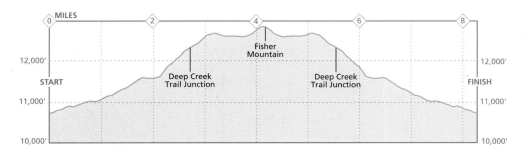

Old CENTER STOCK DRIVEWAY sign off Fisher Mountain Trail

along a ridge, hiking through trees. The wilderness boundary sign appears around the 1.2-mile mark, and you'll have a good view of Fisher Mountain at 2.2 miles. Hike along the edge of the trees for a short distance before entering the woods one last time.

You'll climb above the tree line at 2.4 miles. At 2.7 miles rock cairns mark the unsigned Deep Creek Trail, which leads to the Ivy Creek Trail and then to Goose Lake, about 8 or 9 miles south. Continue climbing straight across the open tundra to a plateau at 3.1 miles. The views are nice from here, but they're even better if you continue to the top of the mountain. You'll drop a bit before reaching the summit. You can see the Fisher Mountain Trail along the west (right) side of the mountain.

To reach the top, continue climbing moderately over trailless terrain. The summit sits 4.1 miles from where you started, at 12,857 feet above sea level. Sit on what seems like the top of the world and be amazed by the 360-degree views. You'll obtain a wonderful perspective on the Weminuche Wilderness and beyond. There's a trail register on top; be sure to sign it.

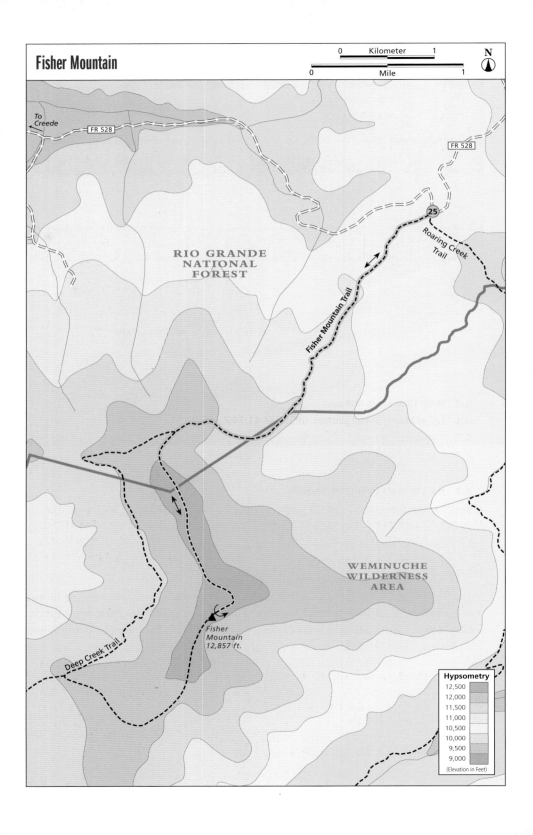

Fisher Mountain

Kilometer

Mile

N

To Creede

FR 528

FR 528

RIO GRANDE
NATIONAL
FOREST

25

Roaring Creek Trail

Fisher Mountain Trail

WEMINUCHE
WILDERNESS
AREA

Deep Creek Trail

Fisher
Mountain
12,857 ft.

Hypsometry

12,500
12,000
11,500
11,000
10,500
10,000
9,500
9,000
(Elevation in Feet)

Mike Vining and Donna Ikenberry with Fisher Mountain in the near distance

Miles and Directions

0.0 North Lime Creek trailhead.

0.1 Fisher Mountain Trail junction. GPS: N37 41.749' / W106 54.909'.

1.2 Wilderness boundary.

2.7 Deep Creek Trail (unsigned) junction. GPS: N37 40.421' / W106 56.581'.

4.1 Fisher Mountain. GPS: N37 39.417' / W106 56.250'.

8.2 Back to North Lime Creek trailhead.

Option: You can make the hike an 10.6-mile loop if you do the following: From the top of Fisher Mountain, hike southwest, descending the Fisher Mountain Trail for 1.5 miles to the Deep Creek Trail. Take the latter, traveling northeast for 2.3 miles to the rock cairns mentioned above (at mile 2.7 of the main hike). Then return to the trailhead the way you came in, traveling northeast and hiking a total of 10.6 miles.

Hike Information

Local information: Creede & Mineral County Chamber of Commerce, Creede; (800) 327-2102; www.creede.com.

Local events/attractions: Creede Repertory Theater in Creede is open every summer and is a big hit with locals and visitors alike; (866) 658-2540; www.creederep.org.

The Underground Mining Museum in Creede is a fascinating place and well worth a visit; (719) 658-0811; www.undergroundmining museum.com.

Raft or fish the Rio Grande.

Accommodations: Creede offers motels, cabins, and bed-and-breakfast inns. One national forest campground—Marshall Park—is located off the road as you drive to the trailhead. It's a fee area with drinking water and vault toilets.

26 Ivy Creek Trail to the Continental Divide

Hike this trail, and you'll find wildflowers and wildlife (including the possibility of seeing moose, pikas, and boreal toads), the shortest and quickest access to Goose Lake, and impressive views near South River Peak and the Continental Divide.

Start: Ivy Creek trailhead
Distance: 24.8 miles out and back
Hiking time: 2- to 3-day backpack
Difficulty: Strenuous due to length and elevation gain of more than 3,690 feet
Canine compatibility: Dogs must be under control.
Nearest town: Creede
Fees and permits: Free registration (available online, at managing agency, or major trailheads) needed for both day hikers and overnight backpackers. Contact the managing agency for current information.
Maps: USGS Spar City and South River Peak; Trails Illustrated Weminuche Wilderness; DeLorme 3D TopoQuad CD-ROM; Maptech Terrain Navigator CD-ROM
Trail contact: Rio Grande National Forest, Divide Ranger District, Creede; (719) 658-2556; www.fs.usda.gov/riogrande
Special considerations: High-water crossings in early summer can be hazardous.

Finding the trailhead: From Creede drive southwest on CO 149 for 6.2 miles. Turn left (south) onto Middle Creek Road (also known as FR 523). Marshall Park Campground is just across the Rio Grande at the turn. Keep driving; after another 3.9 miles you'll reach a fork. Stay to the left (southeast) here, on Lime Creek Road (FR 528). Go another 2.5 miles to the junction of FR 526, FR 527, and FR 528; keep to the right (southwest) as they begin to merge. (A road to Spar City continues straight, or east.) Drive an additional 0.2 mile to reach another junction. Proceed straight (southwest) on FR 526, heading to Ivy Creek. In another 0.8 mile you'll come to the junction of FR 527 and FR 526. Keep straight (south) on FR 526 to reach the Ivy Creek turnoff in 1.8 miles. Drive 0.2 mile, and you'll find trailhead parking. Just beyond is a campground (no fee, 14-day limit) with vault toilets, picnic tables, and fire rings. Site 1 is for small travel trailers or motor homes; the other four are tent camping only. *DeLorme: Colorado Atlas & Gazetteer:* Page 78 C2. GPS: N37 40.935' / W107 00.031'.

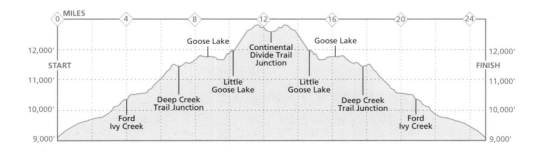

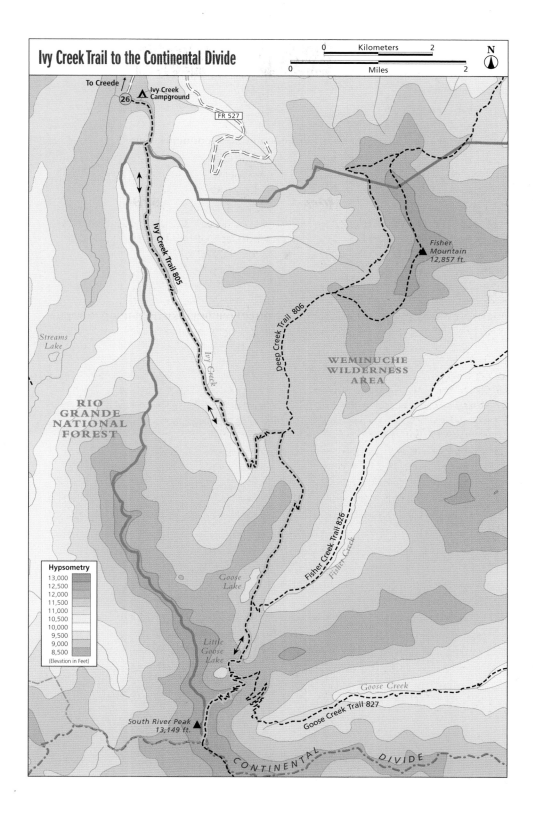

Ivy Creek Trail to the Continental Divide

Kilometers 0 — 2

Miles 0 — 2

N

To Creede

26

Ivy Creek Campground

FR 527

Ivy Creek Trail 805

Fisher Mountain 12,857 ft.

Streams Lake

Ivy Creek

Deep Creek Trail 806

WEMINUCHE WILDERNESS AREA

RIO GRANDE NATIONAL FOREST

Fisher Creek Trail 826

Fisher Creek

Goose Lake

Hypsometry

| 13,000 |
| 12,500 |
| 12,000 |
| 11,500 |
| 11,000 |
| 10,500 |
| 10,000 |
| 9,500 |
| 9,000 |
| 8,500 |

(Elevation in Feet)

Little Goose Lake

Goose Creek

Goose Creek Trail 827

South River Peak 13,149 ft.

CONTINENTAL DIVIDE

Little Goose Lake with Goose Lake in the background

The Hike

Ivy Creek Trail 805 begins among the trees and continues along the creek, climbing moderately to 0.4 mile, where you enter the wilderness. You'll cross Ivy Creek after 0.8 mile and skirt a meadow before entering the trees again and crossing a forested side slope. At 4 miles you'll have to ford Ivy Creek.

Hike across a meadow, and continue climbing moderately. At 4.5 miles you'll enter the trees and climb a side slope. Sixteen switchbacks take you up to huge talus slopes, then back into the trees again. You'll reach a plateau and post-markers at 6.6 miles. Follow the faint path to reach Deep Creek Trail 806 at 7 miles. This route goes north, traversing the west side of Fisher Mountain (see Hike 25 for more information).

Continue south on the Ivy Creek Trail, which leads to Goose Lake. You'll eventually hike back into the trees, climbing at a moderate grade. En route you'll pass a few rock slides, where you may see American pikas. After 8.1 miles you'll descend to a seasonal stream. Afterward you'll hike both in the trees and out of them, with good views into the Fisher Creek drainage as you continue across the wide bench. The trail drops to Goose Lake at 8.7 miles.

To continue to South River Peak and the Continental Divide Trail, hike along the east side of the lake to its southern end. Fisher Creek Trail 826 picks up there, at 9.1 miles; it goes south but soon turns north. Stay on the Ivy Creek Trail, which continues to travel south from the lake. Follow the wooden post-markers. You'll climb a steep grade at times and cross several streams. At 9.5 miles the trail eases up, following the contour line to Little Goose Lake at 10.2 miles.

Numerous switchbacks (another sixteen to be exact) lead to the 11-mile point, where there is a rock cairn on the left (south). Goose Creek Trail 827 merges with the Ivy Creek Trail here. Continue upward via the switchbacks. At 11.8 miles you'll come to a nice spot (12,925 feet is the highest point on this trail) just below the east side of South River Peak, which is 13,149 feet high. To reach the Continental Divide Trail junction, hike another 0.6 mile south.

Miles and Directions

- **0.0** Ivy Creek trailhead.
- **4.0** Ford Ivy Creek.
- **7.0** Deep Creek Trail junction.
- **8.7** Goose Lake. GPS: N37 36.077' / W106 58.155'.
- **10.2** Little Goose Lake.
- **12.4** Continental Divide Trail junction. GPS: N37 33.986' / W106 58.653'.
- **24.8** Back to Ivy Creek trailhead.

Hike Information

Local information: Creede & Mineral County Chamber of Commerce, Creede; (800) 327-2102; www.creede.com.

Local events/attractions: Creede Repertory Theater in Creede is open every summer and is a big hit with locals and visitors alike; (866) 658-2540; www.creederep.org.

The Underground Mining Museum in Creede is a fascinating place and well worth a visit; (719) 658-0811; www.undergroundmining museum.com.

Raft or fish the Rio Grande.

Accommodations: Creede offers motels, cabins, and bed-and-breakfast inns. There's a no-fee campground at the trailhead. A national forest campground—Marshall Park—is located off the road as you drive to the trailhead. It's a fee area with drinking water and vault toilets.

27 Fern Creek to the Continental Divide Trail

You'll find solitude along this trail—at least after you hike away from the Ruby Lakes. There's also abundant wildlife and beautiful scenery. This hike is a great way to access the Continental Divide Trail (CDT) at Trout Lake.

Start: Fern Creek trailhead
Distance: 23.4 miles out and back
Hiking time: 2- to 3-day backpack
Difficulty: Strenuous due to length and elevation gain of more than 3,380 feet
Canine compatibility: Dogs must be under control.
Nearest town: Creede
Fees and permits: Free registration (available online, at managing agency, or major trailheads) needed for both day hikers and overnight backpackers. Contact the managing agency for current information.

Maps: USGS Workman Creek and Little Squaw Creek; Trails Illustrated Weminuche Wilderness; DeLorme 3D TopoQuad CD-ROM; Maptech Terrain Navigator CD-ROM
Trail contact: Rio Grande National Forest, Divide Ranger District, Creede; (719) 658-2556; www.fs.usda.gov/riogrande
Special considerations: The first 4.5 miles of trail, adopted by the Creede OHV Club, are open to foot, horse, ATV, and mountain bike use. A large portion of the trail is above timberline; watch for afternoon thunderstorms. The Papoose Fire ravaged much of the area in June 2013, so use caution when hiking through the burn area.

Finding the trailhead: From Creede go southwest on CO 149 for 16.3 miles. Turn left onto gravel Fern Creek Road, also known as FR 522. After 1.5 miles turn right at the sign for the Fern Creek trailhead. There's plenty of parking and a hitching post for horses at the trailhead. *DeLorme: Colorado Atlas & Gazetteer:* Page 78 B1. GPS: N37 44.291' / W107 06.097'.

The Hike

Sign the register, and begin hiking Fern Creek Trail 815 through the burn area. Several long switchbacks make the initial climb a moderate one. After 0.7 mile you'll get a view to Antelope Park and the winding waters of the Rio Grande.

At 1 mile the grade steepens as you head up the Fern Creek drainage. Sometimes you'll hike near the creek; other times you'll hike above or away from it. At 2.6 miles

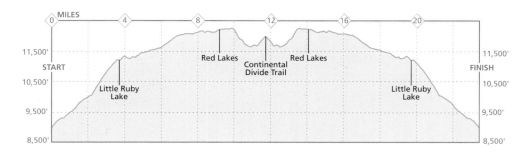

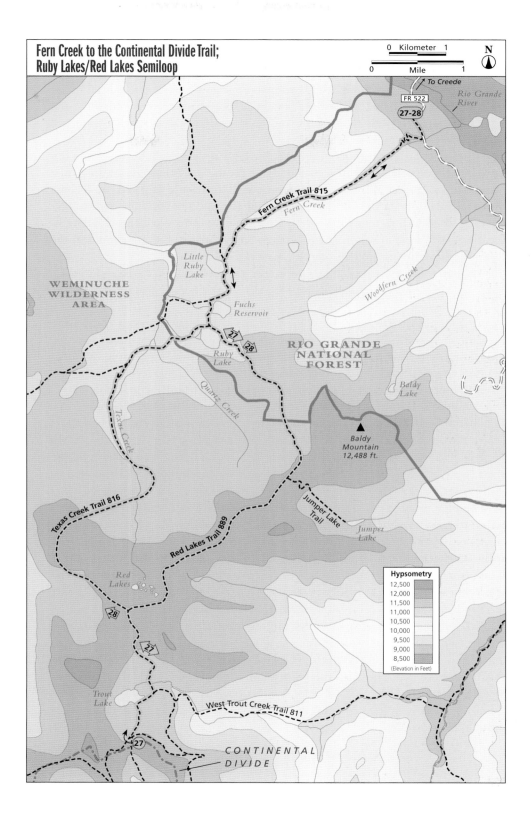

Fern Creek to the Continental Divide Trail;
Ruby Lakes/Red Lakes Semiloop

0   Kilometer   1

0   Mile   1

N

To Creede

FR 522

27-28

Rio Grande
River

Fern Creek Trail 815

Fern Creek

Little
Ruby
Lake

Woodfern Creek

WEMINUCHE
WILDERNESS
AREA

Fuchs
Reservoir

27

28

RIO GRANDE
NATIONAL
FOREST

Ruby
Lake

Baldy
Lake

Quartz Creek

Texas Creek

Baldy
Mountain
12,488 ft.

Jumper Lake
Trail

Texas Creek Trail 816

Red Lakes Trail 889

Jumper
Lake

Red
Lakes

Hypsometry

| 12,500 |
| 12,000 |
| 11,500 |
| 11,000 |
| 10,500 |
| 10,000 |
| 9,500 |
| 9,000 |
| 8,500 |

(Elevation in Feet)

28

27

Trout
Lake

West Trout Creek Trail 811

27

CONTINENTAL
DIVIDE

you'll travel along the west side of a rock slide, a periodic flat area giving you room to breathe between some very steep sections. The rock switches to meadow as you proceed to a junction at 3.8 miles. Unmaintained Texas Creek Trail 816 is off to the right. Look ahead to see Little Ruby Lake, a nice spot surrounded by a meadow and trees. Continue across the flat meadow on the east side of the lake, where you will have a view to high peaks in the northwest.

Head back into the trees at 4 miles. You'll climb at a steep grade. When you top off at 4.3 miles, you will see Fuchs Reservoir on the left (south). Look for Chief Mountain, elevation 13,014 feet, to the southwest. In another 0.3 mile you'll come to a trail junction. At the fork go left (south) to continue to Ruby and Jumper Lakes. (The right fork follows the Fern Creek Trail/Old La Garita Stock Drive to Little Squaw Creek in 4 miles.) You'll reach Ruby Lake at 4.8 miles and find the remains of several cabins there, one of which is fairly intact.

The trail forks at the lake. Texas Creek Trail 816 is once again to the right (west). Take the main route, Red Lakes Trail 889, left (east). There is a sign for it on the lake's northeast side.

At 5.4 miles you'll enter the wilderness. It's a moderate-to-steep climb from here up the drainage. The climb tapers off at 5.7 miles, turning to an easy-to-moderate grade. After 6.7 miles you're up high enough to see west to the Window, the Rio Grande Pyramid, and other points of interest.

You'll reach an unsigned junction with the Jumper Lake Trail at 7 miles. Post-markers head southwest toward the Red Lakes and southeast toward Jumper Lake. Follow the post-markers southwest. You'll have to cross small streams as you travel across the nearly flat tundra. You'll climb gradually, however, reaching a small unnamed lake on the left (east) at 9.1 miles. The closest of the Red Lakes is on the right (west) at 9.2 miles. The lakes are really a pretty series of ponds surrounded by lush grasses.

The hike proceeds to an unsigned junction with Texas Creek Trail 816 at 9.7 miles. To continue to CDT 813, proceed south. You will overlook four unnamed lakes, then begin descending a very steep trail past wildflowers and lichen-covered rocks. Along the way look for pikas. In the distance you'll see Trout Lake and the Continental Divide at the Knife Edge, a narrow sliver of rock. As you descend you'll pass through thick stands of willows.

You'll cross a couple of small streams before you reach West Trout Creek at 10.8 miles. Continue 0.1 mile to an unsigned junction for the West Trout Creek Trail. About 100 yards beyond this crossroads, you'll see a pond on the left. Although you cannot see Trout Lake from this point (you're too low), you can see spur trails that lead to the lake. The main route goes around the lake's east side and proceeds at a steep grade to mile 11.7—the CDT junction. The trail is 12,000 feet high at this point. This is also the junction for the Williams Creek Trail (see Hike 14 for more information).

Miles and Directions

0.0 Fern Creek trailhead.

3.8 Little Ruby Lake. GPS: N37 42.93' / W107 8.37'.

4.8 Ruby Lake.

7.0 Jumper Lake Trail junction.

9.7 Texas Creek Trail junction.

10.9 West Trout Creek Trail junction.

11.7 Continental Divide Trail. GPS: N37 38.247' / W107 9.352'.

23.4 Back to Fern Creek trailhead.

Options: For those interested in an extended trek along the CDT, this is a good way to reach Trout Lake, the ending and starting point for Hikes 35 and 36, respectively.

If you want to make a side trip to Jumper Lake, follow the unsigned trail that meets Red Lakes Trail 889 at mile 7. Climb the ridge to the southeast and then descend to the lake. It's 1 mile to the water, with an elevation gain of 150 feet and a descent of 600 feet. If you want to loop back to Ruby Lake rather than proceed to the CDT, take Texas Creek Trail 816 at mile 9.7 (see Hike 28).

Hike Information

Local information: Creede & Mineral County Chamber of Commerce, Creede; (800) 327-2102; www.creede.com.

Local events/attractions: Creede Repertory Theater in Creede is open every summer and is a big hit with locals and visitors alike; (866) 658-2540; www.creederep.org.

The Underground Mining Museum in Creede is a fascinating place and well worth a visit; (719) 658-0811; www.undergroundmining museum.com.

Raft or fish the Rio Grande.

Accommodations: Creede offers motels, cabins, and bed-and-breakfast inns. One national forest campground—Marshall Park—is located off CO 149, about 6.5 miles southwest of Creede, as you drive to the trailhead. It's a fee area with drinking water and vault toilets.

28 Ruby Lakes/Red Lakes Semiloop

You'll find solitude along this trail—at least once you hike away from the Ruby Lakes—and abundant wildlife.

See map page 123
Start: Fern Creek trailhead
Distance: 19.7-mile semiloop
Hiking time: 2- to 3-day backpack
Difficulty: Strenuous due to length and elevation gain of more than 3,200 feet
Canine compatibility: Dogs must be under control.
Nearest town: Creede
Fees and permits: Free registration (available online, at managing agency, or major trailheads) needed for both day hikers and overnight backpackers. Contact the managing agency for current information.

Maps: USGS Workman Creek and Little Squaw Creek; Trails Illustrated Weminuche Wilderness; DeLorme 3D TopoQuad CD-ROM; Maptech Terrain Navigator CD-ROM
Trail contact: Rio Grande National Forest, Divide Ranger District, Creede; (719) 658-2556; www.fs.usda.gov/riogrande
Special considerations: The first 4.5 miles of trail, adopted by the Creede OHV Club, are open to foot, horse, ATV, and mountain bike use. A large portion of the trail is above timberline; watch for afternoon thunderstorms. The Papoose Fire ravaged much of the area in June 2013, so use caution when hiking through the burn area.

Finding the trailhead: From Creede go southwest on CO 149 for 16.3 miles. Turn left onto gravel Fern Creek Road, also known as FR 522. After 1.5 miles turn right at the sign for the Fern Creek trailhead. There's plenty of parking and a hitching post for horses at the trailhead. *DeLorme: Colorado Atlas & Gazetteer:* Page 78 B1. GPS: N37 44.291' / W107 06.097'.

The Hike

Sign the register, and begin hiking Fern Creek Trail 815 through the burned forest. Several long switchbacks make the initial climb a moderate one. After 0.7 mile you'll get a view to Antelope Park and the winding waters of the Rio Grande.

At 1 mile the grade steepens as you head up the Fern Creek drainage. Sometimes you'll hike near the creek; other times you'll hike above or away from it. After 2.6 miles you'll travel along the west side of a rock slide, a periodic flat area giving you

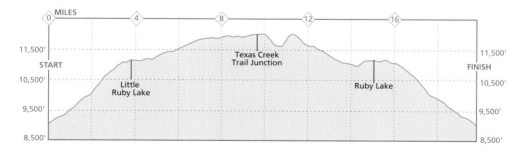

room to breathe between some very steep sections. The rock switches to meadow as you proceed to a junction at 3.8 miles. Unmaintained Texas Creek Trail 816 is off to the right. Look ahead to see Little Ruby Lake. Continue across the flat meadow on the east side of the lake, where you will have a view to high peaks in the northwest.

Head back into the trees at 4 miles. You'll climb at a steep grade. When you top off at 4.3 miles, you will see Fuchs Reservoir on the left (south). Look for Chief Mountain, elevation 13,014 feet, to the southwest. In another 0.3 mile you'll come to a trail junction. At the fork go left (south) to continue to Ruby and Jumper Lakes. (The right fork follows the Fern Creek Trail/Old La Garita Stock Drive to Little Squaw Creek in 4 miles.) You'll reach Ruby Lake at 4.8 miles and find the remains of several cabins there, one of which is fairly intact.

The trail forks at the lake. Texas Creek Trail 816 is once again to the right (west). Take the main route, Red Lakes Trail 889, left (east). There is a sign for it on the lake's northeast side.

At 5.4 miles you'll enter the wilderness. It's a moderate-to-steep climb from here up the drainage. The climb tapers off at 5.7 miles, turning to an easy-to-moderate grade. After 6.7 miles you're up high enough to see west to the Window, the Rio Grande Pyramid, and other points of interest.

You'll reach an unsigned junction with the Jumper Lake Trail at 7 miles. Post-markers head southwest toward the Red Lakes and southeast toward Jumper Lake. Follow the post-markers southwest. You'll have to cross small streams as you travel across the nearly flat tundra. You'll climb gradually, however, reaching a small unnamed lake on the left (east) at 9.1 miles. The closest of the Red Lakes is on the right (west) at 9.2 miles. The lakes are really a pretty series of ponds surrounded by lush grasses.

The hike proceeds to an unsigned junction with Texas Creek Trail 816 at 9.7 miles. Turn onto this trail and hike around the Red Lakes, generally going northwest. The trail is faint or nonexistent at times, but if you look closely, you'll find post-markers and rock cairns to show you the way. As you hike, look southwest for a close-up view of Chief Mountain and the Little Squaw Creek drainage.

After 11.4 miles you'll reach a small lake on the left. You'll also wonder which way to turn, given that there are no visible markers or cairns and the lake is not shown on maps. Head due east; you'll come to a post-marker at 11.6 miles. If you continue north, as others have done, you will find that the trail quickly fades away. There is a lone post-marker in that direction, but it is for another, unknown trail—not Trail 816.

Beyond this point the trail is obvious at times, nonexistent at others. Don't worry: Post-markers and rock cairns define the way. You'll begin a gradual descent to the Texas Creek drainage, crossing a stream after 11.8 miles. A moderate descent soon has you paralleling Texas Creek, traveling through thick willows. Continue down a meadow. You'll cross two branches of the creek at 12.4 miles, hiking on its east side for 0.1 mile until you cross back to the west side.

The trail heads out into the open, but remains near the trees, as you cross a couple of streams and gradually descend. After 13.8 miles you'll reach a post-marker and sign pointing the way to Ruby Lake. Though you won't see another marker or cairn, there is a well-worn trail across the creek and up the hill. Follow it. You'll cross the meadow to the east, then ford Texas and Quartz Creeks before the 14.1-mile point, when you'll begin a steep climb.

You'll leave the wilderness at 14.3 miles; the trail lessens in severity after this point. You'll reach Ruby Lake at 14.9 miles. Return to the trailhead the way you hiked in, reaching it after a total of 19.7 miles.

Miles and Directions

- **0.0** Fern Creek trailhead.
- **3.8** Little Ruby Lake. GPS: N37 42.93' / W107 8.37'.
- **4.8** Ruby Lake.
- **7.0** Jumper Lake Trail junction.
- **9.7** Texas Creek Trail junction.
- **13.8** Post-marker to Ruby Lake.
- **14.9** Ruby Lake.
- **19.7** Back to Fern Creek trailhead.

Options: You may want to make a side trip to Jumper Lake. To do so, take the unsigned trail that meets Red Lakes Trail 889 at mile 7. Climb the ridge to the southeast, then descend to Jumper Lake. It's 1 mile away, with an elevation gain of 150 feet and a descent of 600 feet.

From mile 9.7 on the Red Lakes Trail, you can hike south to reach the Continental Divide Trail (CDT) near Trout Lake (see Hike 27). For CDT routes to and from Trout Lake, see Hikes 35 and 36.

Hike Information

Local information: Creede & Mineral County Chamber of Commerce, Creede; (800) 327-2102; www.creede.com.

Local events/attractions: Creede Repertory Theater in Creede is open every summer and is a big hit with locals and visitors alike; (866) 658-2540; www.creederep.org.

The Underground Mining Museum in Creede is a fascinating place and well worth a visit; (719) 658-0811; www.undergroundmining museum.com.

Raft or fish the Rio Grande.

Accommodations: Creede offers motels, cabins, and bed-and-breakfast inns. One national forest campground—Marshall Park—is located off the road as you drive to the trailhead. It's a fee area with drinking water and vault toilets.

29 Squaw Pass

Hike all the way to Squaw Pass, or take a day hike just a few miles up the trail. You might see some wildlife. Hike in the proper season, and you'll find wildflowers and colorful aspens as well.

Start: Squaw Creek trailhead
Distance: 19.6 miles out and back
Hiking time: 2- to 3-day backpack
Difficulty: Strenuous due to length and elevation gain of more than 2,000 feet; moderate if you cover only the first few miles as a day hike
Canine compatibility: Dogs must be under control.
Nearest town: Creede
Fees and permits: Free registration (available online, at managing agency, or major trailheads) needed for both day hikers and overnight backpackers. Contact the managing agency for current information.
Maps: USGS Weminuche Pass, Little Squaw Creek, and Cimarrona Peak; Trails Illustrated Weminuche Wilderness; DeLorme 3D Topo-Quad CD-ROM; Maptech Terrain Navigator CD-ROM
Trail contact: Rio Grande National Forest, Divide Ranger District, Creede; (719) 658-2556; www.fs.usda.gov/riogrande

Finding the trailhead: From Creede drive southwest on CO 149 for about 20 miles. Turn left (south) onto Rio Grande Reservoir Road, also known as FR 520. It's paved in the beginning, but after 0.3 mile the road surface turns to maintained gravel. Drive another 11.1 miles, and make another left (south) at the signed junction for Thirtymile Campground and the Weminuche and Squaw Creek trailheads. Keep right upon entering the area, reaching the trailhead parking area in 0.2 mile. If you're going into the wilderness on horseback, there's a stock-unloading area with hitching posts and corrals 0.6 mile before the campground entrance. Stock unloading is not permitted in the campground. *DeLorme: Colorado Atlas & Gazetteer:* Page 77 C7. GPS: N37 43.398' / W107 15.543'.

The Hike

From the parking area follow the signs south about 200 yards to a wilderness sign and trail register. After signing in at the register, which provides access to the Weminuche Trail as well (see Hike 30), head straight south on Squaw Creek Trail 814 (also known as Big Squaw Trail). (***Note:*** The trail heading west from the register is the Weminuche

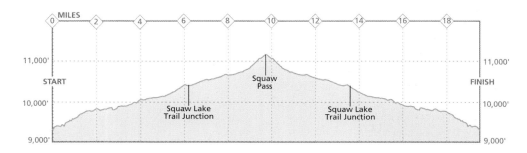

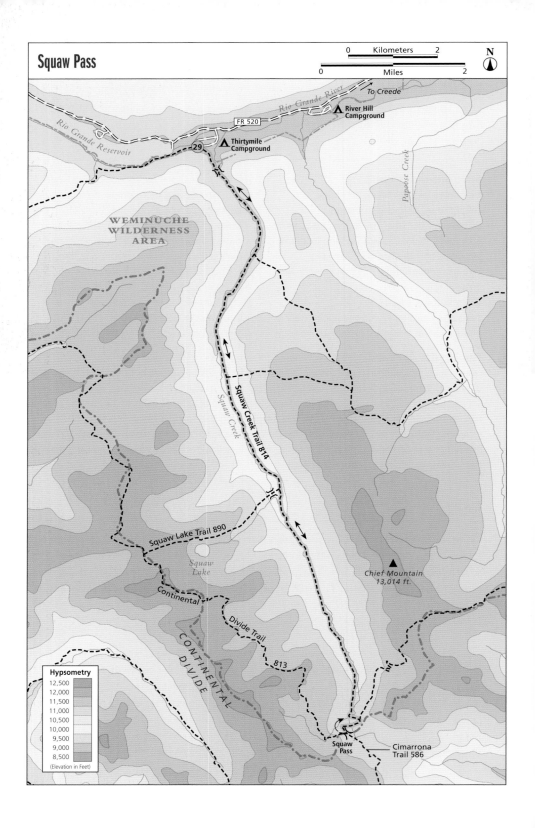

Squaw Pass

0 Kilometers 2
0 Miles 2

N

Rio Grande River
To Creede
▲ River Hill Campground

Rio Grande Reservoir
FR 520
Papoose Creek

29 ▲ Thirtymile Campground

WEMINUCHE WILDERNESS AREA

Squaw Creek Trail 814

Squaw Creek

Squaw Lake Trail 890

Squaw Lake

▲ Chief Mountain 13,014 ft.

Continental

Divide Trail

813

CONTINENTAL DIVIDE

Squaw Pass

Cimarrona Trail 586

Hypsometry
12,500
12,000
11,500
11,000
10,500
10,000
9,500
9,000
8,500
(Elevation in Feet)

Johnna Heberling Bambrey backpacking the Squaw Creek Trail

Trail; see Hike 30 for more information.) You'll soon climb through conifers and aspens at a moderate-to-steep grade. After 0.3 mile you'll see Squaw Creek to the left. In another 0.1 mile you'll drop a bit, descending to a bridge across Squaw Creek at 0.6 mile. Just beyond you enter the wilderness.

The trail climbs and occasionally descends as you follow Squaw Creek through a semi-narrow canyon. As you continue, the canyon opens up. You'll see an amazing array of colorful aspens here in the fall. You'll exit the trees at 1.8 miles, ascending at an easy grade through vast meadows stretching to Squaw Pass. Along the way you'll cross many small streams, some with evidence of active beavers.

At 6.1 miles you'll reach a junction and a bridge over Squaw Creek. The Squaw Lake Trail heads west over the creek and ascends a steep grade to Squaw Lake, which is 1,600 feet higher than this point. Your route continues south through the meadow; follow wooden post-markers as you ascend. You'll occasionally hike amid trees, but expect to stay mostly in the open, where you may see elk or even a moose.

At 8.6 miles the trail increases its pitch, climbing at a moderate-to-steep grade for more than half a mile. You'll arrive at last at the unsigned junction, where your route merges with Continental Divide Trail (CDT) 813. Follow the wooden post-markers as you proceed south across a rocky slope. Look for pikas here. At 9.8 miles you'll reach Squaw Pass. From here the CDT takes off to the west and up a ridge, and the Cimarrona Trail 586 heads south about 10 miles to the Cimarrona trailhead.

Gray jay (Perisoreus Canadensis)

Miles and Directions

0.0   Squaw Creek trailhead.

0.6   Wilderness boundary.

6.1   Squaw Lake Trail junction. GPS: N37 38.980' / W107 14.248'.

9.8   Continental Divide Trail and Squaw Pass. GPS: N37 36.125' / W107 12.995'.

19.6   Back to Squaw Creek trailhead.

Hike Information

Local information: Creede & Mineral County Chamber of Commerce, Creede; (800) 327-2102; www.creede.com.

Local events/attractions: Creede Repertory Theater in Creede is open every summer and is a big hit with locals and visitors alike; (866) 658-2540; www.creederep.org.

The Underground Mining Museum in Creede is a fascinating place and well worth a visit; (719) 658-0811; www.undergroundmining museum.com.

Raft or fish the Rio Grande.

One of the best burger joints around is at Freeman's General Store. Open in summer, you'll find it 2.1 miles east of the CO 149/FR 520 junction on CO 149.

Accommodations: Creede offers motels, cabins, and bed-and-breakfast inns. Thirtymile Campground, a national forest facility, is located at the trailhead. This fee area provides water and vault toilets. You'll pass River Hill Campground, another national forest facility and fee area with water and vault toilets, about 1.4 miles before you reach the trailhead. There are also primitive campsites—no fee—en route.

30 Weminuche Pass Area

Spend a day hiking to Weminuche Pass, and you'll find lush meadows and wildflowers. The route provides access to the Continental Divide Trail (CDT).

Start: Weminuche trailhead
Distance: 9.6 miles out and back
Hiking time: About 4 to 8 hours or 2-day backpack
Difficulty: Moderate, with a few steep sections
Canine compatibility: Dogs must be under control.
Nearest town: Creede
Fees and permits: Free registration (available online, at managing agency, or major trailheads) needed for both day hikers and overnight backpackers. Contact the managing agency for current information.
Maps: USGS Weminuche Pass; Trails Illustrated Weminuche Wilderness; DeLorme 3D TopoQuad CD-ROM; Maptech Terrain Navigator CD-ROM
Trail contact: Rio Grande National Forest, Divide Ranger District, Creede; (719) 658-2556; www.fs.usda.gov/riogrande

Finding the trailhead: From Creede drive southwest on CO 149 for about 20 miles. Turn left (south) onto Rio Grande Reservoir Road, also known as FR 520. It's paved in the beginning, but after 0.3 mile the road surface turns to maintained gravel. Drive another 11.1 miles, and make another left (south) at the signed junction for Thirtymile Campground and the Weminuche and Squaw Creek trailheads. Keep right upon entering the area, reaching a parking area in 0.2 mile. If you're going into the wilderness on horseback, there's a stock-unloading area 0.6 mile before the campground entrance. Stock unloading is not permitted in the campground. *DeLorme: Colorado Atlas & Gazetteer:* Page 77 C7. GPS: N37 43.398' / W107 15.543'.

The Hike

From the parking area follow the signs south about 200 yards to a wilderness sign and trail register. After signing in at the register, which provides access to the Squaw Creek Trail as well (see Hike 29), hike west on Weminuche Trail 818. You'll hike past some old cabin remains after 0.3 mile and pass the Rio Grande Reservoir dam and spillway later. You'll enter the wilderness at 0.8 mile.

The trail grade stays fairly level as you begin your hike, with some gentle ups and downs. At 1.3 miles you will begin hiking at a more moderate grade, with short, steep

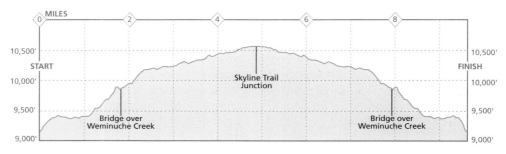

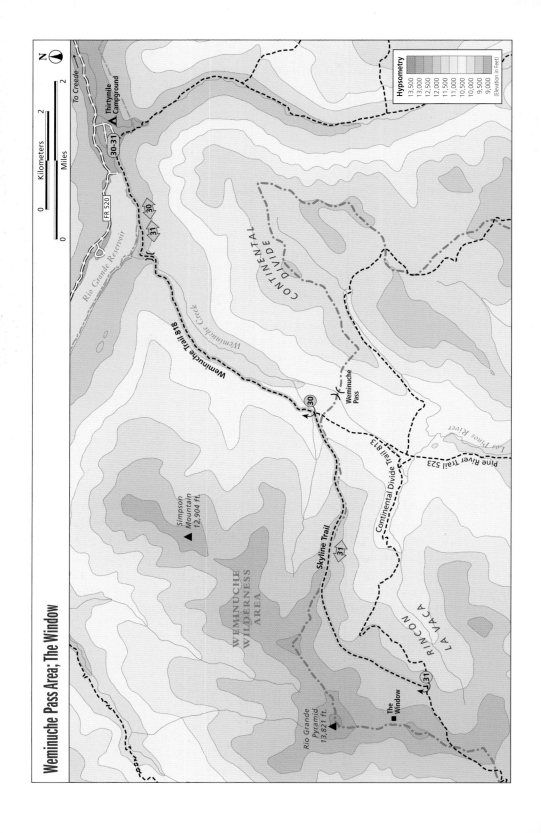

Weminuche Pass Area; The Window

Weminuche Pass area from the Skyline Trail

ascents through a mix of spruce and aspens. Turn south at mile 1.5, heading up the Weminuche Creek drainage.

Cross a bridge over the creek at 1.8 miles, then continue climbing. At 2 miles the trail eases up some, climbing through meadows ringed with aspens and spruce. You'll cross a couple of streams as you proceed.

At 4 miles you'll have to ford an unnamed stream that flows from Simpson Mountain, to the west. Continue another 0.8 mile and cross Weminuche Creek; you may have to get your feet wet here early in the season. Just after crossing the creek, you'll come to a junction with the Skyline Trail, which leads to the Window and the Rio Grande Pyramid (see Hike 31 for more information). From this point Weminuche Pass is 0.3 mile southeast, with a drop of about 60 feet in elevation.

Miles and Directions

0.0 Weminuche trailhead.

0.8 Wilderness boundary.

1.8 Bridge over Weminuche Creek. GPS: N37 42.820' / W107 17.274'.

4.8 Skyline Trail junction. GPS: N37 41.087' / W107 19.289'.

9.6 Back to Weminuche trailhead.

Options: At 10,565 feet above sea level, Weminuche Pass is the lowest point on the Weminuche portion of the Continental Divide. The true point for Weminuche Pass is about 0.3 mile southwest of the 4.8-mile trail junction, at GPS N37 40.849' / W107 19.027'. If you're interested in connecting with the Continental Divide Trail (see Hikes 36 and 37), you can hike the Skyline Trail and access the CDT near the Window (see Hike 31)—or you can continue south another 1.4 miles on the Pine River Trail.

Hike Information

Local information: Creede & Mineral County Chamber of Commerce, Creede; (800) 327-2102; www.creede.com.

Local events/attractions: Creede Repertory Theater in Creede is open every summer and is a big hit with locals and visitors alike; (866) 658-2540; www.creederep.org.

The Underground Mining Museum in Creede is a fascinating place and well worth a visit; (719) 658-0811; www.undergroundmining museum.com.

Raft or fish the Rio Grande.

One of the best burger joints around is at Freeman's General Store. Open in summer, you'll find it 2.1 miles east of the CO 149/FR 520 junction on CO 149.

Accommodations: Creede offers motels, cabins, and bed-and-breakfast inns. Thirtymile Campground, a national forest facility, is located at the trailhead. This fee area provides water and vault toilets. You'll pass River Hill Campground, another national forest facility and fee area with water and vault toilets, about 1.4 miles before you reach the trailhead. There are also primitive campsites—no fee—en route.

31 The Window

You will find lush meadows, wildflowers, and grand views on this hike. The route provides access to the Rio Grande Pyramid and the Continental Divide Trail (CDT).

See map page 134
Start: Weminuche trailhead
Distance: 19.4 miles out and back
Hiking time: 2- to 3-day backpack
Difficulty: Strenuous due to length and elevation gain of more than 3,000 feet
Canine compatibility: Dogs must be under control.
Nearest town: Creede
Fees and permits: Free registration (available online, at managing agency, or major trailheads) needed for both day hikers and overnight backpackers. Contact the managing agency for current information.
Maps: USGS Weminuche Pass and Rio Grande Pyramid; Trails Illustrated Weminuche Wilderness; DeLorme 3D TopoQuad CD-ROM; Maptech Terrain Navigator CD-ROM
Trail contact: Rio Grande National Forest, Divide Ranger District, Creede; (719) 658-2556; www.fs.usda.gov/riogrande

Finding the trailhead: From Creede drive southwest on CO 149 for about 20 miles. Turn left (south) onto Rio Grande Reservoir Road, also known as FR 520. It's paved in the beginning, but after 0.3 mile the road surface turns to maintained gravel. Drive another 11.1 miles, and make another left (south) at the signed junction for Thirtymile Campground and the Weminuche and Squaw Creek trailheads. Keep right upon entering the area, reaching a parking area in 0.2 mile. If you're going into the wilderness on horseback, there's a stock-unloading area 0.6 mile before the campground entrance. Stock unloading is not permitted in the campground. *DeLorme: Colorado Atlas & Gazetteer:* Page 77 C7. GPS: N37 43.398' / W107 15.543'.

The Hike

From the parking area follow the signs south about 200 yards to a wilderness sign and trail register. After signing in at the register, which provides access to the Squaw Creek Trail as well (see Hike 29), hike west on Weminuche Trail 818. You'll hike past some old cabin remains after 0.3 mile and pass the Rio Grande Reservoir dam and spillway later. You'll enter the wilderness at 0.8 mile.

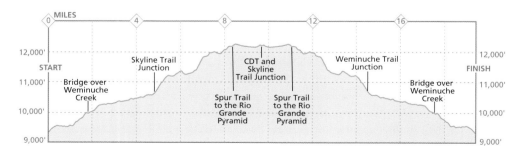

Mike Vining hiking the Skyline Trail with the Rio Grande Pyramid in the background

The trail stays fairly level as you begin your hike, with some gentle ups and downs. At 1.3 miles you will begin hiking at a more moderate grade, with some short, steep ascents through mixed spruce and aspens. Turn south at mile 1.5, heading up the Weminuche Creek drainage. Cross a bridge over the creek at 1.8 miles, then continue climbing.

At 2 miles the trail eases up, climbing gently through meadows ringed with aspens and spruce. You'll cross a couple of streams as you proceed. At 4 miles you'll have to ford an unnamed stream that flows from Simpson Mountain, to the west. Continue to 4.8 miles and a Weminuche Creek crossing; you may have to get your feet wet here early in the season. Just after crossing the creek, you'll meet the Skyline Trail, which leads to the Rio Grande Pyramid and the landmark rock formation known as the Window.

Hike the moderate, though sometimes steep, Skyline Trail through the trees. You'll soon head across a semiopen slope, with a vast meadow to the east. Eventually you will see the Window and the Rio Grande Pyramid to the west. The trail then eases up, passing through willows before reaching a tiny lake at 7 miles. From here you'll climb gradually, passing a spur trail leading to the top of the Rio Grande Pyramid (elevation 13,821 feet) at 8.3 miles. You'll reach the junction of the Skyline Trail and the CDT at a point near the Window after a total of 9.7 miles.

Miles and Directions

0.0 Weminuche trailhead.

0.8 Wilderness boundary.

1.8 Bridge over Weminuche Creek. GPS: N37 42.820' / W107 17.274'.

4.8 Skyline Trail junction. GPS: N37 41.087' / W107 19.289'.

8.3 Spur trail to Rio Grande Pyramid.

9.7 Skyline Trail and CDT junction just east of the Window. GPS: N37 39.808' / W107 23.090'.

19.4 Back to Weminuche trailhead.

Options: At 10,565 feet above sea level, Weminuche Pass is the lowest point on the Weminuche portion of the Continental Divide. The true point for Weminuche Pass is about 0.3 mile southwest of the 4.8-mile trail junction, at GPS N37 40.849' / W107 19.027'. If you're interested in connecting with the Continental Divide Trail, see Hikes 36 and 37. Another option is to continue south for 1.4 miles on the Pine River Trail.

The climb from the main trail up to the top of the Rio Grande Pyramid is outstanding, with amazing above-tree-line views and many pikas. Beware, however; the climb is very steep, gaining 1,524 feet in 0.9 mile. Add that to the steep climb from Weminuche Pass, and you'll gain 2,540 feet in 2.3 miles. The top 700 feet of the mountain consists of huge rock boulders. Use caution! The 360-degree view from the top of the highest point in the eastern San Juans is worth the effort to get there.

Hike Information

Local information: Creede & Mineral County Chamber of Commerce, Creede; (800) 327-2102; www.creede.com.

Local events/attractions: Creede Repertory Theater in Creede is open every summer and is a big hit with locals and visitors alike; (866) 658-2540; www.creederep.org.

The Underground Mining Museum in Creede is a fascinating place and well worth a visit; (719) 658-0811; www.undergroundmining museum.com.

Raft or fish the Rio Grande.

One of the best burger joints around is at Freeman's General Store. Open in summer, you'll find it 2.1 miles east of the CO 149/FR 520 junction on CO 149.

Accommodations: Creede offers motels, cabins, and bed-and-breakfast inns. Thirtymile Campground, a national forest facility, is located at the trailhead. This fee area provides water and vault toilets. You'll pass River Hill Campground, another national forest facility and fee area with water and vault toilets, about 1.4 miles before you reach the trailhead. There are also primitive campsites—no fee—en route.

32 Ute Creek Semiloop

This semiloop provides access to vast meadows and wildflowers. It is a great way to link up with the Continental Divide Trail (CDT). Be sure to search along the river for American dippers and wandering garter snakes.

Start: Ute Creek trailhead
Distance: 25.9-mile semiloop
Hiking time: 3- to 4-day backpack
Difficulty: Strenuous due to length and elevation gain of more than 3,000 feet
Canine compatibility: Dogs must be under control.
Nearest town: Creede
Fees and permits: Free registration (available online, at managing agency, or major trailheads) needed for both day hikers and overnight backpackers. Contact the managing agency for current information.

Maps: USGS Finger Mesa and Rio Grande Pyramid; Trails Illustrated Weminuche Wilderness; DeLorme 3D TopoQuad CD-ROM; Maptech Terrain Navigator CD-ROM
Trail contact: Rio Grande National Forest, Divide Ranger District, Creede; (719) 658-2556; www.fs.usda.gov/riogrande
Special considerations: Hikers must camp at least 200 feet from West Ute Lake; campfires are not permitted. In addition, livestock must be kept 200 feet away from the lake. Fording the Rio Grande can be dangerous until mid to late summer.

Finding the trailhead: From Creede drive southwest on CO 149 for about 20 miles. Turn left (south) onto Rio Grande Reservoir Road, also known as FR 520. It's paved in the beginning but turns to maintained gravel after 0.3 mile. Drive another 11.1 miles, and you'll see a signed junction for Thirtymile Campground and the Weminuche and Squaw Creek trailheads. Do not turn here. Instead, continue along the north side of the Rio Grande Reservoir for another 5.9 miles to a sign for the Ute Creek trailhead. The trailhead is on the south side of the road in 0.2 mile. There's an outhouse, a stock-unloading area, hitching posts, and plenty of room to park or spend the night. *DeLorme: Colorado Atlas & Gazetteer:* Page 77 B7. GPS: N37 45.580' / W107 20.570'.

The Hike

From the trail register Ute Creek Trail 819 goes right along the Rio Grande via a raised path. Follow the path for about 500 feet, then ford the river. There's a trail sign on the south side of the river, which can be a dangerous crossing until midsummer. At

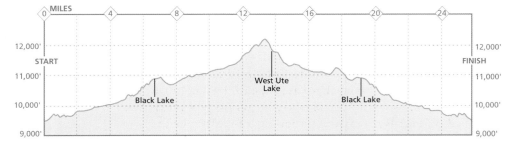

this point the trail climbs moderately. You'll enter the wilderness, with its thick aspen groves, at 0.3 mile. These trees can be absolutely gorgeous in late summer and early fall.

The trail has a mostly easy, sometimes moderate grade as you continue. You'll cross a stream at 0.5 mile, then head up the Ute Creek drainage at 1.1 miles. An occasional switchback helps ease the way. At mile 2.5 there's a grand view up the Ute Creek valley to the high country.

You'll switch between hiking in the open and hiking in the trees (conifers and aspens), paralleling Ute Creek at times. You'll cross several streams before reaching Black Lake at 6.7 miles. At 7 miles you'll come to a fork. The route on the left (south) follows Middle Ute Creek. The route on the right (west) is West Ute Trail 825; it will be your return trail for this loop. For now hike south into the broad, vast meadows of the Middle Ute drainage, descending at a moderate-to-steep grade.

You'll cross several creeks before you reach the East Ute Creek Trail junction on the left (southeast) at 7.8

Aspens in the fall

miles. Continue straight (south) on Middle Ute Creek Trail 819. You'll climb an easy-to-moderate grade, with the Window and the Rio Grande Pyramid visible to the east. The trail is mostly in the open, but you'll pass through an occasional stand of trees. The route crosses more streams as you climb to another junction at 9.8 miles. Here Ute Lake Trail 905 takes off to the left (southeast); the Middle Ute continues straight (southwest). Hike straight up the Middle Ute to reach the CDT junction at 11.4 miles. The CDT used to traverse the side slope visible west of this point, but it has been rerouted.

From the CDT junction you can head south to Twin Lakes (1 mile away). If you wish to continue the loop, however, climb the fairly steep trail to the 12.8-mile point. Here you'll meet the Middle Ute Lake Trail; go right (north). It's a moderate-to-steep climb to the ridgetop at 13.3 miles, where you'll have a grand view. You can see west to the Grenadier Range and other portions of the Weminuche.

Ute Creek Semiloop

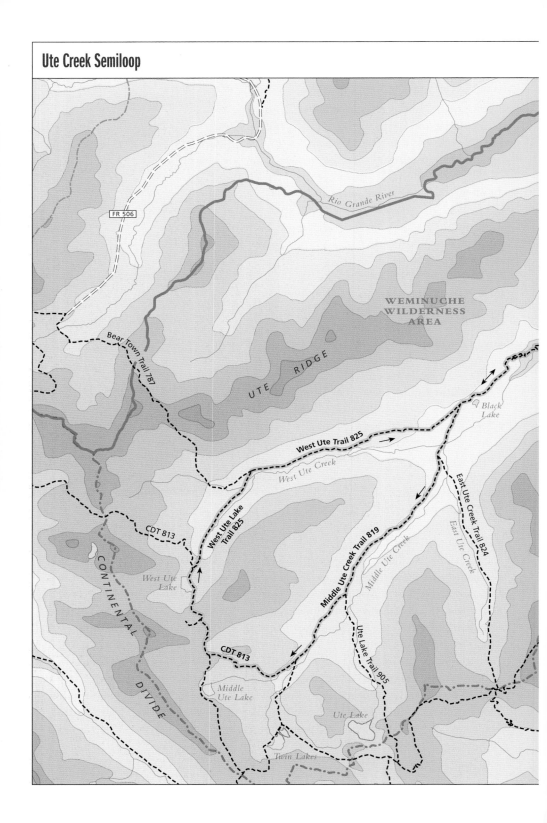

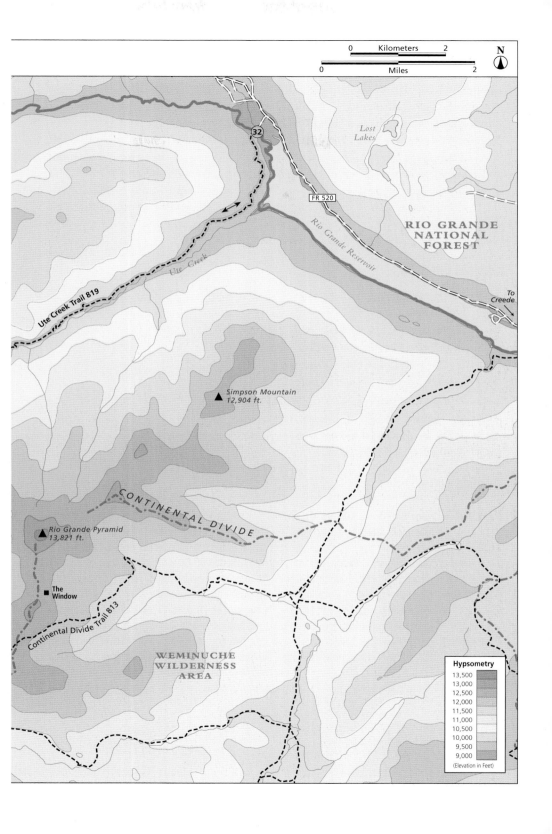

0   Kilometers   2

0   Miles   2

N

Lost
Lakes

32

FR 520

Rio Grande Reservoir

RIO GRANDE
NATIONAL
FOREST

To
Creede

Ute Creek

Ute Creek Trail 819

Simpson Mountain
12,904 ft.

CONTINENTAL DIVIDE

Rio Grande Pyramid
13,821 ft.

The
Window

Continental Divide Trail 813

WEMINUCHE
WILDERNESS
AREA

Hypsometry

13,500
13,000
12,500
12,000
11,500
11,000
10,500
10,000
9,500
9,000
(Elevation in Feet)

Descend the slope, passing a small lake before reaching West Ute Lake at 13.9 miles. From there continue to the junction of West Ute Trail 825 and the CDT at 14.6 miles. Keep straight (north) on Trail 825. You'll hike through the trees, descending to a vast meadow that extends down West Ute Creek for miles. Be sure to look west to Nebo Mountain and Nebo Pass before you have gone too far.

Ford West Ute Creek at 15.3 miles. At 15.5 miles you'll come to a fork in the trail. From here you can climb to Starvation Pass, about 2 miles away (see Hike 33 for more information). Note that on some maps, this trail is mistakenly shown as the CDT. The latter is to the west and makes its way across the north side of Mount Nebo.

The trail crosses several streams and passes as you descend to Middle Ute Creek Trail 819, meeting it at 18.9 miles. From here return the way you came in, passing Black Lake and arriving at the trailhead at 25.9 miles.

Miles and Directions

0.0 Ute Creek trailhead.

0.3 Wilderness boundary.

6.7 Black Lake. GPS: N37 42.404' / W107 24.803'.

7.8 East Ute Creek Trail junction; continue south.

9.8 Ute Lake Trail junction; continue southwest.

11.4 Continental Divide Trail junction; head west.

13.9 West Ute Lake. GPS: N37 40.026' / W107 28.726'.

14.6 CDT and West Ute Lake Trail junction; continue north.

18.9 Middle Ute Creek and West Ute Creek Trail junction; proceed northeast.

25.9 Back to Ute Creek trailhead.

Hike Information

Local information: Creede & Mineral County Chamber of Commerce, Creede; (800) 327-2102; www.creede.com.

Local events/attractions: Creede Repertory Theater in Creede is open every summer and is a big hit with locals and visitors alike; (866) 658-2540; www.creederep.org.

The Underground Mining Museum in Creede is a fascinating place and well worth a visit; (719) 658-0811; www.undergroundmining museum.com.

Raft or fish the Rio Grande.

One of the best burger joints around is at Freeman's General Store. Open in summer, you'll find it 2.1 miles east of the CO 149/FR 520 junction on CO 149.

Accommodations: Creede offers motels, cabins, and bed-and-breakfast inns. En route to the trailhead, you'll pass two national forest facilities. Both River Hill Campground and Thirtymile Campground are fee areas; water and vault toilets are provided. Lost Trail Campground is about 1 mile beyond the trailhead. It's a free place to camp, with vault toilets.

33 Starvation Pass

This trail features stunning views, an array of wildflowers, and the opportunity to see wildlife.

Start: Unmarked trailhead south of old Beartown site
Distance: 4.4 miles out and back
Hiking time: About 3 to 5 hours
Difficulty: Moderate, though hike may feel strenuous due to the lofty elevation
Canine compatibility: Dogs must be under control.
Nearest town: Creede
Fees and permits: Free registration (available online, at managing agency, or major

trailheads) needed for both day hikers and overnight backpackers. Contact the managing agency for current information.
Maps: USGS Storm King Peak and Rio Grande Pyramid; Trails Illustrated Weminuche Wilderness; DeLorme 3D TopoQuad CD-ROM; Maptech Terrain Navigator CD-ROM
Trail contact: Rio Grande National Forest, Divide Ranger District, Creede; (719) 658-2556; www.fs.usda.gov/riogrande

Finding the trailhead: From Creede drive southwest on CO 149 for about 20 miles. Turn left (south) onto Rio Grande Reservoir Road, also known as FR 520. It's paved in the beginning but turns to gravel after 0.3 mile. Follow it another 11.1 miles, and you'll see a signed junction for Thirtymile Campground. Continue past this turnoff along the north side of the Rio Grande Reservoir for another 5.9 miles. You'll come to a sign for the Ute Creek trailhead. Keep going straight.

From here the road conditions change; the well-maintained gravel route becomes a narrow, bumpy, sometimes steep, four-wheel-drive road. If you have a good vehicle, drive another 0.8 mile to the Lost Trail Campground, then proceed an additional 8.5 miles to a junction for Stony Pass. A sign claims that the pass is 6 miles away via FR 520 and that Beartown is 4 miles distant via FR 506. Both are very rough, four-wheel-drive roads.

Turn left (southwest) onto FR 506, and continue to the unsigned trailhead, which is just south of the old Beartown site. You'll drive another 5.1 miles, then turn onto a spur road taking off to the east. The road crosses two streams en route to the trailhead, another 0.1 mile away. If you reach the sign for Hunchback Pass, you've gone too far. Turn around and head back 0.4 mile to the spur road. *DeLorme: Colorado Atlas & Gazetteer:* Page 77 C5. GPS: N37 42.912' / W107 30.486'.

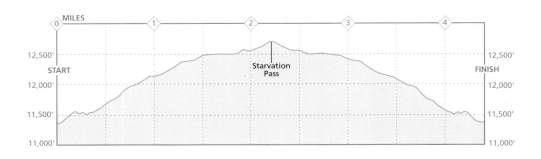

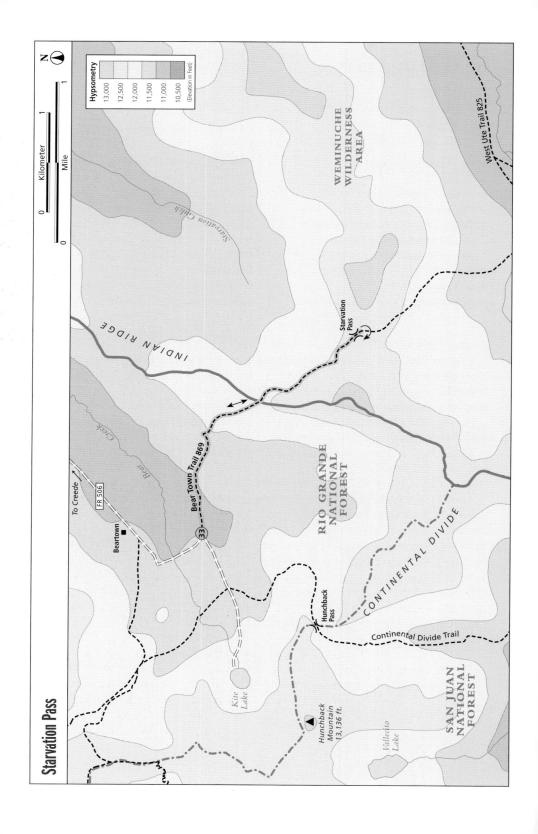

Starvation Pass

The Hike

There is a Weminuche Wilderness sign and a well-defined (though unsigned) trail south of the parking area at the end of the road. Hike on this trail into the trees. Moderate-to-steep switchbacks lead the way for 0.9 mile. You'll emerge from the trees to terrific views. These continue as you climb the sometimes steep grade to the top of Starvation Pass at 2.2 miles. From here you'll see high peaks all around you. Look south to West Ute Lake, northwest to Stony Pass.

If you'd like to descend to the West Ute Trail (see Hike 32 for more information), with views of the Window and the Rio Grande Pyramid en route, continue less than 2 miles. On the way you'll lose about 1,400 feet in elevation.

Please note that on some maps this trail is mistakenly shown as the Continental Divide Trail. The CDT is to the west and makes its way across the north side of Mount Nebo.

Alpine forget-me-nots (Myosotis alpestris)

Miles and Directions

0.0 Unmarked trailhead.
0.9 Emerge from the trees.
2.2 Starvation Pass. GPS: N37 42.094' / W107 29.204'.
4.4 Back to trailhead.

Hike Information

Local information: Creede & Mineral County Chamber of Commerce, Creede; (800) 327-2102; www.creede.com.

Local events/attractions: Creede Repertory Theater in Creede is open every summer and is a big hit with locals and visitors alike; (866) 658-2540; www.creederep.org.

The Underground Mining Museum in Creede is a fascinating place and well worth a visit; (719) 658-0811; www.undergroundmining museum.com.

Raft or fish the Rio Grande.

One of the best burger joints around is at Freeman's General Store. Open in summer, you'll find it 2.1 miles east of the CO 149/FR 520 junction on CO 149.

Accommodations: Creede offers motels, cabins, and bed-and-breakfast inns. En route to the trailhead, you'll pass three national forest facilities. Both River Hill Campground and Thirtymile Campground are fee areas; water and vault toilets are provided. Lost Trail Campground is a free place to camp, with vault toilets.

The Continental Divide Trail in the Weminuche Wilderness

On its 3,100-mile journey from Mexico to Canada, the Continental Divide Trail (CDT) crosses 85 miles of the Weminuche Wilderness, gaining more than 17,000 feet in elevation and dropping about 15,000 feet over its route. It's a strenuous trail that is usually easy to follow. On occasion it is difficult to find or nearly nonexistent. It stays above the tree line much of the way. Water may be scarce at times. Late-afternoon thunderstorms can threaten hikers, and snow can be deep in places, even into July.

What can you expect? I spent ten days backpacking the CDT with my then fiancé and now husband, Mike, and we discovered one stunning vista after another. Starting at Wolf Creek Pass, we enjoyed hiking at an average elevation of 12,000 feet, surveying landmarks such as the Rio Grande Pyramid and the Window when we were still miles away. We also spied herds of elk, watched a ptarmigan and her babies, and delighted in a potpourri of colorful wildflowers. Imagine our joy at reaching Stony Pass, knowing that we had hiked 85 miles and that a hot shower and Mexican food were in our near future! Though we were glad to reach our destination, we were both a bit sad to have to say good-bye to our high-elevation odyssey.

July, August, and September are the best months for hiking the CDT, though you may encounter snow any month of the year. Hike too early in the season, and you'll be postholing through thigh-deep snow. (The Forest Service claims that some hikers have hit 20-foot drifts.) Worst of all, you'll miss the lovely wildflower display. Mike and I hiked the trail during the last part of July and found little snow. We did encounter boggy sections, however, because of daily thundershowers that increased in severity as the days passed by.

We hiked the entire Weminuche section of the CDT in one long backpack, but you don't have to do the whole trail at once. For your convenience, I've divided the trail into four sections, choosing what I think are the best places to link up and leave the CDT. You can hike them as I've suggested or use your imagination and put sections together. You may want to link up with and leave the trail at other points. The choice is yours.

The hikes vary in miles but are similar in beauty. All are worthwhile. **Note:** Although I started the hiking miles at 0.0 for each segment, I also noted the accumulated CDT miles in parentheses in the Miles and Directions log. For example, the second segment (Hike 35) begins at Sawtooth Mountain; it is listed as 0.0 (12.5) under the Miles and Directions heading.

When hiking the CDT, you'll sometimes find that water is scarce. Most of it is off the trail a few hundred yards to a mile or so. Carry extra water while hiking through these areas.

34 Wolf Creek Pass to Sawtooth Mountain

If you love being up high, then the Continental Divide Trail (CDT) is for you. There are stunning views, mountain lakes, wildlife, and wildflowers.

Start: CDT trailhead at Wolf Creek Pass
Distance: 12.5 miles point to point
Hiking time: About 6 to 8 hours
Difficulty: Strenuous due to length, vertical gain of approximately 3,000 feet, and lofty elevation
Canine compatibility: Dogs must be under control.
Nearest town: South Fork
Fees and permits: Free registration (available online, at managing agency, or major trailheads) needed for both day hikers and overnight backpackers. Contact the managing agency for current information.
Maps: USGS Wolf Creek and Mount Hope; Trails Illustrated Weminuche Wilderness;

DeLorme 3D TopoQuad CD-ROM; Maptech Terrain Navigator CD-ROM
Trail contacts: San Juan National Forest, Pagosa Ranger District, Pagosa Springs; (970) 264-2268; www.fs.usda.gov/sanjuan. Rio Grande National Forest, Divide Ranger District, Creede; (719) 658-2556; www.fs.usda.gov/riogrande.
Special considerations: You may not camp—or picket, hobble, tether, or graze pack or riding stock—within 200 feet of Archuleta Lake. Campfires are also prohibited. Watch for late-afternoon thunderstorms. Snow can be deep in places into July.

Finding the trailhead: The southern end of the Weminuche Wilderness portion of the CDT is at Wolf Creek Pass. To get there drive 19 miles southwest of South Fork on US 160 or 22.6 miles northeast of Pagosa Springs on US 160. The marked trailhead is across from the sign for Wolf Creek Pass, elevation 10,857 feet. Look for a path that soon disappears into the trees. *DeLorme: Colorado Atlas & Gazetteer:* Page 88 A3. GPS: N37 28.998' / W106 48.109'.

If Lobo Overlook is open, you can save yourself a mile and a gain of approximately 800 feet by driving to the radio tower and overlook. About 0.1 mile east of Wolf Creek Pass, look for a turnoff on the north side of the road. From here a gravel road leads to the 11,680-foot-high overlook, almost 3 miles away. Park near the radio tower to access Lobo Trail 878.

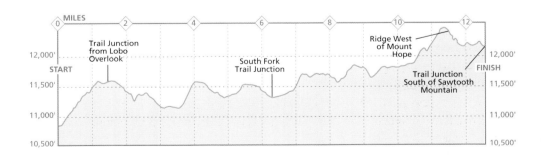

Rock Lake

The Hike

From Wolf Creek Pass, CDT 813 begins on the north side of US 160. A trail marker shows the way, and you may also see remains of a series of small wooden steps. You'll quickly move into the trees; switchbacks help make the moderate-to-steep climb a little easier to bear. The first rise tops off at 1.1 miles, where there are some nice views. You'll descend 40 feet or so before reaching the trail from Lobo Overlook at 1.5 miles. (If you begin the hike at Lobo Overlook, you'll hike 0.5 mile from the trailhead to this point.)

You'll climb and descend as you make your way to the wilderness boundary at 2.7 miles. The roller coaster–like terrain continues past a couple of meadows. You'll see a small lake on the left (and another on the right) at 5.2 miles. Set in rock, the lake on the right is appropriately named Rock Lake. (A sign claims this is Lake Joyce, but it is not. Look for tiger salamanders in the grassy area at the north end of the lake.)

Beyond Rock Lake the trail climbs at a steep grade to 5.5 miles. You now begin hiking off and on the true Continental Divide, always staying near the top. At 6.1 miles you'll be able to see Big Meadows Reservoir to the northeast. You'll then descend along an eastern side slope, crossing a large talus slope before heading back into the trees. The South Fork Trail 750 junction appears at 6.4 miles.

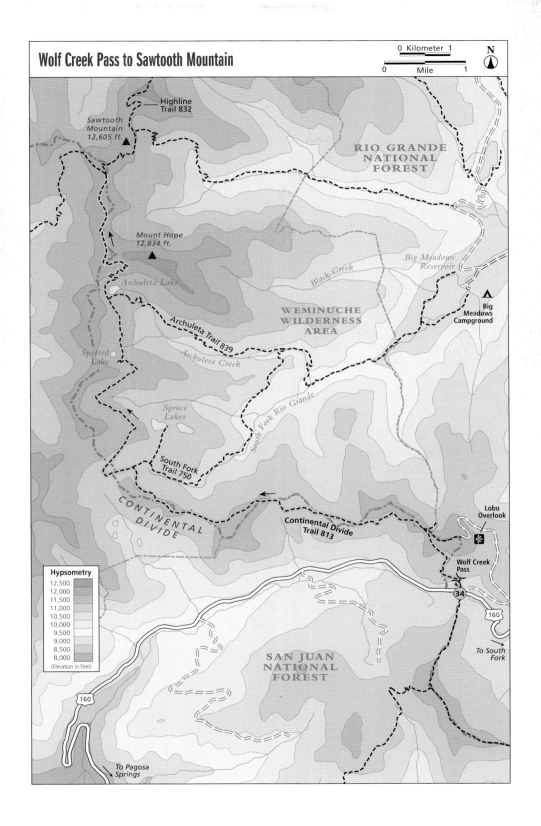

Wolf Creek Pass to Sawtooth Mountain

0 Kilometer 1

0 Mile 1

N

Highline Trail 832

Sawtooth Mountain 12,605 ft.

RIO GRANDE NATIONAL FOREST

Mount Hope 12,834 ft.

Big Meadows Reservoir

Archuleta Lake

Black Creek

WEMINUCHE WILDERNESS AREA

Archuleta Trail 839

Big Meadows Campground

Spotted Lake

Archuleta Creek

Spruce Lakes

South Fork Rio Grande

South Fork Trail 750

CONTINENTAL DIVIDE

Continental Divide Trail 813

Lobo Overlook

Wolf Creek Pass

34

160

Hypsometry

	Elevation (ft)
	12,500
	12,000
	11,500
	11,000
	10,500
	10,000
	9,500
	9,000
	8,500
	8,000

(Elevation in Feet)

SAN JUAN NATIONAL FOREST

To South Fork

160

To Pagosa Springs

Continue on the CDT, hiking across a meadow and into the trees. You'll climb at a moderate-to-steep grade. Long switchbacks, one descent, and an occasional stream crossing make the climb bearable. At 8.7 miles you'll come to a ridge above Spotted Lake. There are grand views of Mount Hope, the Hope Creek drainage, and more from this point. Traverse an open slope; it is decorated with wildflowers come summer. The trail switchbacks down to the lake at 9.2 miles.

Beyond Spotted Lake you'll climb moderately past some meadows. Look for elk. You'll eventually top out on another ridge, then descend gradually to a fork with Archuleta Trail 839 at 10 miles. Continue north on the CDT; a series of steep switchbacks follows, offering views of both the South San Juans and the wilderness. You'll come to the top of a ridge at 11.4 miles. From here Mount Hope's 12,834-foot summit seems close enough to touch.

To finish out this section, descend easily to 12.5 miles and a junction with Highline Trail 832 just south of Sawtooth Mountain.

Miles and Directions

0.0 Wolf Creek Pass.

1.5 Trail junction from Lobo Overlook (Lobo Trail 878).

2.7 Wilderness boundary.

6.4 South Fork Trail junction.

10.0 Archuleta Trail junction.

11.4 High point on ridge near Mount Hope. GPS: N37 32.654' / W106 52.675'.

12.5 Highline Trail junction just south of Sawtooth Mountain.

Options: Sawtooth Mountain is accessible from two other trails: Hope Creek Trail (Hike 21) and the Highline Trail (Hike 24). Try the latter if you like being up high. Starting at the Hunters Lake trailhead, the Highline Trail climbs less than 1,580 feet.

Beginning with this hike, you can travel all the way to Stony Pass. Hike 35 starts where Hike 34 ends, just south of Sawtooth Mountain; it takes you 25.3 miles to Trout Lake. Hike 36 starts at Trout Lake and travels 19.5 miles to the Pine River Trail near Weminuche Pass. Hike 37 picks up at this trail and goes 27.7 miles to Stony Pass. Consult these hikes for a full itinerary.

Hike Information

Local information: South Fork Chamber of Commerce, South Fork; (719) 873-5556; www.southforkcolorado.org.

Local events/attractions: Attend the Little Britches Rodeo (June), Logger Days Festival (July), Rhythms of the Rio Music Festival (August), or Chili Cookoff (October).

Raft or fish the Rio Grande.

Accommodations: South Fork has a number of private campgrounds and motels. One national forest campground—Big Meadows—is about 13 miles southwest of South Fork, off Big Meadow Reservoir Road (FR 410). It's a fee area with drinking water and vault toilets.

35 Sawtooth Mountain to Trout Lake

The Continental Divide Trail (CDT) has spectacular views, high mountain lakes, and wonderful wildflowers. Look for wildlife, including elk.

Start: Junction of CDT and Highline Trail south of Sawtooth Mountain

Distance: 25.3 miles point to point (additional mileage to reach starting point; see Finding the Trailhead)

Hiking time: 3- to 4-day backpack (excluding hike time to starting point)

Difficulty: Strenuous due to length, vertical gain of more than 5,000 feet, and lofty elevation

Canine compatibility: Dogs must be under control.

Nearest town: South Fork

Fees and permits: Free registration (available online, at managing agency, or major trailheads) needed for both day hikers and overnight backpackers. Contact the managing agency for current information.

Maps: USGS South River Peak, Palomino Mountain, and Cimarrona Peak; Trails Illustrated Weminuche Wilderness; DeLorme 3D TopoQuad CD-ROM; Maptech Terrain Navigator CD-ROM

Trail contacts: San Juan National Forest, Pagosa Ranger District, Pagosa Springs; (970) 264-2268; www.fs.usda.gov/sanjuan. Rio Grande National Forest, Divide Ranger District, Creede; (719) 658-2556; www.fs.usda.gov/riogrande.

Special considerations: The trail is easy to follow, but it's above the tree line for some of the way; watch for late-afternoon thunderstorms. Snow can linger in places, especially around the Knife Edge; use caution.

Finding the trailhead: Sawtooth Mountain is accessible from two lovely trails: the Hope Creek Trail (Hike 21) and the Highline Trail (Hike 24). To reach the trailhead for either, drive southwest from the junction of US 160 and CO 149 in South Fork. Follow US 160 for 11.7 miles. Turn right onto Big Meadow Reservoir Road (FR 410), which is paved for 0.4 mile and then turns to gravel. After 1.4 miles you'll come to a fork. A sign says Shaw Lake via Forest Road 430 to the right. Take FR 430, keeping right at the next fork in 0.2 mile. From here it is 1.2 miles on FR 430 to the Hope Creek trailhead (GPS: N37 33.252' / W106 48.161') and 9.6 miles to the Hunters Lake turnoff. For the latter turn left, and you'll reach the Hunters Lake trailhead in 0.1 mile. *DeLorme: Colorado Atlas & Gazetteer:* Page 78 D3. GPS: N37 36.935' / W106 50.366'.

From the Hope Creek trailhead: Hike Trail 838. You'll cross a stream at 0.6 mile and enter a meadow at 1 mile. Travel another 0.3 mile and enter the wilderness. There are more stream and meadow crossings as you proceed. The trail gets a little steeper, but occasional switchbacks (like the one at 3.7 miles) help ease the way. At 4.2 miles you'll cross a large meadow. At 4.9 miles the trail reaches a scenic basin semi-surrounded by mountains. You'll reach the tree line at 5.6 miles. The trail meets Highline Trail 832 (also known as Highland Trail) at 5.8 miles. From there it's another 0.9 mile southwest on the Highline Trail to the junction with the CDT. This hike takes approximately 3 hours.

From the Hunters Lake trailhead: This route is for those who like to be up high. Take Trail 800. You'll cross a stream at 0.2 mile, reach the north end of Hunters Lake at 0.5 mile, and reach the south end at 1 mile. Watch for tree blazes and rock cairns as you head south. You'll enter the Weminuche Wilderness at 1.2 miles and see a junction with the unsigned Lake Creek Trail. Keep going straight. You will hike into spruce trees and climb moderately. At 2 miles you'll start to switchback up to Highline Trail 832 (also called Highland Trail). At the trail junction (mile 2.1), go left and continue through trees to the beginning of the Stairsteps (volcanic rocks). You'll climb a steep 400 feet in a little more than half a mile and reach one of the highest points on the trail at about 2.7 miles. Follow the rock cairns across the nearly level plateau to reach another trail junction at 3.2 miles. Stay on the Highline Trail, traveling south toward the Continental Divide. Continue following rock cairns to a point near Sawtooth Mountain. Switchback down to a junction with the Hope Creek Trail. From there it's another 0.9 mile southwest to the junction with the CDT. This hike takes 3 to 4 hours.

The Hike

From the junction of CDT 813 and Highline Trail 832 south of Sawtooth Mountain, head northwest at a gradual descent. At 0.6 mile you'll see post-markers off to the left (south) that lead to Elk Creek, Beaver Meadow, and eventually Beaver Creek. To the right (north) you will see the Goose Creek drainage.

You'll climb and descend at an easy-to-moderate grade. You'll walk past wildflowers if you're there in midsummer. From 1.1 miles the trail is fairly level and open, allowing for grand views. You'll reach the junction for the Sawtooth Trail (to the north) at 1.6 miles. It drops to Goose Creek Trail 827 in nearly 3 miles and 2,000 vertical feet.

Stay on the CDT. After 2 miles you'll begin a moderately steep descent, reaching a mostly tree-covered saddle at 2.5 miles. In another 0.2 mile you'll see the remains of an old cabin (including a stove) on the left, just off the trail. Proceed through the trees from the saddle, climbing back into the open at the 3-mile point. Cross another saddle, then climb up a steep grade. At 4 miles you'll cross yet another saddle.

Next you'll descend at a moderate-to-easy grade, reaching a low point on a saddle at 4.6 miles. From here the trail follows the contour lines. You'll skirt a bench where there is a small creek. You'll then begin a series of switchbacks to the top of a saddle at 6.5 miles and 12,860 feet above sea level. You'll have fantastic views of the wilderness and beyond from this point, the highest place along the Weminuche portion of the CDT. You'll see the Rio Grande Pyramid, the Grenadiers, and the Needles.

It's a short, steep descent to 6.7 miles and another saddle. After 7.1 miles you'll come to a junction with Goose Creek Trail 827, which goes off to the right (see Hike 26 for more information). This trail leads past the 13,149-foot summit of South River Peak, about 0.5 mile north.

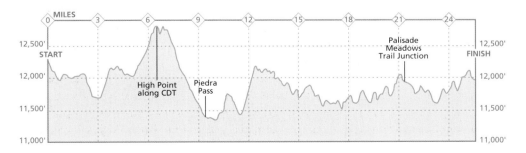

The CDT stays to the left (west) at the junction. You'll descend, cross a stream at 8.6 miles, and enter the trees just afterward. At 9.4 miles you'll reach a junction with the Rainbow Trail—aka West Fork San Juan Trail 561—which leads left to the West Fork trailhead, 12 miles south (see Hike 19 for more information). The junction is Piedra Pass, and it has abundant water and lovely views.

From Piedra Pass the CDT climbs easily to 9.6 miles and a junction with Turkey Creek Trail 580, which heads into the drainage to the south/southwest. (It is 20.1 miles back to the Turkey Creek trailhead; see Hike 18 for more information.) You'll see a sign for the East Fork Piedra River. Post-markers will help you stay on the CDT, which runs parallel to the Turkey Creek Trail but at a higher elevation.

You'll gradually climb to 9.7 miles and cross a stream. It's a moderate uphill to the 10-mile mark, where the CDT curves west. You'll hike mostly in the trees, crossing occasional meadows. At 10.7 miles you'll cross an immense talus slope and emerge into the open. From this point the trail alternately climbs and descends, sometimes steeply, to the 13-mile point and the East Fork Trout Creek Trail junction. Look for the CDT just up the hill.

Next you'll climb to meet the Middle Fork Trail atop a plateau. At 14 miles the trail descends slightly through a boggy area. Follow post-markers to the edge of the basin, where you'll descend an easy-to-moderate grade. At 14.4 miles you'll begin a short, steep ascent to the top. The route continues across side slopes—some open, some covered with trees—throughout most of your journey to Trout Lake.

The trail climbs and descends in turn, reaching a picturesque basin at 15.6 miles. Within the basin you'll find small tarns. Descend to 16 miles, then begin the same thing all over again—lots of ups and downs, sometimes in the woods, sometimes not, sometimes steep, sometimes not. The trail tends to stay on top of the Continental Divide, though you will drop on the north and south sides at times. At 18.1 miles there will be a body of water on your right; it's a 300-foot descent to this lake. (The Middle Fork Piedra River Trail picks up somewhere in this area, but it is difficult to find from the CDT.)

At 18.8 miles you'll emerge into the open. Stay on the Continental Divide, continuing the roller-coaster walk. At one point you'll climb to 11,950 feet above sea level. At 20.1 miles you'll cross a saddle and have good views all around. Look north into the Middle Trout Creek drainage; you may see a herd of elk.

Proceed along the exposed Continental Divide to 20.9 miles. The CDT will drop onto a saddle and then head north. At 21.2 miles a trail to the left (south) leads to Palisade Meadows. Go straight ahead. After traversing the Continental Divide for another mile, you'll descend a side slope where there is lots of vegetation, plus a stream crossing. You will see Cherokee Lake to the north at 23.5 miles. A side trail descends a short distance to the lake.

Beyond Cherokee Lake the CDT crosses open tundra, climbing to the rock promontory/sliver called the Knife Edge at 24.4 miles. There are incredible views from here. If you hike during prime wildflower season, you'll see an impressive display as you continue to Trout Lake. Continue west, hiking across the Knife Edge, which can

Sawtooth Mountain to Trout Lake

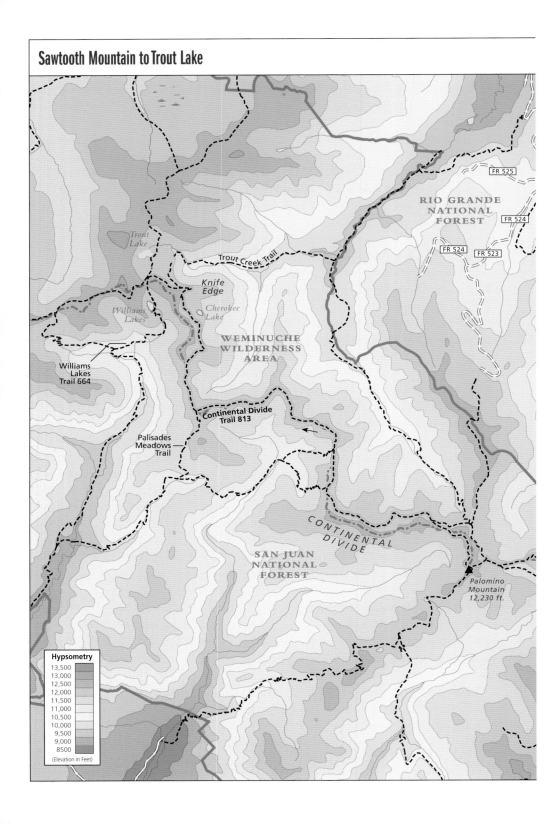

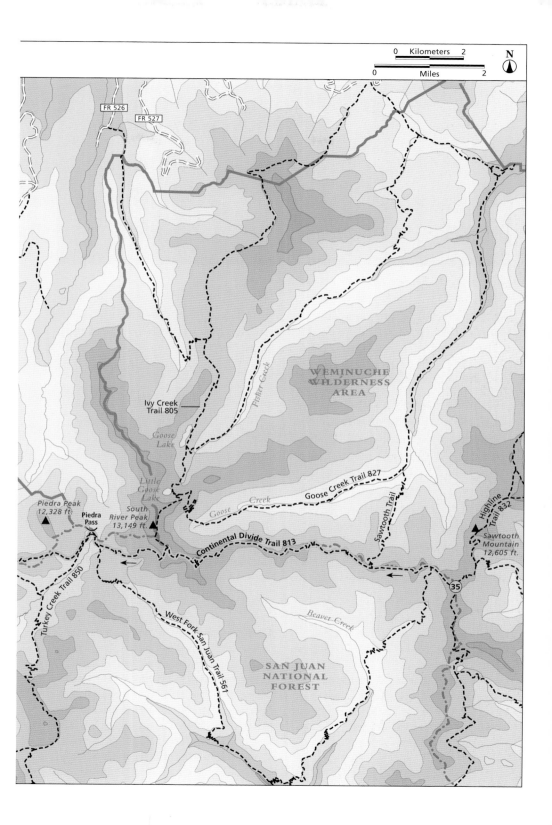

0   Kilometers   2

0   Miles   2

FR 526

FR 527

WEMINUCHE
WILDERNESS
AREA

Fisher Creek

Ivy Creek
Trail 805

Goose
Lake

Little
Goose
Lake

Goose Creek Trail 827

Goose   Creek

Sawtooth Trail

Highline
Trail 832

Piedra Peak
12,328 ft.

South
River Peak
13,149 ft.

Piedra
Pass

Sawtooth
Mountain
12,605 ft.

Continental Divide Trail 813

Turkey Creek Trail 850

West Fork San Juan Trail 561

Beaver Creek

35

SAN JUAN
NATIONAL
FOREST

Hiker on the Continental Divide near South River Peak

be covered with slippery snow until mid-July or later. Descend to the Trout Lake/ Williams Lakes Trails at 25.3 miles. The lakes are less than a mile away; Trout Lake is to the right (north), and Williams Lakes are to the left (south).

Miles and Directions (accumulated CDT miles)

0.0 (12.5)   Junction just south of Sawtooth Mountain.

1.6 (14.1)   Sawtooth Trail junction.

6.5 (19.0)   High point along CDT. GPS: N37 33.825' / W106 58.106'.

9.4 (21.9)   Piedra Pass. GPS: N37 34.251' / W107 0.053'.

13.0 (25.5)   East Fork Trout Creek Trail junction.

21.2 (33.7)   Palisade Meadows Trail junction. GPS: N37 36.094' / W107 8.304'.

23.5 (36.0)   Cherokee Lake.

25.3 (37.8)   Trout Lake Trail junction. GPS: N37 38.247' / W107 9.352'.

Option: You can continue hiking all the way to Stony Pass. Hike 36 starts at Trout Lake and travels 19.5 miles to the Pine River Trail near Weminuche Pass. Hike 37 picks up at the Pine River Trail and goes 27.7 miles to Stony Pass. Consult these hikes for a full itinerary.

Hike Information

Local information: South Fork Chamber of Commerce, South Fork; (719) 873-5556; www .southforkcolorado.org.

Local events/attractions: Attend the Little Britches Rodeo (June), Logger Days Festival (July), Rhythms of the Rio Music Festival (August), or Chili Cookoff (October).

Raft or fish the Rio Grande.

Accommodations: South Fork has a number of private campgrounds and motels. One national forest campground—Big Meadows—is about 13 miles southwest of South Fork, off Big Meadow Reservoir Road (FR 410). It's a fee area with drinking water and vault toilets. Another national forest facility, Marshall Park Campground, is 6.5 miles southwest of Creede, right off CO 149. It, too, is a fee area; facilities include water and outhouses.

36 Trout Lake to Weminuche Pass

Hike this section of the Continental Divide Trail (CDT), and you'll see that it continues to provide stunning views, high mountain lakes, abundant wildflowers, and wildlife that includes bighorn sheep near Hossick Peak.

Start: Junction of CDT and Trout Lake Trail south of Trout Lake

Distance: 19.5 miles point to point (additional mileage to reach starting point; see Finding the Trailhead)

Hiking time: 2- to 3-day backpack (excluding hike time to starting point)

Difficulty: Strenuous due to length, vertical gain of more than 3,000 feet, and lofty elevation

Canine compatibility: Dogs must be under control.

Nearest town: Creede

Fees and permits: Free registration (available online, at managing agency, or major trailheads) needed for both day hikers and overnight backpackers. Contact the managing agency for current information.

Maps: USGS Little Squaw Creek, Granite Lake, Cimarrona Peak, and Weminuche Pass; Trails Illustrated Weminuche Wilderness; DeLorme 3D TopoQuad CD-ROM; Maptech Terrain Navigator CD-ROM

Trail contacts: San Juan National Forest, Pagosa Ranger District, Pagosa Springs; (970) 264-2268; www.fs.usda.gov/sanjuan. San Juan National Forest, Columbine Ranger District, Bayfield; (970) 884-2512; www.fs.usda.gov/sanjuan. Rio Grande National Forest, Divide Ranger District, Creede; (719) 658-2556; www.fs.usda.gov/riogrande.

Finding the trailhead: If you have completed Hike 35, you are already at the starting point for this hike. Otherwise you can access the CDT south of Trout Lake from the Fern Creek trailhead (Hike 27). This will add 11.7 miles and 6 to 8 hours of hiking time to the trip. To reach the Fern Creek trailhead from Creede, go southwest on CO 149 for 16.3 miles. Turn left onto gravel Fern Creek Road, also known as FR 522. After 1.5 miles turn right at the sign for the Fern Creek trailhead. *DeLorme: Colorado Atlas & Gazetteer:* Page 78 B1. GPS: N37 44.291' / W107 06.097'.

Begin hiking Fern Creek Trail 815 through the burn area. At 1 mile the grade will steepen as you head up the Fern Creek drainage. You'll hike near the creek at times; at other times you'll hike above or away from it. After 2.6 miles you'll travel along the west side of a rock slide. The rock switches to meadow as you continue to a junction at 3.8 miles. Unmaintained Texas Creek Trail 816 is to the right. Look ahead to see Little Ruby Lake, and continue across the flat meadow on the east side of it. Head back into the trees at 4 miles. You'll climb at a steep grade, topping off at 4.3 miles, where you will see Fuchs Reservoir on the left. In another 0.3 mile you'll come to a trail junction. At the fork go left (south); you'll reach Ruby Lake at 4.8 miles. The trail forks here. Texas Creek Trail 816 is once again to the right.

The main route heads left (east) to a sign for Red Lakes Trail 889, on the lake's northeast side. At 5.4 miles you'll enter the wilderness. The moderate-to-steep climb tapers off at 5.7 miles. You'll reach an unsigned junction with the Jumper Lake Trail at 7 miles. Post-markers head southeast toward Jumper Lake and southwest toward the Red Lakes; follow the southwest route. You'll cross a few streams and gradually climb to a small, unnamed lake on the left at 9.1 miles. The closest of the Red Lakes is on the right (west) at 9.2 miles. Proceed to the unsigned junction with Texas

Creek Trail 816 at 9.7 miles. To continue to CDT 813, descend to the south. You'll cross a couple of small streams before you reach West Trout Creek at 10.8 miles and an unsigned junction with the West Trout Creek Trail at 10.9 miles. You will see spur trails that lead to Trout Lake (though you're still too low to see the lake itself). The trail will take you around the east side of the lake and climb steeply to the CDT at 11.7 miles (and an elevation of 12,000 feet).

The Hike

At its junction with the Trout Lake Trail, go west on the CDT, following post-markers across the tundra. Look for ptarmigan and wildflowers in the area. You'll reach the top of a ridge at 0.7 mile and descend to a narrow saddle at 1.3 miles. From here there are excellent views into the Little Squaw Creek drainage. The trail climbs for the next 0.5 mile, staying near the top of the Continental Divide (mostly on the north side); it then descends to 2.5 miles and the Williams Creek Trail, which leads to the west fork of the creek. There are a couple of small lakes here.

The CDT climbs again to 3.6 miles and the top of a ridge just south of Chief Mountain. From here you can see west to the Needles, the Rio Grande Pyramid, and the Window. Descend into the Squaw Creek drainage; you will drop at a generally moderate (but sometimes steep) grade and reach the trees at 4.7 miles. After 5 miles the trail parallels a pretty stream, crossing it at 5.1 miles. The unsigned Squaw Creek Trail merges from the right at 5.6 miles (see Hike 29 for more information on this route).

Continue left (south) along a talus slope. You'll reach the meadowy realm of Squaw Pass at 5.9 miles. Beyond the pass the CDT begins a short, steep climb to a bench to the west. You'll hike in the trees, then switchback up at 6.1 miles. The trail exits the trees at 6.6 miles, where there's a stream. The grade becomes more gradual here. At 7.3 miles there is a lake on the right.

Hike another 0.5 mile, then begin a steep descent to another basin at 8.5 miles. The trail passes a number of small lakes before crossing a stream at 9.1 miles. From there you'll climb a moderate-to-steep grade to 10.7 miles and a ridge that hosts wildflowers and offers beautiful views. Continue climbing to 10.9 miles, where you will see Squaw Lake on the right. At 11.4 miles you'll reach the highest point on this section of the CDT, 12,780 feet above sea level.

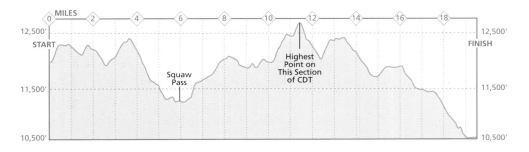

Mike Vining backpacking the CDT

The trail descends at a steep grade to 11.8 miles and the Squaw Lake Trail junction. Proceed on the CDT, dropping into a low part of the basin before climbing a steep slope. You'll reach the top of the next ridge at 13 miles and then hike across a wide, high plateau that is fairly level. The trail then begins a moderate (but sometimes steep) descent in the open. At 14.9 miles you'll pass the head of Snowslide Canyon and see many ponds in the area. A moderate climb begins at 15.2 miles, and at 15.5 miles you'll reach a junction with the Snowslide Canyon Trail. This is also the top of the ridge.

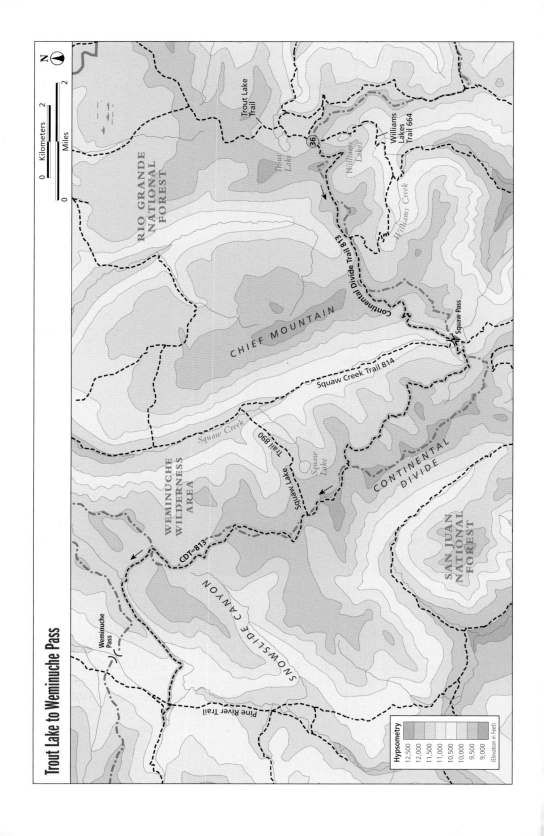

Trout Lake to Weminuche Pass

N

Kilometers
0   2

Miles
0   2

RIO GRANDE NATIONAL FOREST

Trout Lake Trail

Trout Lake

36

Williams Lakes

Williams Lakes Trail 664

Williams Creek

Continental Divide Trail 813

CHIEF MOUNTAIN

Squaw Pass

Squaw Creek Trail 814

Squaw Creek

Trail 890

Squaw Lake

CONTINENTAL DIVIDE

WEMINUCHE WILDERNESS AREA

CDT-813

SAN JUAN NATIONAL FOREST

SNOWSLIDE CANYON

Weminuche Pass

Pine River Trail

Hypsometry

	Elevation in Feet
	12,500
	12,000
	11,500
	11,000
	10,500
	10,000
	9,500
	9,000

(Elevation in Feet)

> Look closely when you're in the alpine or tundra region, and you will see miniature wildflowers. For instance, mountain bluebells, also known as tall chiming bells, may grow to 4 feet at a lower elevation, but they are mere inches high in the alpine area.

The trail descends steeply at first, then moderately, into the trees at 15.7 miles. Along the way you'll emerge for more views of the Window, the Rio Grande Pyramid, and other formations. At 16.5 miles you'll cross the North Fork Pine River. Look for lots of wildflowers in season. You'll cross the river again soon after.

The route descends moderately to the trees at 18.3 miles, then continues to Fuchs Diversion Ditch at 18.7 miles. You'll reach the meadow near Weminuche Pass just beyond the ditch. The CDT crosses the meadow (look for post-markers) and jumps a canal at 19.1 miles. It meets the Pine River (Los Pinos) Trail, which is unsigned, at 19.5 miles. Follow post-markers to take the CDT west from here. At an elevation of 10,565 feet, this is the lowest part of the CDT in the Weminuche.

Miles and Directions (accumulated CDT miles)

0.0 (37.8)	Junction Trout Lake Trail and CDT.
2.5 (40.3)	Williams Creek Trail junction.
3.6 (41.4)	Top of ridge.
5.9 (43.7)	Squaw Pass. GPS: N37 36.125' / W107 12.995'.
11.4 (49.2)	Highest point of this CDT section.
15.5 (53.3)	Snowslide Canyon Trail junction.
19.5 (57.3)	Pine River Trail near Weminuche Pass. GPS: N37 40.096' / W107 19.844'.

Option: You can continue hiking to Stony Pass from here. Hike 37 picks up at the Pine River Trail and goes 27.7 miles to the pass. Consult that hike for a full itinerary.

Hike Information

Local information: Creede & Mineral County Chamber of Commerce, Creede; (800) 327-2102; www.creede.com.

Local events/attractions: Creede Repertory Theater in Creede is open every summer and is a big hit with locals and visitors alike; (866) 658-2540; www.creederep.org.

The Underground Mining Museum in Creede is a fascinating place and well worth a visit; (719) 658-0811; www.undergroundmining museum.com.

Raft or fish the Rio Grande.

One of the best burger joints around is at Freeman's General Store. Open in summer, you'll find it 2.1 miles east of the CO 149/FR 520 junction on CO 149.

Accommodations: Creede offers motels, cabins, and bed-and-breakfast inns. One national forest campground—Marshall Park—is located off the road as you drive to the trailhead at Fern Creek. Another, Thirtymile Campground, is located at the trailhead to Weminuche Pass. Both are fee areas with water and vault toilets.

37 Weminuche Pass to Stony Pass

If you've hiked from Wolf Creek Pass to this point, you've seen some of the most wonderful parts of the Weminuche Wilderness. Continue hiking to Stony Pass, and you'll witness spectacular scenes, see-forever views, high mountain lakes, wildlife, and wildflowers.

Start: Junction of Continental Divide Trail (CDT) and Pine River Trail near Weminuche Pass
Distance: 27.7 miles point to point (additional mileage to reach starting point; see Finding the Trailhead)
Hiking time: 3- to 4-day backpack (excluding hike time to starting point)
Difficulty: Strenuous due to length, vertical gain of more than 6,000 feet, and lofty elevation
Canine compatibility: Dogs must be under control.
Nearest town: Silverton
Fees and permits: Free registration (available online, at managing agency, or major trailheads) needed for both day hikers and overnight backpackers. Contact the managing agency for current information.

Maps: USGS Weminuche Pass, Rio Grande Pyramid, Storm King Peak, and Howardsville; Trails Illustrated Weminuche Wilderness; DeLorme 3D TopoQuad CD-ROM; Maptech Terrain Navigator CD-ROM
Trail contacts: San Juan National Forest, Columbine Ranger District, Bayfield; (970) 884-2512; www.fs.usda.gov/sanjuan. Rio Grande National Forest, Divide Ranger District, Creede; (719) 658-2556; www.fs.usda.gov/riogrande.
Special considerations: Hikers must camp at least 200 feet from West Ute Lake; campfires are not permitted. In addition, livestock must be kept 200 feet away from the lake. The trail is easy to follow in most places, but difficult to follow in other places. The CDT is above the tree line much of the way, so watch for late-afternoon thunderstorms. Snow can be deep in places as late as July.

Finding the trailhead: If you have completed Hike 36, you are already at the starting point for this hike. Otherwise you can hike 6.2 miles from Thirtymile Campground to Weminuche Pass (Hike 30); this will add 2 to 4 hours to the trip. To reach the campground trailhead from Creede, drive southwest on CO 149 for 20 miles. Turn left onto Rio Grande Reservoir Road, also known as FR 520. It is paved but turns to maintained gravel after 0.3 mile. Drive another 11.1 miles, and turn left at the signed junction for Thirtymile Campground and the Weminuche and Squaw Creek trailheads. Keep right upon entering the area; you will reach a parking area in 0.2 mile. *DeLorme: Colorado Atlas & Gazetteer:* Page 77 C7. GPS: N37 43.398' / W107 15.543'.

From the parking area follow the signs south about 200 yards to a wilderness sign and trail register. After signing in at the register, which provides access to the Squaw Creek Trail as well (see Hike 29), hike west on Weminuche Trail 818, hiking toward the Rio Grande Reservoir. You'll pass old cabin remains after 0.3 mile and then the dam and spillway. You'll enter the wilderness at 0.8 mile. The trail grade stays fairly level (with gentle ups and downs) until mile 1.3. Here the grade becomes moderate, with short, steep ascents through a mix of trees. After 1.5 miles you'll turn south, heading up the Weminuche Creek drainage. Cross a bridge over the creek at 1.8 miles. At 2 miles the trail eases up; you will climb through meadows and cross a few streams as you proceed.

At 4 miles you'll have to ford an unnamed stream that flows from Simpson Mountain, to the west. Continue another 0.8 mile, and you'll cross Weminuche Creek. (You may have to get your feet wet here early in the season.) Just after crossing the creek, you'll come to a junction with the Skyline Trail. Stay on Trail 818 to the Weminuche Pass area and continue to the Pine River Trail/CDT junction, which is south another 1.4 miles.

The Hike

From the junction of Pine River (Los Pinos) Trail 523 and the CDT near Weminuche Pass, follow the CDT post-markers to where you ford the Rincon La Vaca. Just beyond this river the CDT begins a steep climb through the trees. After 0.5 mile you'll enter a meadow and hike parallel to Rincon La Vaca. There are good views of the Window and the Rio Grande Pyramid here.

The trail crosses several small streams as you hike to the west end of the meadow, where you'll begin a steep climb. At 1.1 miles you'll enter the trees; there is a pond on the left just beyond. At 1.6 miles you'll descend a bit, switching between meadow and trees as you parallel a stream. A very steep slope begins at 2.1 miles. The trail skirts a talus slope, with a pretty waterfall off to the side at 2.3 miles.

At 2.5 miles you'll come to a fork: One trail heads southwest, the other northwest. Go left (southwest) and continue the steep climb. At 2.9 miles the trail eases, climbing more gradually. The Window and the Rio Grande Pyramid will remain visible as you ascend through willows.

At 3.2 miles the trail crosses a stream, and at 3.3 miles Skyline Trail 564 joins the CDT from the right. The Skyline trail is unsigned, but post-markers point the way up the ridge to the northeast. Continue on the CDT, crossing nearly flat terrain and a couple of streams. Just after the last crossing, you'll reach a small lake that mirrors the Window.

From this lake you'll climb an easy-to-moderate grade to a ridgetop at 4.6 miles. There is a good view into the Ute drainages from here, with an abundance of wildflowers to keep you occupied on the descent. The drop is a moderate one, but the grade steepens as you near the head of the East Ute Creek drainage.

The East Ute Creek Trail 824 junction is at 5.6 miles. Follow the rock cairns to a junction where a spur trail heads left (southeast) to the Rincon La Osa. Continue

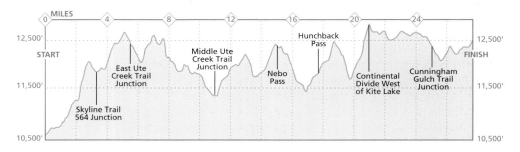

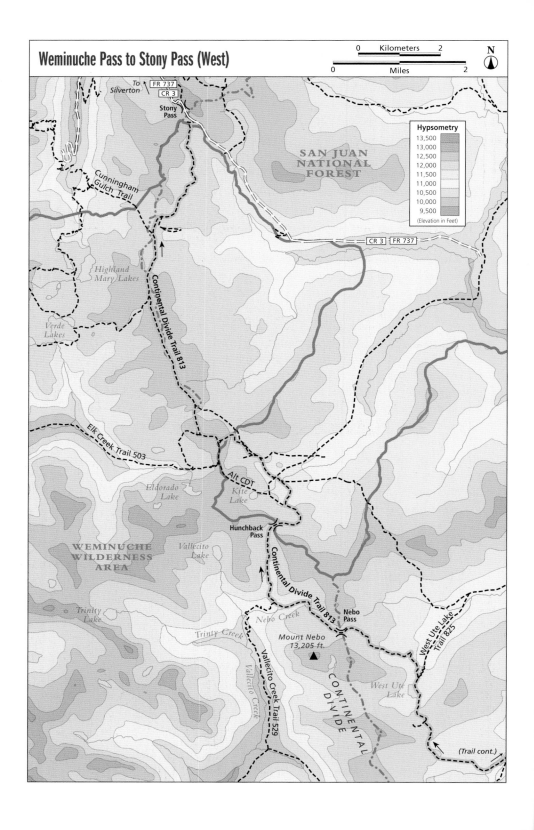

Weminuche Pass to Stony Pass (West)

To
Silverton   FR 737
CR 3
Stony
Pass

SAN JUAN
NATIONAL
FOREST

Hypsometry

13,500
13,000
12,500
12,000
11,500
11,000
10,500
10,000
9,500
(Elevation in Feet)

Cunningham Gulch Trail

CR 3   FR 737

Highland
Mary Lakes

Continental Divide Trail 813

Verde
Lakes

Elk Creek Trail 503

Alt CDT

Eldorado
Lake

Kite
Lake

WEMINUCHE
WILDERNESS
AREA

Hunchback
Pass

Vallecito
Lake

Continental Divide Trail 813

Trinity
Lake

Nebo Creek

Nebo
Pass

West Ute Lake
Trail 825

Trinity Creek

Mount Nebo
13,205 ft.

West Ute
Lake

Vallecito Creek Trail 529

Vallecito Creek

CONTINENTAL
DIVIDE

(Trail cont.)

Weminuche Pass to Stony Pass (East)

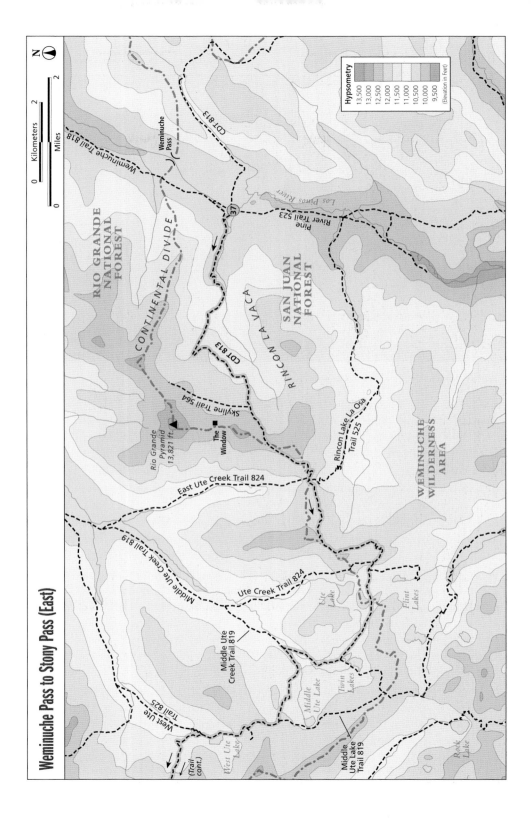

Hypsometry

| 13,500 |
| 13,000 |
| 12,500 |
| 12,000 |
| 11,500 |
| 11,000 |
| 10,500 |
| 10,000 |
| 9,500 |

(Elevation in Feet)

N

0 Kilometers 2

0 Miles 2

Weminuche Trail 818

Weminuche Pass

CDT 813

RIO GRANDE NATIONAL FOREST

CONTINENTAL DIVIDE

Los Pinos River

37

Pine River Trail 523

RINCON LA VACA

SAN JUAN NATIONAL FOREST

CDT 813

Skyline Trail 564

Rio Grande Pyramid 13,821 ft.

The Window

East Ute Creek Trail 824

Rincon Lake La Osa Trail 525

WEMINUCHE WILDERNESS AREA

Middle Ute Creek Trail 819

Ute Creek Trail 824

Ute Lake

Flint Lakes

Middle Ute Creek Trail 819

West Ute Trail 825

(Trail cont.)

West Ute Lake

Middle Ute Lake

Twin Lakes

Middle Ute Lake Trail 819

Rock Lake

View west from the Rio Grande Pyramid

right (northwest) on the CDT. You will climb an easy-to-moderate grade to a stream at 6.3 miles. Continue to a nice view of Ute Lake from the ridge. You'll regain the top of the Continental Divide at 7.5 miles.

Proceed along the ridge to a junction at 7.7 miles. Here yet another trail heads east to Rincon La Osa. To continue on the CDT, hike southwest and drop to the Ute Lakes area. (Once again, the topographic map is in error.) The trail descends steeply to a junction at 8 miles. Take the left (northwest) fork and head directly toward Ute Lake, still descending sharply. At 8.2 miles there is a junction on the left (south) with the Flint Lakes Trail. Just beyond this crossroads is another branch of Ute Lake Trail 905; it's to the right and northwest. Keep straight and to the southwest.

Pass Ute Lake. You'll climb at an easy-to-moderate grade for a short distance, then begin dropping. At 8.7 miles there's a good view of the basin ahead; you'll see Twin Lakes and several high peaks after the 9-mile mark. The trail then descends steeply to a fork at 9.5 miles, where the rerouted CDT breaks from its older version. Keep going straight (north) on the new CDT.

Descend to the junction of the Middle Ute Creek Trail at 10.6 miles. Head west from here, climbing a fairly steep trail to the Middle Ute Lake Trail junction at 12 miles. Post-markers show you the way to both trails. You can see back to the Rio Grande Pyramid and the Window from here. It's a moderate-to-steep climb to the top of a ridge at 12.5 miles.

Descend the ridge. You'll pass a small lake, reach West Ute Lake at 13.1 miles, and find a junction at 13.8 miles. Here West Ute Trail 825 continues north. Stay on the CDT, which goes left (northwest). Just beyond the junction you'll cross a stream. (**Note:** The CDT over Nebo Pass is not shown on topographic maps.) The trail stays in the trees at first, then emerges into the open, where there is an abundance of wildflowers.

The trail ascends at an easy-to-moderate grade to 13.9 miles, where you'll cross a creek. It then climbs at a steep—sometimes very steep—grade, crossing the most northerly of two creeks at 14.6 miles. Pass a little lake on the left. At 14.9 miles you'll cross another creek and then reach the top of Nebo Pass at 12,450 feet above sea level. There are wonderful views of the Grenadiers from here. Descend just a bit for a fantastic view of Nebo Lake with the peaks in the background.

From Nebo Pass descend moderately to 15.7 miles, where you'll cross yet another stream. A steep switchback leads down to 15.8 miles and Nebo Creek. Almost immediately after crossing the creek, you'll cross again and hike along its south side.

After 16 miles the trail eases, but it soon becomes difficult to find. It follows Nebo Creek (actually using the creek bed as a trail) for 100 yards or so, then crosses to the north side of the creek and heads into the trees. At 16.4 miles it moves away from Nebo Creek, descending moderately to an unsigned junction with Vallecito Creek Trail 529.

You'll see lots of willows, wildflowers, and other vegetation as you hike north up a side stream that eventually flows into Vallecito Creek. It's a steep climb to 16.9 miles, where you cross the stream. You will cross several more side streams before climbing a steep grade to the top of Hunchback Pass at 17.8 miles. This pass sits at 12,493 feet above sea level, reaching into the heavens. From here you can see south to the Guardian, the most prominent peak in view, and farther south into the Needle Mountains.

At this point you'll pass out of the wilderness and descend a moderate-to-steep slope. You will cross several streams and pass old mining remains en route to a junction with a four-wheel-drive road at 19.4 miles. There's a trail register here; be sure to sign in or out.

If you want to stay on the primary CDT, see Hike 4 (page 29) for more information. If you want to continue this hike, which follows an alternate CDT, go left (west) up the four-wheel-drive road. (The two trails merge in about 2 miles.) It's a steep climb up to Kite Lake at 19.9 miles. You'll find an old mining cabin and a couple of mine shafts. Just before reaching the lake, look for a rock cairn marking a trail to the right (north). Climb the steep (sometimes very steep) grade, crossing a stream en route to 12,800 feet at 20.9 miles. You are standing on the Continental Divide. Take in the impressive view of Eldorado Lake, with Peak Two behind it. You can also see the Elk Creek drainage and lakes north of it.

Turn right (north) onto the trail. You'll reach a high point of 12,840 feet, then begin a short but steep descent over rocky terrain. You'll meet Elk Creek Trail 503 at

21.3 miles (see Hike 4 for more information). Hike 0.3 mile to another junction at 21.6 miles. Here the Colorado Trail and the primary CDT take off to the right (east); you go left (northwest) on the CDT.

Follow post-markers to 21.7 miles, then stay north past a few pretty lakes. Rock cairns lead the way as you roll up and down to the 23.5-mile point. Look for two rock cairns here, one to the west and the other to the east. Follow the trail that passes between the two. At 23.9 miles you'll reach an unsigned junction with the trail to Verde Lakes; pass it. The terrain still rolls as you continue to a small lake on the left at 24.3 miles. Descend steeply to a small lake on the right. At 25.1 miles look for a sign pointing the way to the CDT. You'll also see an unmarked, well-defined trail heading to the northwest. It leads down into Cunningham Gulch (see Option 2).

The last portion of the CDT used to be tough to follow, but the Forest Service rerouted the trail a few years ago and it's now in good shape. From this point the trail heads to the northeast and climbs and descends, roller coaster fashion, with some switchbacks along the way. It pretty much travels north, eventually winding around the east side of Stony Pass Peak. You will arrive at the Stony Pass trailhead at 27.7 miles. If you've hiked the whole CDT route in the Weminuche, you've come 85 miles!

Miles and Directions (accumulated CDT miles)

0.0 (57.3)	Pine River Trail near Weminuche Pass.
3.3 (61.0)	Skyline Trail 564 junction.
5.6 (62.9)	East Ute Creek Trail junction.
7.7 (65.0)	Junction atop ridge.
9.5 (66.8)	Rock Lake Trail junction.
12.0 (69.3)	Middle Ute Lake Trail junction.
13.8 (71.1)	West Ute Lake Trail junction.
14.9 (72.2)	Nebo Pass.
17.8 (75.1)	Hunchback Pass. GPS: N37 42.284' / W107 31.206'.
21.3 (78.6)	Elk Creek Trail junction.
25.1 (82.4)	Cunningham Gulch Trail junction. GPS: N37 45.229' / W107 33.385'.
27.7 (85.0)	Stony Pass. GPS: 37 47.686' / W107 32.844'.

Option 1: Mile 9.5 marks the junction of the old and new (rerouted) CDT. The trip described above continues on the new trail. If you'd like to hike the old CDT—which stays true to the Continental Divide—go west past the north end of Twin Lakes, then climb the moderate-to-steep slope to the Rock Lake Trail junction. From there head north on the Middle Ute Lake Trail, traversing a side slope bursting with summer wildflowers. Once the trail was difficult to find because of thick willows, but it was cleared in summer 1998 and is now a pleasure to hike. After 2.2 miles you'll reach the 12-mile junction mentioned in the main text.

Option 2: If you don't have four-wheel drive, you can't get to Stony Pass. But you can hike an alternate route, ending this section by hiking the Cunningham Gulch Trail. The unsigned but defined route you passed at mile 25.1 is a nice trail. It descends 1,380 feet and ends 2.1 miles later at the Highland Mary Lakes trailhead (see Hike 1 for more details).

THE CONTINENTAL DIVIDE TRAIL

The CDT is a National Scenic Trail and a link between the Weminuche and South San Juan Wilderness Areas. Hiking the trail through both areas is an experience you don't want to miss—it's all about amazing views, wildflowers, alpine tundra, and other natural beauties. The 3,100-mile trail is still in the making (it's about 72 percent complete), but it is traveled by a select few who through-hike it each year. The CDT started as a dream in the 1960s, when it was identified as a way to traverse the backbone of our country. When it is complete, the trail will pass through twenty-five national forests, twenty wilderness areas, three national parks, and one national monument. Certainly the trail is one of the most awesome and spectacular pathways in the country. Spanning Mexico and Canada, it travels through New Mexico, Colorado, Wyoming, Idaho, and Montana. Hike the CDT in the Weminuche and South San Juan Wilderness Areas, and you'll see one of the most gorgeous parts of the trail.

Option 3: If you want to do a day hike, I recommend starting at Stony Pass and traveling south as far as you desire. You could also choose to hike the full trail in reverse, from Stony Pass to Weminuche Pass. Stony Pass is accessible from Silverton. From the junction of US 550 and CO 110 at the southwest end of town, drive northeast on CO 110 (Greene Street). After 1 mile go right (east) on San Juan CR 2. The road is paved for the first 2 miles, then it turns to maintained gravel. After another 2.1 miles turn right (south) onto San Juan CR 4 toward Stony Pass. After an additional 1.7 miles, the road forks again. Keep left on San Juan CR 3 (FR 737) for 4.1 miles to the top of Stony Pass (elevation 12,588 feet). The four-wheel-drive road is rough and very narrow in some places. The trailhead is a couple hundred yards east of the pass, near the remains of an old cabin on the right side of the road. *DeLorme: Colorado Atlas & Gazetteer:* Page 77 B5. GPS: 37 47.686' / W107 32.844'.

Hike Information

Local information: Silverton Chamber of Commerce, Silverton; (970) 387-5654 or (800) 752-4494; www.silvertoncolorado.com.
Local events/attractions: Ride the Durango & Silverton Narrow Gauge Railroad, Durango; (970) 247-2733 or (877) 872-4607; www.durangotrain.com.

Walk around historic downtown Silverton.

Accommodations: Silverton offers a variety of private campgrounds and motels. If you're starting the hike from Weminuche Pass, you'll find a campground at the trailhead. Thirtymile Campground is a national forest facility. It's a fee area; facilities include water and vault toilets.

The South San Juan Wilderness

The South San Juan Wilderness is located in the San Juan Mountains, the largest single range (10,000-plus square miles) in the US Rockies. The South San Juans are separated from the main portion of the range by US 160 and by the Rio Grande and the San Juan River.

The South San Juan area was designated wilderness by an act of Congress in December 1980, and additional acreage was added with the passage of the Colorado Wilderness Act of 1993. The wilderness encompasses 158,790 acres. It is often called Colorado's wildest corner and is known for its sweeping vistas, solitude, bottomlands, spacious U-shaped valleys, glaciated uplands, jagged mountains and pinnacles, and high, gentle hills. It is also home to the headwaters of three rivers: the Conejos, the San Juan, and the Blanco.

The South San Juan Wilderness also embraces the lofty realms of the Continental Divide. Stretching from Elwood Pass, which is southeast of the more famous Wolf Creek Pass, and continuing southeast to Cumbres Pass, which isn't too far north of the New Mexico border, the trail stretches for more than 50 miles. Forty of these miles are in the wilderness. Within its borders you'll find more than thirty lakes, most of which were carved by glaciers.

Wildlife is abundant in the South San Juans. There are elk, deer, coyotes, bighorn sheep, mountain lions, beavers, snowshoe hares, and many small animals, including squirrels, chipmunks, and pikas. Birdlife includes golden eagles, bald eagles, and a variety of hawks, among other species. If there are grizzly bears in Colorado, they would most likely be in the remote and rugged southern San Juans. (The last known great grizzly was killed in the region in 1979.) Even wolverines, thought to be extinct in the state, may still live here. Circumstantial evidence points to their unceasing existence. In addition, the last gray wolf in the state was probably killed here in 1943, yet there have been wolf sightings in Colorado in recent years.

The South San Juan Wilderness, which ranges in elevation from 8,000 to 13,000-plus feet, receives light use, especially compared with other wildernesses of the San Juan Mountains. Popular for all sorts of outdoor activities, including animal watching and photography, the wilderness's 180 miles of trails make access relatively easy.

Although there are no 14,000-foot peaks (better known as fourteeners) in the area, the wilderness is home to two Colorado county high points. At 13,300 feet, Summit Peak is the highest point in Archuleta County and in all the wilderness. At 13,172 feet, Conejos Peak soars above all of Conejos County.

38 Summit Peak via Quartz Creek

Summit Peak can be reached via many routes. This one is perhaps the longest and most strenuous, but it's a good hike all the same. The views are tremendous once you climb out of the drainage. Best of all, most all of the hike is located in the wilderness.

Start: Quartz Creek trailhead
Distance: 17.6 miles out and back
Hiking time: About 8 to 10 hours or 2- to 3-day backpack
Difficulty: Strenuous due to length and elevation gain of more than 4,000 feet
Canine compatibility: Dogs must be under control.
Nearest town: Pagosa Springs

Fees and permits: None
Maps: USGS Summit Peak; Trails Illustrated South San Juan/Del Norte; DeLorme 3D TopoQuad CD-ROM; Maptech Terrain Navigator CD-ROM
Trail contact: San Juan National Forest, Pagosa Ranger District, Pagosa Springs; (970) 264-2268; www.fs.usda.gov/sanjuan

Finding the trailhead: From the junction of US 84 and US 160 on the east edge of Pagosa Springs, travel northeast on US 160 for 9.7 miles to FR 667 (also known as East Fork Road), which leads right (east) to the East Fork Campground. (Shortly after turning off US 160, you'll pass the campground.) Drive the gravel road for about 9.2 miles to Quartz Meadow Road (FR 684), a four-wheel-drive-recommended route that can be very slippery when wet. Turn right (south) onto FR 684, fording the East Fork San Juan River, and then proceed 3 miles to the trailhead. Please note that high-clearance, four-wheel-drive vehicles are preferred for both roads because of several creek and river crossings. During some periods river crossings are impossible for any vehicle. *DeLorme: Colorado Atlas & Gazetteer:* Page 88 A3. GPS: N37 23.352' / W106 44.984'.

The Hike

There's an easier way to get to the top of Summit Peak (see *Hiking Colorado's Summits,* Globe Pequot Press), but you won't travel through nearly 8 miles of wilderness via that route. Quartz Creek Trail is the best choice for a true wilderness adventure.

From the trailhead, where there are no amenities, only a trail sign, hike Quartz Creek Trail 571, which starts in a nearly flat drainage. You'll reach the wilderness boundary after 1.4 miles and enter the trees. The trail eventually turns to the southeast and climbs at a more moderate grade. At 3.1 miles you'll ford Quartz Creek, which is fairly narrow at this point. Then you'll climb a steep slope before reaching a set of switchbacks that make the grade more moderate and enable you to see a number of waterfalls along the way.

At 4.7 miles the trail enters a beautiful, stream-filled basin with pockets of trees and some relatively flat areas. Wind around the basin, which is decorated with wildflowers in summer; you'll find more switchbacks leading above the tree line toward a saddle at 12,240 feet. The switchbacks end short of the saddle, but scattered rock cairns will help you find your way.

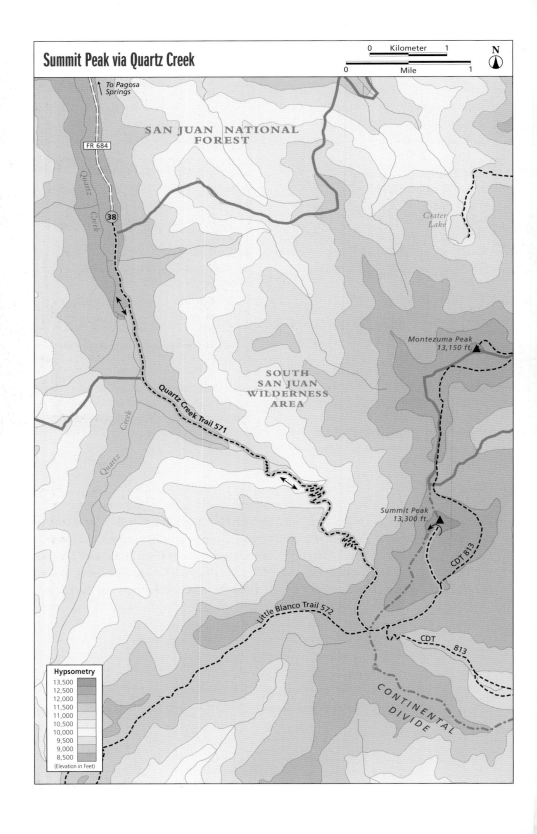

Summit Peak via Quartz Creek

0 Kilometer 1

0 Mile 1

N

To Pagosa Springs

FR 684

Quartz Creek

38

SAN JUAN NATIONAL FOREST

Crater Lake

Montezuma Peak 13,150 ft.

SOUTH SAN JUAN WILDERNESS AREA

Quartz Creek

Quartz Creek Trail 571

Summit Peak 13,300 ft.

CDT 813

Little Blanco Trail 572

CDT 813

CONTINENTAL DIVIDE

Hypsometry

13,500
12,500
12,000
11,500
11,000
10,500
10,000
9,500
9,000
8,500
(Elevation in Feet)

Mike Vining hiking Summit Peak

You'll reach the saddle and a junction for Little Blanco Trail 572 at 7.1 miles. Head northeast and drop down the east side to Continental Divide Trail 813 at 7.4 miles. (If you're interested in the Little Blanco Trail, see Hike 40 for more information.) The trail is unmarked in this area, but you'll see post–markers and rock cairns as you travel northeast to 8 miles and a point south of Summit Peak. From here even the most gentle grade is moderate to steep; hike to a saddle and then take the southwest ridge to the top at 8.8 miles. From the summit of Summit Peak, expect fantastic views of the wilderness and beyond.

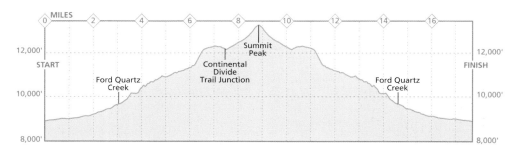

Summit Peak (left) and Montezuma Peak (right) from Long Trek Mountain

Miles and Directions

0.0 Quartz Creek trailhead.

7.1 Little Blanco Trail junction. GPS: N37 20.142' / W106 42.452'.

7.4 Continental Divide Trail junction. GPS: N37 20.185' / W106 41.386'.

8.0 Point south of Summit Peak. GPS: N37 20.464' / W106 41.807'.

8.8 Summit Peak.

17.6 Back to Quartz Creek trailhead.

Hike Information

Local information: Pagosa Springs Chamber of Commerce, Pagosa Springs; (970) 264-2360 or (800) 252-2204; www.pagosachamber.com.

Local events/attractions: The Pagosa Hot Springs, reputed to be the world's hottest mineral springs, are known for their healing qualities. Contact the Springs Resort at (800) 225-0934, www.pagosahotsprings.com; Healing Waters Resort & Spa at (800) 832-5523, www.pshotsprings.com; or Overlook Mineral Springs Spa at (970) 264-4040, www.overlook hotsprings.com, for more information.

Chimney Rock National Monument (designated a national monument by President Barack Obama in September 2012) is open mid-May through the end of September. Call (970) 883-5359 or go to www.chimneyrockco.org.

Accommodations: Pagosa Springs has a number of private campgrounds and motels. Also, you'll pass the East Fork Campground, a national forest facility, en route to the trailhead. It's a fee area with water and vault toilets.

39 Little Blanco Trail to Quartz Lake

The Little Blanco Trail provides a beautiful way to access the Continental Divide. Once you climb to the top of the nearest ridge, you are in alpine country, where the views are just as awesome as expansive. Wildflowers dot the trail in the summer months, and aspens on the lower section of the hike are ablaze in the fall. If the Divide is your destination, consider spending the night at Quartz Lake and making it a day hike from there.

Start: Little Blanco trailhead
Distance: 9.4 miles out and back
Hiking time: About 6 to 8 hours or overnight backpack
Difficulty: Strenuous due to length and elevation gain of 2,400 feet
Canine compatibility: Dogs must be under control.
Nearest town: Pagosa Springs

Fees and permits: Free trail registration at the trailhead
Maps: USGS Blackhead Peak; Trails Illustrated South San Juan/Del Norte; DeLorme 3D TopoQuad CD-ROM; Maptech Terrain Navigator CD-ROM
Trail contact: San Juan National Forest, Pagosa Ranger District, Pagosa Springs; (970) 264-2268; www.fs.usda.gov/sanjuan

Finding the trailhead: From the junction of US 84 and US 160 on the east edge of Pagosa Springs, travel south on US 84 for 0.3 mile. Turn left (east) onto Mill Creek Road (Archuleta CR 302), which is a gravel road. Drive it 6.3 miles to a fork; keep right (northeast) on what is now called Nipple Mountain Road, or FR 665. (The left fork, FR 662, dead-ends.) After 9.7 miles you'll see a sign for Little Blanco Trail. There are no facilities at the trailhead, just a trail register and plenty of room to park. There are places to camp en route. *DeLorme: Colorado Atlas & Gazetteer:* Page 88 B3. GPS: N37 18.120' / W106 48.334'.

The Hike

You'll find a sign at the trailhead. Although it describes Quartz Lake as being 4 miles away, you should know that it is 4.7 miles and a climb of 2,400 feet in elevation. The trip is worth every inch of effort needed to get there.

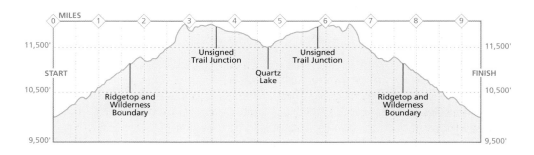

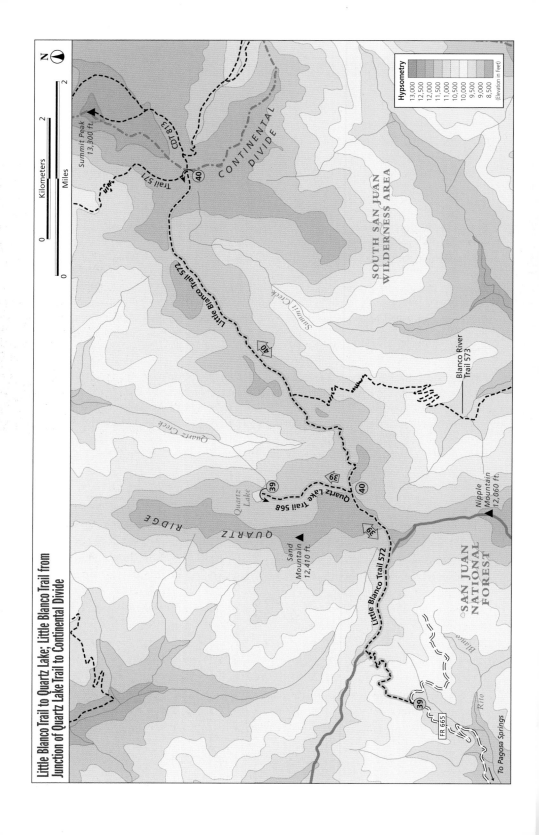

Little Blanco Trail to Quartz Lake; Little Blanco Trail from Junction of Quartz Lake Trail to Continental Divide

Mike Vining enjoying the view from the Little Blanco Trail

Begin hiking Little Blanco Trail 572 by ascending a steep slope covered with aspens and some pines. Moderate switchbacks make the going easier as you first travel north, then east. As you climb, look west to Pagosa Springs and north to the Weminuche Wilderness; once you top a ridge at 1.7 miles, look east to the lovely realms of the South San Juan Wilderness. Although the wilderness begins at this point, there is no sign denoting the boundary.

From here continue east along a vast ridge, with occasional views south to Nipple Mountain and the massive bulk of Blackhead Peak. The trail steepens as you continue to 2.9 miles and a jagged pass just south of Sand Mountain. The views only get better as you continue over fairly level ground to 3.6 miles and an unsigned trail junction. From here you can continue east to the Continental Divide (see Hike 40 for more information), but Quartz Lake is north. Hike Quartz Lake Trail 568, mostly descending (though there's one quick uphill) to the lake at 4.7 miles and 11,500 feet. Look for wildlife in the area, including golden eagles, deer, and coyotes.

Miles and Directions

0.0 Little Blanco trailhead.

3.6 Unsigned trail junction. GPS: N37 18.695' / W106 46.030'.

4.7 Quartz Lake. GPS: N37 19.470' / W106 46.015'.

9.4 Back to Little Blanco trailhead.

Hike Information

Local information: Pagosa Springs Chamber of Commerce, Pagosa Springs; (970) 264-2360 or (800) 252-2204; www.pagosachamber.com.
Local events/attractions: The Pagosa Hot Springs, reputed to be the world's hottest mineral springs, are known for their healing qualities. Contact the Springs Resort at (800) 225-0934, www.pagosahotsprings.com; Healing Waters Resort & Spa at (800) 832-5523, www.pshotsprings.com; or Overlook Mineral Springs Spa at (970) 264-4040, www.overlook hotsprings.com, for more information.

Chimney Rock National Monument (designated a national monument by President Barack Obama in September 2012) is open mid-May through the end of September. Call (970) 883-5359 or go to www.chimneyrockco.org.
Accommodations: Pagosa Springs has a number of private campgrounds and motels. There are also primitive places to camp en route to the trailhead.

40 Little Blanco Trail from Junction of Quartz Lake Trail to Continental Divide

This is one of many ways to access the Continental Divide, and it's a beauty. The hike is rich in alpine country, where the views are magnificent. Wildflowers dot the trail in the summer months. If the Divide is your destination, consider spending the night at Quartz Lake and making it a day hike from there.

See map page 178
Start: Junction of Little Blanco and Quartz Lake Trails
Distance: 9.2 miles out and back (additional mileage to reach starting point; see Finding the Trailhead)
Hiking time: About 5 to 8 hours or overnight backpack if you camp at Quartz Lake (excluding hike time to reach starting point)
Difficulty: If you hike out and back the same day, strenuous due to length and elevation gain of more than 2,400 feet; moderate if you camp overnight

Canine compatibility: Dogs must be under control.
Nearest town: Pagosa Springs
Fees and permits: None
Maps: USGS Blackhead Peak and Summit Peak; Trails Illustrated South San Juan/ Del Norte; DeLorme 3D TopoQuad CD-ROM; Maptech Terrain Navigator CD-ROM
Trail contact: San Juan National Forest, Pagosa Ranger District, Pagosa Springs; (970) 264-2268; www.fs.usda.gov/sanjuan

Finding the trailhead: Your starting point, the junction of the Little Blanco and Quartz Lake Trails, is a 3.6-mile hike from the Little Blanco trailhead. To reach the trailhead from eastern Pagosa Springs, go to the junction of US 84 and US 160. Travel south on US 84 for 0.3 mile. Turn left onto Mill Creek Road (Archuleta CR 302), which is a gravel road. Drive it 6.3 miles to a fork; keep right on what is now called Nipple Mountain Road, or FR 665. (The left fork, FR 662, dead-ends.) After 9.7 miles you'll see a sign for Little Blanco Trail. *DeLorme: Colorado Atlas & Gazetteer:* Page 88 B3. GPS: N37 18.120' / W106 48.334'.

Begin hiking Little Blanco Trail 572 by ascending a steep slope covered with aspens and pines. Moderate switchbacks make the going easier as you first travel north, then east. You will top a ridge at 1.7 miles. Although the wilderness begins at this point, there is no sign denoting the boundary. Continue east along a vast ridge. The trail steepens as you continue to 2.9 miles and a jagged pass just south of Sand Mountain. Continue over fairly level ground to 3.6 miles and an unsigned trail junction about 1 mile south of Quartz Lake. This trip will take you 3 to 4 hours.

The Hike

From the unsigned junction of the Little Blanco and Quartz Lake Trails, hike east on Little Blanco Trail 572. The trail often climbs and descends, but you will eventually reach the highest point along the trail at the Continental Divide. Note that you'll

The Continental Divide Trail from the Little Blanco Trail

gain 1,289 feet en route to the Divide and descend 1,036 feet. Rock cairns and post-markers point the way.

The trail is above the tree line for much of the way, which means the views of the South San Juan Wilderness—and beyond to the Weminuche and La Garita Wildernesses—are superb. The wildflowers are gorgeous in summer. Be sure to look for wildlife, including elk, deer, golden eagles, and ferruginous hawks. You will reach a signed trail junction at 1.6 miles. Blanco River Trail 573 heads south from this point, ending more than 8 miles later at the Blanco River trailhead.

Continue on the Little Blanco Trail, traveling northeast while the trail skirts the base of 12,000-foot-plus mountains. Summit Peak and Montezuma Peak are obvious to the northeast. Summit Peak is the highest point in Archuleta County and in all the wilderness. You will reach a saddle and signed trail junction at 4.6 miles and 12,245 feet. Although this is the Continental Divide, Continental Divide Trail 813 is another 0.2 mile and 120-foot drop to the east.

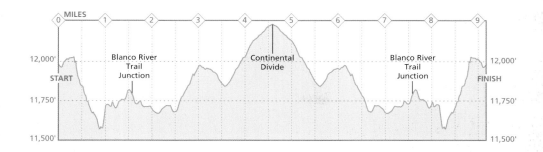

Miles and Directions

0.0 Unsigned trail junction. GPS: N37 18.695' / W106 46.030'.

1.6 Blanco River Trail 573 junction. GPS: N37 19.245' / W106 44.955'.

4.6 Junction with Continental Divide. GPS: N37 20.142' / W106 42.452'.

9.2 Back to unsigned trail junction.

Hike Information

Local information: Pagosa Springs Chamber of Commerce, Pagosa Springs; (970) 264-2360 or (800) 252-2204; www.pagosachamber.com.

Local events/attractions: The Pagosa Hot Springs, reputed to be the world's hottest mineral springs, are known for their healing qualities. Contact the Springs Resort at (800) 225-0934, www.pagosahotsprings.com; Healing Waters Resort & Spa at (800) 832-5523, www.pshotsprings.com; or Overlook Mineral Springs Spa at (970) 264-4040, www.overlook hotsprings.com, for more information.

Chimney Rock National Monument (designated a national monument by President Barack Obama in September 2012) is open mid-May through the end of September. Call (970) 883-5359 or go to www.chimneyrockco.org.

Accommodations: Pagosa Springs has a number of private campgrounds and motels.

41 Fish Lake Trail

The trail to Fish Lake is blessed with many switchbacks—welcome help as you ascend the thousands of feet needed to gain access to the Continental Divide. Once you are above the tree line, the views are tremendous. There's no doubt that you'll be glad you made the hike to the lofty realms of the South San Juan Wilderness.

Start: Fish Creek trailhead
Distance: 24.4 miles out and back
Hiking time: 2- to 3-day backpack
Difficulty: Strenuous due to length and elevation gain of approximately 4,000 feet
Canine compatibility: Dogs must be under control.
Nearest town: Pagosa Springs

Fees and permits: Free trail registration at the trailhead
Maps: USGS Summit Peak and Elephant Head Rock; Trails Illustrated South San Juan/ Del Norte; DeLorme 3D TopoQuad CD-ROM; Maptech Terrain Navigator CD-ROM
Trail contact: San Juan National Forest, Pagosa Ranger District, Pagosa Springs; (970) 264-2268; www.fs.usda.gov/sanjuan

Finding the trailhead: From the junction of US 84 and US 160 on the east edge of Pagosa Springs, travel south/southeast on US 84 for 8 miles. At this point turn left (northeast) onto Blanco Basin Road (also called Archuleta CR 326). It's a gravel road that leads through Blanco Basin. After 9.7 miles make a right, cross the Blanco River via a bridge, and drive southeast on FR 660, also called Castle Creek Road. After 6.7 miles you'll reach the end of FR 660 and the Fish Creek trailhead. There are no facilities at the trailhead, but there's plenty of room to camp. *DeLorme: Colorado Atlas & Gazetteer:* Page 88 C4. GPS: N37 13.222' / W106 43.441'.

The Hike

From the trailhead, where you should sign in at the trail register, ford Fish Creek (you might have to get your feet wet early in the season). You will reach a junction within 100 yards. Signs point the way to Fish Creek Trail 575, which heads right (south), and to Fish Lake Trail 574, which heads left (north). Take the latter, hiking northwest and descending about 200 feet. The trail parallels Fish Creek, though you are not often next to it. Cross a small side stream, then cross North Fork Fish Creek at 1.4 miles.

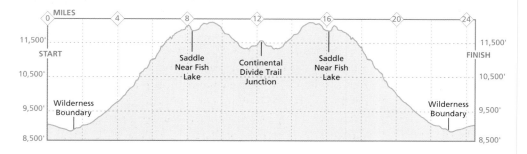

Junction of the Fish Lake Trail and the Continental Divide Trail

You will enter the wilderness at 1.5 miles and begin a more northeasterly hike. The trail travels through fir, aspen, and pine trees (even a few ponderosa pines) and through meadows. Though they are not shown on area maps, switchbacks make travel up the steep slope easier.

The trail crosses North Fork Fish Creek three more times: at 1.9, 3, and 5 miles. Otherwise the stream is usually a steep hike away from the trail. At 5 miles the trail heads in a more southeasterly direction. At 6.3 miles you'll find one of the few "flat" spots in the area. There is water on the west side of the trail, and it is not too difficult to reach—but it may be a seasonal stream created by snowmelt.

From this point continue ascending, exiting the trees as you switchback up the steep slope. The trail eases and heads in a more easterly direction to a saddle at 8.1 miles. Before you reach it, look northeast to Gunsight Pass. From the saddle you will see Fish Lake, set in a bowl and just as pretty as can be. A trail skirts the southern end of the lake and easily crosses the headwaters of Fish Creek. Continue southeast, up the

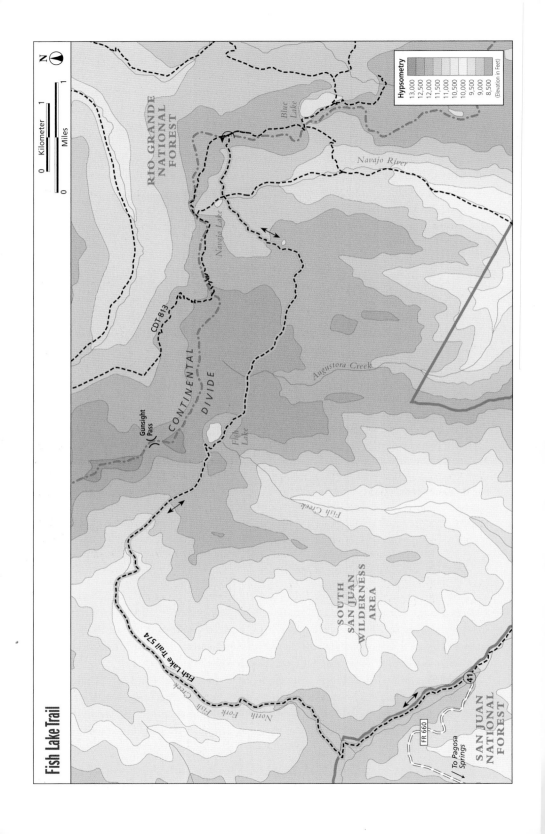

Fish Lake Trail

opposite side of the lake. The trail is difficult to follow at times, but cairns are present, so look for them. Near the top of the plateau you will see the path.

The trail proceeds across wide-open tundra, crossing small Augustora Creek en route. At about 9.7 miles begin descending into a gentle drainage. You will reach a wonderful unnamed lake at 10.8 miles. There are broad vistas along the way and the opportunity to see wildlife and wildflowers.

Continue dropping to a creek crossing. You will pass a small pond before reaching what may as well be called Navajo Lake at 11.6 miles. Though unnamed on area maps, this body of water feeds and gives life to the Navajo River. To complete the Fish Lake Trail, travel east, gaining in elevation as you head through trees and meadows. You will reach Continental Divide Trail 813 at 12.2 miles, where you'll see a sign for Trail 574 pointing back the way you came.

Miles and Directions

0.0   Fish Creek trailhead.
1.5   Wilderness boundary. GPS: N37 14.224' / W106 44.121'.
8.1   Saddle west of Fish Lake. GPS: N37 15.252' / W106 41.283'.
10.8 Unnamed lake. GPS: N37 14.768' / W106 39.182'.
12.2 Continental Divide Trail junction. GPS: N37 15.155' / W106 38.102'.
24.4 Back to Fish Creek trailhead.

Hike Information

Local information: Pagosa Springs Chamber of Commerce, Pagosa Springs; (970) 264-2360 or (800) 252-2204; www.pagosachamber.com.
Local events/attractions: The Pagosa Hot Springs, reputed to be the world's hottest mineral springs, are known for their healing qualities. Contact the Springs Resort at (800) 225-0934, www.pagosahotsprings.com; Healing Waters Resort & Spa at (800) 832-5523, www.pshotsprings.com; or Overlook Mineral Springs Spa at (970) 264-4040, www.overlook hotsprings.com, for more information.

Chimney Rock National Monument (designated a national monument by President Barack Obama in September 2012) is open mid-May through the end of September. Call (970) 883-5359 or go to www.chimneyrockco.org.
Accommodations: Pagosa Springs has a number of private campgrounds and motels. There's room for primitive camping at the trailhead.

42 Flattop Mountain

The trail to Flattop Mountain leads through lush woods where wildflowers are abundant. You may see animal life. Best of all, the views from on top are magnificent. Along the way hikers can make a quick side trip to Opal Lake, a popular place for fishing and viewing birdlife.

Start: Opal Lake trailhead
Distance: 8.2 miles out and back
Hiking time: About 4 to 6 hours
Difficulty: Strenuous due to elevation gain of approximately 3,000 feet
Canine compatibility: Dogs must be under control.
Nearest town: Pagosa Springs

Fees and permits: None
Maps: USGS Harris Lake and Elephant Head Rock; Trails Illustrated South San Juan/ Del Norte; DeLorme 3D TopoQuad CD-ROM; Maptech Terrain Navigator CD-ROM
Trail contact: San Juan National Forest, Pagosa Ranger District, Pagosa Springs; (970) 264-2268; www.fs.usda.gov/sanjuan

Finding the trailhead: From the junction of US 84 and US 160 on the east edge of Pagosa Springs, travel south/southeast on US 84 for 8 miles. At this point turn left (northeast) onto Blanco Basin Road. It's a gravel road that leads through Blanco Basin. After 9.5 miles make a right, cross the Blanco River via a bridge, and drive southeast on FR 660, also called Castle Creek Road. After 3.3 miles you'll see Opal Lake Road (FR 023) on the right (south). Continue on FR 023 for an additional 0.7 mile to the Opal Lake trailhead. There are no facilities at the trailhead, but there's a place to camp nearby. *DeLorme: Colorado Atlas & Gazetteer:* Page 88 C4. GPS: N37 12.235' / W106 45.739'.

The Hike

The Forest Service asks that you not sign in at the register if you are hiking to the top of Flattop Mountain. The spur trail leading to the summit is not a system trail, and the Forest Service typically does not promote nonsystem trails.

Begin hiking up Trail 564, which offers a moderate grade most of the time, though you will find an occasional steep section. Pass by a swamp-like area and

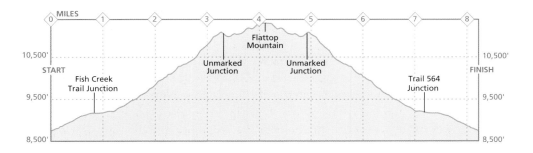

View north from Flattop Mountain

continue through the trees, a mixed forest of firs, spruce, and aspens. The forest floor hosts a variety of lush plants.

You will enter the wilderness after 0.3 mile and reach a trail junction at 0.9 mile. Here Fish Creek Trail 575 runs east and south. If you take the southern fork, you'll pass a side trail to Opal Lake and eventually reach the Leche Creek Trail. (See Hike 43 for more information. A sign also indicates that this is the way to V-Rock.) To continue to Flattop Mountain, hike east on the faint trail. It leads through aspens and a lot of vegetation.

After 1.7 miles you will cross an unnamed stream that eventually meets South Creek. Then you will ascend a series of generally moderate (though sometimes steep) switchbacks that lead through a pretty forest to a saddle at 3.2 miles. Step off the Fish Creek Trail at this point and head north on an unmaintained trail; it will peter out every now and then. As you proceed, remember to keep the ridge in sight. The trail skirts the ridge, on the east side most of the time, and reaches the top at 3.9 miles. Travel over the rocky ridge for almost 0.2 mile to the true summit at 11,463 feet. Amazing views abound from the top. Stay away from the western edge, as it drops straight off. And be sure to sign the summit register.

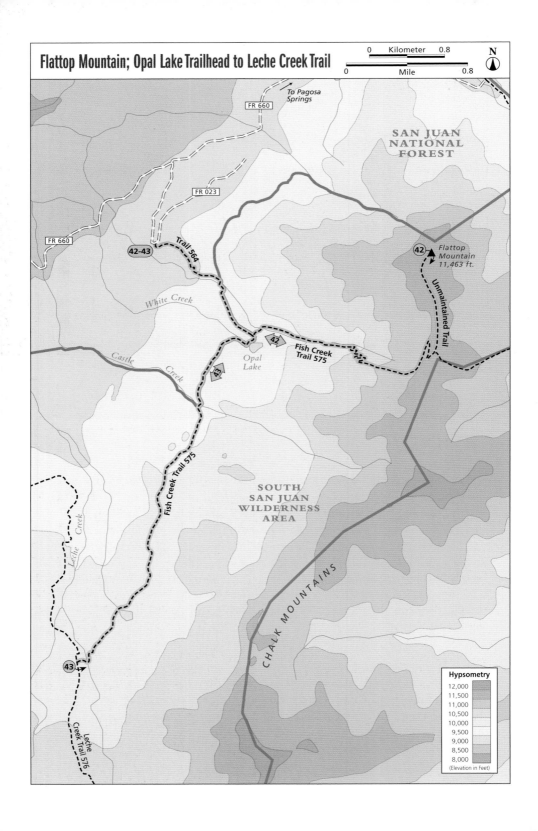

Witch's butter (Tremella mesenterica)

Miles and Directions

0.0 Opal Lake trailhead.

0.9 Junction with Fish Creek Trail 575. GPS: N37 11.823' / W106 45.272'.

3.2 Saddle south of Flattop Mountain. GPS: N37 11.659' / W106 43.733'.

4.1 Flattop Mountain.

8.2 Back to Opal Lake trailhead.

Hike Information

Local information: Pagosa Springs Chamber of Commerce, Pagosa Springs; (970) 264-2360 or (800) 252-2204; www.pagosachamber.com.

Local events/attractions: The Pagosa Hot Springs, reputed to be the world's hottest mineral springs, are known for their healing qualities. Contact the Springs Resort at (800) 225-0934, www.pagosahotsprings.com; Healing Waters Resort & Spa at (800) 832-5523, www.pshotsprings.com; or Overlook Mineral Springs Spa at (970) 264-4040, www.overlook hotsprings.com, for more information.

Chimney Rock National Monument (designated a national monument by President Barack Obama in September 2012) is open mid-May through the end of September. Call (970) 883-5359 or go to www.chimneyrockco.org.

Accommodations: Pagosa Springs has a number of private campgrounds and motels. There's also a primitive place to camp near the trailhead.

43 Opal Lake Trailhead to Leche Creek Trail

Bring your camera: Colorado columbine and other wildflowers grace this route, and you may see elk and deer. Opal Lake is a popular stop, as it offers good fishing and hosts a variety of birdlife.

See map page 190
Start: Opal Lake trailhead
Distance: 8 miles out and back
Hiking time: About 4 to 6 hours
Difficulty: Strenuous due to length
Canine compatibility: Dogs must be under control.
Nearest town: Pagosa Springs

Fees and permits: Free trail registration at the trailhead
Maps: USGS Harris Lake and Elephant Head Rock; Trails Illustrated South San Juan/ Del Norte; DeLorme 3D TopoQuad CD-ROM; Maptech Terrain Navigator CD-ROM
Trail contact: San Juan National Forest, Pagosa Ranger District, Pagosa Springs; (970) 264-2268; www.fs.usda.gov/sanjuan

Finding the trailhead: From the junction of US 84 and US 160 on the east edge of Pagosa Springs, travel south/southeast on US 84 for 8 miles. At this point turn left (northeast) onto Blanco Basin Road. It's a gravel road that leads through Blanco Basin. After 9.5 miles make a right turn, cross the Blanco River via a bridge, and drive southeast on FR 660, also called Castle Creek Road. After 3.3 miles you'll see Opal Lake Road (FR 023) on the right (south). Continue on FR 023 for an additional 0.7 mile to the Opal Creek trailhead. There are no facilities at the trailhead, but there's a place to camp nearby. *DeLorme: Colorado Atlas & Gazetteer:* Page 88 C4. GPS: N37 12.235' / W106 45.739'.

The Hike

Sign in at the register, and take Trail 564. Although the grade is moderate most of the time, you will find an occasional steep section. Pass by a swamp-like area and proceed through the trees, a mixed forest of firs, spruce, and aspens. The forest floor supports an array of lush plants.

You will enter the wilderness at 0.3 mile and reach a junction at 0.9 mile. Here Fish Creek Trail 575 takes off to the east and south. The trail to the east is the route

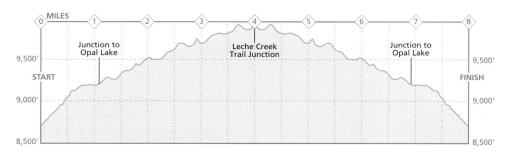

to Flattop Mountain (see Hike 42 for more information). Take the southern route, hiking to another junction at 1.1 miles. A side trail leads 0.1 mile to pretty Opal Lake, a popular spot for fishing.

Hike south on the Fish Creek Trail, passing through an open meadow. Be sure to look for animal life. The trail continues through an occasional meadow, forests of aspens and evergreens, and rocky slopes dotted with wildflowers, including Colorado columbine. At 3.4 miles you will pass a lake that feeds Leche Creek.

Proceed to a small stream at 3.8 miles. Keep to the right, and you will reach Leche Creek at 3.9 miles. The trail can be a bit confusing in this area. Cross Leche Creek and stay on the trail that heads southwest for another 0.1 mile to the junction with Leche Creek Trail 576.

Great blue heron (Ardea herodias)

Miles and Directions

0.0 Opal Lake trailhead.

0.9 Junction with Fish Creek Trail 575. GPS: N37 11.823' / W106 45.272'.

1.1 Junction with side trail to Opal Lake. GPS: N37 11.713' / W106 45.213'.

3.9 Leche Creek crossing. GPS: N37 9.781' / W106 46.185'.

4.0 Junction with Leche Creek Trail 576. GPS: N37 9.724' / W106 46.230'.

8.0 Back to Opal Lake trailhead.

Hike Information

Local information: Pagosa Springs Chamber of Commerce, Pagosa Springs; (970) 264-2360 or (800) 252-2204; www.pagosachamber.com.

Local events/attractions: The Pagosa Hot Springs, reputed to be the world's hottest mineral springs, are known for their healing qualities. Contact the Springs Resort at (800) 225-0934, www.pagosahotsprings.com; Healing Waters Resort & Spa at (800) 832-5523, www.pshotsprings.com; or Overlook Mineral Springs Spa at (970) 264-4040, www.overlook hotsprings.com, for more information.

Chimney Rock National Monument (designated a national monument by President Barack Obama in September 2012) is open mid-May through the end of September. Call (970) 883-5359 or go to www.chimneyrockco.org.

Accommodations: Pagosa Springs has a number of private campgrounds and motels. There's also a primitive place to camp near the trailhead.

44 Navajo Peak/Leche Creek Trails Shuttle Hike

The highlight of hiking these trails comes in the form of trees, and there are lots of them! Aspens—quaking visual treats of gold, yellow, and orange—come alive in late September, when fall colors are at their peak in this part of the country. This area is also a mecca for animal life, including black bear, elk, and deer. Although you can hike the trail from either direction, it's best to start at the Navajo Peak trailhead and end at the Leche Creek trailhead because you'll gain less elevation going south to north. A shuttle is advised, but if one isn't available, try hiking half of the trail from either end.

Start: Navajo Peak trailhead or Leche Creek trailhead

Distance: 11.2-mile shuttle

Hiking time: About 5 to 7 hours or overnight backpack

Difficulty: Strenuous due to length and elevation gain of more than 1,700 feet

Canine compatibility: Dogs must be under control.

Nearest town: Pagosa Springs

Fees and permits: Free trail registration at the trailhead

Maps: USGS Chromo, Chama Peak, and Harris Lake; Trails Illustrated South San Juan/Del Norte; DeLorme 3D TopoQuad CD-ROM; Maptech Terrain Navigator CD-ROM

Trail contact: San Juan National Forest, Pagosa Ranger District, Pagosa Springs; (970) 264-2268; www.fs.usda.gov/sanjuan

Finding the trailhead: To reach the southernmost trailhead at Navajo Peak, from Pagosa Springs head to the junction of US 84 and US 160, which is on the east edge of town. From there drive south/southeast on US 84 for approximately 24 miles to the community of Chromo, where you'll find a small store. (The junction is also about 24 miles northwest of Chama, New Mexico, via US 64 and US 84.) Near the store turn left (east) onto Archuleta CR 382, also known as Navajo River Road. The road is paved for almost a mile and then turns to gravel. Travel 7.8 miles on CR 382, then turn left (north) onto Price Lakes Road (FR 731); stay on this dirt road for 7.6 miles to the trailhead. A sign points the way to Navajo Peak Trail. There are plenty of places to camp en route and at the trailhead. *DeLorme: Colorado Atlas & Gazetteer:* Page 88 D3. GPS: N37 05.198' / W106 45.289'.

To reach the northernmost trailhead, head to the same junction of US 84 and US 160 on the east edge of Pagosa Springs. Now travel south/southeast on US 84 for 8 miles. At this point turn left (northeast) onto Blanco Basin Road. It's a gravel road that leads through Blanco Basin. After 9.5 miles make a right, cross the Blanco River via a bridge, and drive southeast on FR 660, also called Castle Creek Road. After 0.4 mile you'll see FR 668 on the right (south). Drive FR 668 for 0.5 mile to a fork; keep left (southeast) for an additional 0.2 mile to the signed trailhead. There are no facilities at the trailhead, just plenty of room to park. Look for the actual trail up the road, about 200 feet southeast of the parking area. *DeLorme: Colorado Atlas & Gazetteer:* Page 88 C3. GPS: N37 12.156' / W106 47.480'.

American black bear (Ursus americanus)

The Hike

From the trailhead, where there is a trail register, hike Navajo Peak Trail 577, entering the wilderness after 0.6 mile. You will hike north and then west, gradually climb past aspen groves and evergreens, then descend easy-to-moderate grades through various meadows. There are spacious views of aspens, so fall is the perfect time to hike this trail. Cross the Little Navajo River at 2.8 miles; shortly thereafter the trail heads north. Be sure not to take one of the cow paths west! Cow trails are numerous throughout the area and can make navigation difficult. Expect to be confused at times.

Climb the moderate grade (which includes occasional steep sections) to a signed trail junction at 3.4 miles. The Navajo Peak Trail leads west to Buckles Lake Road. You continue north on Leche Creek Trail 576. An occasional rock cairn marks the way. Although the path is usually obvious, sometimes it is difficult to see or even non-existent. Continue north, and you eventually will reach a high point at 5.8 miles and 10,430 feet. It's all downhill from there.

At 6 miles you will reach a junction with V-Rock Trail 578, which leads south-west to Buckles Lake Road. To continue on the Leche Creek Trail, head north. Look

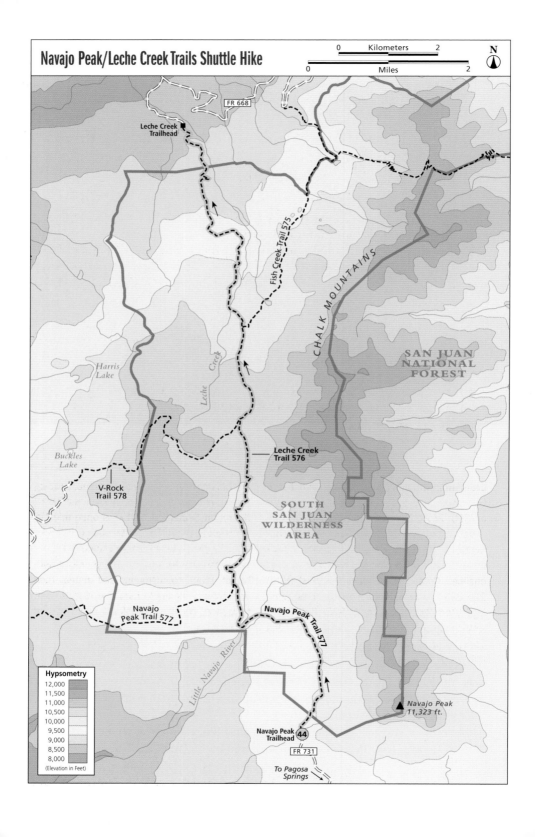

Navajo Peak/Leche Creek Trails Shuttle Hike

0 Kilometers 2

0 Miles 2

N

Leche Creek
Trailhead

FR 668

Fish Creek Trail 575

CHALK MOUNTAINS

SAN JUAN
NATIONAL
FOREST

Harris
Lake

Leche Creek

Buckles
Lake

V-Rock
Trail 578

Leche Creek
Trail 576

SOUTH
SAN JUAN
WILDERNESS
AREA

Navajo
Peak
Trail 577

Navajo Peak Trail 577

Little Navajo River

Navajo Peak
11,323 ft.

Navajo Peak
Trailhead

44

FR 731

To Pagosa
Springs

Hypsometry

	Elevation
	12,000
	11,500
	11,000
	10,500
	10,000
	9,500
	9,000
	8,500
	8,000

(Elevation in Feet)

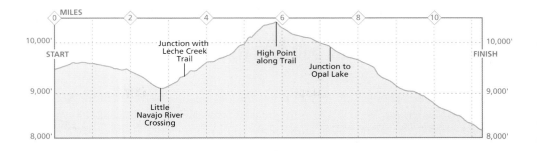

east for occasional views of the rugged Chalk Mountains. The trail descends at a mostly moderate grade through firs and aspens.

You will reach another trail junction at 7.3 miles. Fish Creek Trail 575 heads northeast to Opal Lake (see Hike 43 for more information). Proceed northwest and then north on the Leche Creek Trail; you will reach the trailhead after 11.2 miles. The parking area is about 50 yards to the northwest.

Miles and Directions

0.0   Navajo Peak trailhead.
0.6   Wilderness boundary.
3.4   Navajo Peak/Leche Creek Trails junction. GPS: N37 6.869' / W106 46.264'.
6.0   V-Rock Trail 578 junction. GPS: N37 8.707' / W106 46.260'.
11.2 Leche Creek trailhead.

Hike Information

Local information: Pagosa Springs Chamber of Commerce, Pagosa Springs; (970) 264-2360 or (800) 252-2204; www.pagosachamber.com.
Local events/attractions: The Pagosa Hot Springs, reputed to be the world's hottest mineral springs, are known for their healing qualities. Contact the Springs Resort at (800) 225-0934, www.pagosahotsprings.com; Healing Waters Resort & Spa at (800) 832-5523, www.pshotsprings.com; or Overlook Mineral Springs Spa at (970) 264-4040, www.overlook hotsprings.com, for more information.

Chimney Rock National Monument (designated a national monument by President Barack Obama in September 2012) is open mid-May through the end of September. Call (970) 883-5359 or go to www.chimneyrockco.org.
Accommodations: Pagosa Springs has a number of private campgrounds and motels. There are primitive places to camp en route to both trailheads, and it's possible to camp at both trailheads, too.

The Continental Divide Trail in the South San Juan Wilderness

The Continental Divide Trail (CDT) passes through the lovely realms of the South San Juan Wilderness on its 3,100-mile journey from Mexico to Canada. This trail provides one of the premier hikes in the entire country, for there is nothing like being on top of the Continental Divide. Why? Because hiking the Continental Divide means being up high each and every day. It means seeing forever, seeing little in the way of man and much in the way of nature.

The best months for hiking the trail are July, August, and September. Snow can linger into July (though you may encounter it any month of the year). Hike too early in the season, and the trail may be difficult to find. You may also spend a lot of time punching through the snow. Hike too late in the season, and you may get caught in a big snowstorm.

Mike and I hiked the entire South San Juan section of the CDT in one long backpack, but you may choose to break up the trip. You also may want to hike other trails that lead to the CDT. While doing research for this book, we were on the CDT many times, traveling various trails that linked up with it. You can hike the southern end of the trail from Cumbres Pass or drive to the trailhead at Elwood Pass and hike the northern end of the CDT. The possibilities are endless. The most important thing is that you get out on the trail and enjoy it.

Special note: When hiking the CDT, you'll sometimes find that water is scarce. Most of it can be found a few hundred yards to a mile off the CDT. Carry extra water while hiking through these areas.

45 Continental Divide Trail (Cumbres Pass to Elwood Pass) Shuttle Hike

The Continental Divide Trail (CDT) through the South San Juan Wilderness is one of the most memorable backpacks a hiker can make, with stunning views, breathless scenes, and wildflowers galore. Although you can hike north to south, I describe the hike from south to north for several reasons. First, my husband and I live closer to Elwood Pass, and we wanted to end up closer to home. More importantly, I think the hike just gets more and more beautiful as you hike to the north. I guess you could say I like to save the best for last! *Note:* Snow conditions in early summer and early fall may make hiking the trail difficult.

Start: Continental Divide trailhead at Cumbres Pass (or do the hike in reverse and start at the Continental Divide trailhead at Elwood Pass)
Distance: 51.4-mile shuttle
Hiking time: 5- to 7-day backpack
Difficulty: Strenuous due to length and high elevation
Canine compatibility: Dogs must be under control.
Nearest towns: Chama, New Mexico, and South Fork, Colorado

Fees and permits: Free trail registration at the trailhead
Maps: USGS Cumbres, Archuleta Creek, Victoria Lake, Elephant Head Rock, Summit Peak, and Elwood Pass; Trails Illustrated Weminuche Wilderness; DeLorme 3D TopoQuad CD-ROM; Maptech Terrain Navigator CD-ROM
Trail contact: Rio Grande National Forest, Conejos Peak Ranger District, La Jara; (719) 274-8971; www.fs.usda.gov/riogrande

Finding the trailhead: To reach the trailhead at Cumbres Pass, drive northeast from Chama, New Mexico, on NM/CO 17 for about 12 miles to a place near Cumbres Pass, which is in Colorado. (The CDT crosses the highway about 300 yards west of the pass.) Look for room to park on the south side of the road. There's also a post-marker on the south side for Continental Divide Trail 813. A post-marker on the north side of the road bears the number 813. If you'd prefer parking off the main highway, continue northeast 0.3 mile to the turnoff for Trujillo Meadows Reservoir. Turn left (north) onto FR 118, a dirt road; after 0.1 mile make another left (west) onto FR 119.1A. A sign points the way to the Continental Divide National Scenic Trail. Pass a small pond and a parking area with an outhouse at 0.2 mile. There's room to camp here. It's best to park here and continue another 0.1 mile on foot via the road to a trail register and a train trestle. *DeLorme: Colorado Atlas & Gazetteer:* Page 89 D6. GPS: N37 01.118' / W106 27.078'.

To reach Elwood Pass, from South Fork head southwest on US 160 for 7.3 miles. Then travel south/southeast on Park Creek Road (FR 380), which is gravel, for 18.2 miles. At this point FR 380 continues straight (west); you make a right turn where there is a sign for Elwood Pass. The four-wheel-drive road is known as FR 667. It's about 100 yards north to the trailhead. *DeLorme: Colorado Atlas & Gazetteer:* Page 89 A4. GPS: N37 24.333' / W106 38.656'.

The Hike

If you parked off CO 17, you'll hike under the train trestle and reach a sign that says NO MOTOR VEHICLES in about 200 feet. A trail register marks the start of the South San Juan Wilderness portion of CDT 813. From the obscure trailhead hike 0.2 mile to an unmarked trail junction. The trail that merges with the CDT was probably made by cattle; like many of the unmarked paths in the wilderness, you'll just have to ignore it.

The CDT continues north and then west, traversing open slopes with wildflowers and a mixed forest of aspens and evergreens. You will cross a couple of intermittent streams en route. The trail climbs and descends a fairly easy grade. At 1 mile there's an unmarked junction; keep right, hiking up switchbacks complete with guardrails. Cross Wolf Creek at 2.8 miles. Just before the crossing look for a lovely little waterfall upon entering the drainage.

Past Wolf Creek the trail alternates between more open slopes and forested areas. In the open look for falcons and Swainson's hawks; in the forest look for grouse. The trail sometimes parallels private property. At 4.5 miles it heads in a northerly direction, and at 5.3 miles it crosses an old logging road.

Shortly after you'll begin to climb an open ridge with good views. At 5.8 miles a sign on the ridge points the way to Flat Peak (sometimes called Flat Mountain) and the Dipping Lakes. It's easy to see an old trail traveling over the top of the peak in front of you, but fortunately the CDT contours around to the west.

At 7.7 miles you will reach a saddle; cross to the east side and continue north. If you're in need of water by the 9-mile mark, head off the trail when it begins to climb up the ridge and go due north to a small lake. (If you stay on the trail, you'll see this lake as you climb above it to the west.) At 10.8 miles the trail goes directly over the top of Flat Peak, elevation 12,187 feet. It's a short, steep climb to the summit. From the top you'll see two wilderness peaks: Conejos Peak to the north and Summit Peak to the northwest. To the east you'll see across the San Luis Valley to the Sangre de Cristo Mountains; look south, and you'll see to New Mexico.

From Flat Peak descend an easy grade to a spacious, flat area where domestic sheep sometimes graze. You'll pass a few tarns as you travel north. The trail is mostly well marked by rock cairns and some posts. If you can't see the next rock cairn, stop and look for one; you're bound to eventually find it.

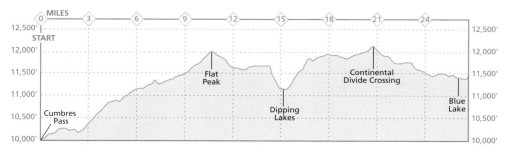

Hikers and their dog on the CDT

Continue hiking in the open. At 14.2 miles you will begin dropping into the trees and then descend a moderate (occasionally steep) slope to the first of the Dipping Lakes at 15.1 miles. The second Dipping Lake has a more spacious feel; it's approximately 0.2 mile away. Meadows abound in the area.

From the west end of the Dipping Lakes, begin a moderate climb to a trail junction at 15.7 miles. Elk Creek Trail 731 goes north and then east from here. (For more information on the trail, see Hike 48.) As you continue to ascend, you'll travel west above the tree line and across open, rocky plateaus where the views are stunning. Look for ptarmigan in this part of the country. The trail is always easy to follow, as rock cairns are prolific.

You will reach a junction near Trail Lake at 19.4 miles. You won't see the lake at this point (it's just over the ridge to the west), but there are two small lakes near the junction. Signposts are marked 813 and 727. Although a sign reads LAGUNA VENADO, the map shows the trail as the Valle Victoria. Someone did scratch in the correct words on the sign for the trail that heads east from here (see Hike 48 for more information).

Climb north/northwest from Trail Lake across open terrain. Rock cairns mark the way as you climb the moderate slope. At 20.8 miles you'll touch the true Continental

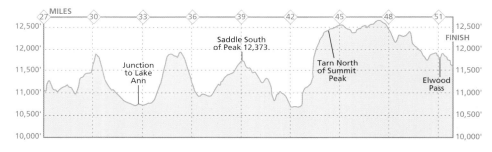

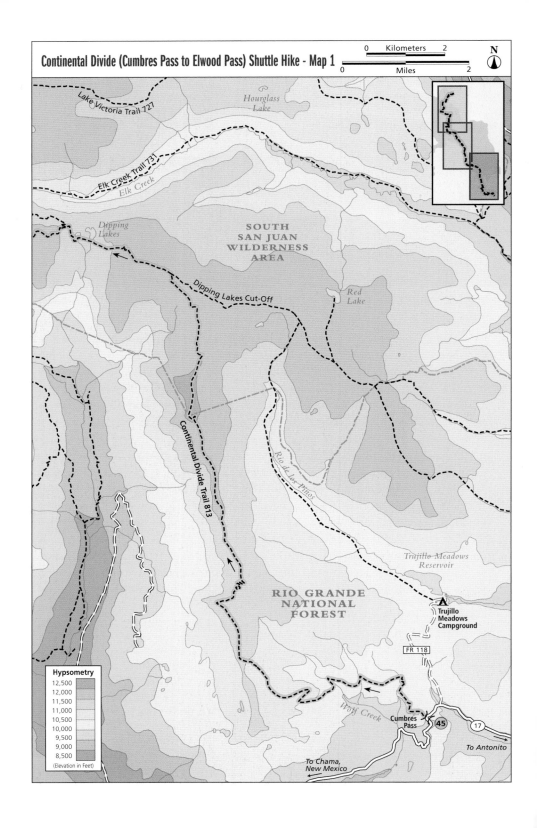

Kilometers

Miles

N

Lake Victoria Trail 727

Hourglass Lake

Elk Creek Trail 731

Elk Creek

Dipping Lakes

SOUTH
SAN JUAN
WILDERNESS
AREA

Dipping Lakes Cut-Off

Red Lake

Continental Divide Trail 813

Rio de los Pinos

Trujillo Meadows
Reservoir

RIO GRANDE
NATIONAL
FOREST

Trujillo
Meadows
Campground

FR 118

Wolf Creek

Cumbres
Pass

45

17

To Antonito

To Chama,
New Mexico

Hypsometry

| 12,500 |
| 12,000 |
| 11,500 |
| 11,000 |
| 10,500 |
| 10,000 |
| 9,500 |
| 9,000 |
| 8,500 |

(Elevation in Feet)

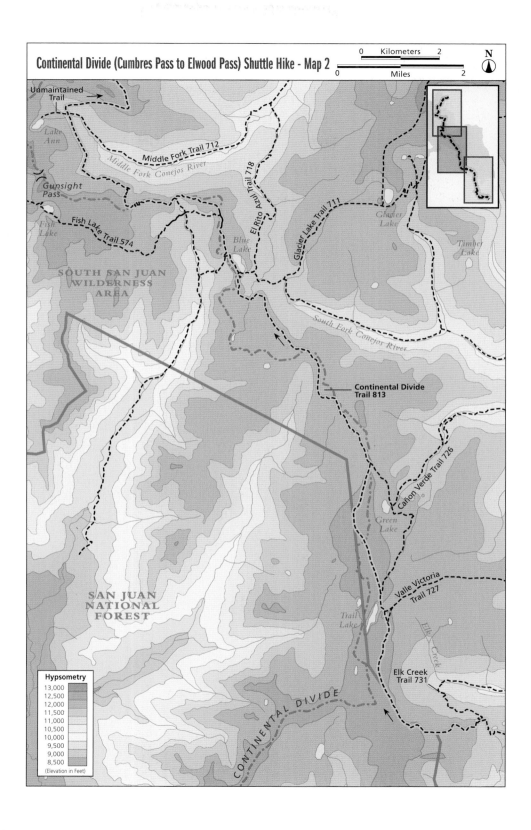

Continental Divide (Cumbres Pass to Elwood Pass) Shuttle Hike - Map 2

Unmaintained Trail

Lake Ann

Middle Fork Trail 712

Middle Fork Conejos River

Gunsight Pass

Fish Lake

Fish Lake Trail 574

El Rito Azul Trail 718

Glacier Lake Trail 711

Glacier Lake

Timber Lake

Blue Lake

SOUTH SAN JUAN WILDERNESS AREA

South Fork Conejos River

Continental Divide Trail 813

Cañon Verde Trail 726

Green Lake

SAN JUAN NATIONAL FOREST

Valle Victoria Trail 727

Trail Lake

Elk Creek

Elk Creek Trail 731

CONTINENTAL DIVIDE

Hypsometry

Elevation
13,000
12,500
12,000
11,500
11,000
10,500
10,000
9,500
9,000
8,500

(Elevation in Feet)

0 Kilometers 2
0 Miles 2

N

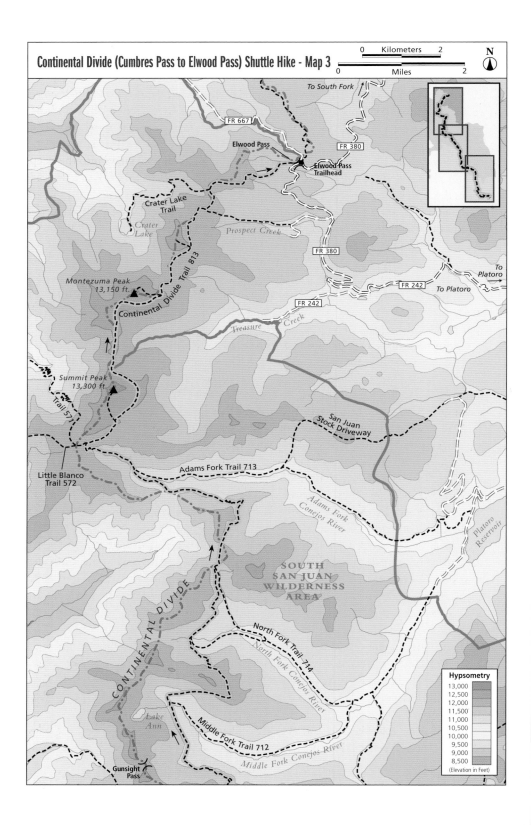

0   Kilometers   2

0   Miles   2

N

To South Fork

FR 667

Elwood Pass

FR 380

Elwood Pass
Trailhead

Crater Lake
Trail

Crater
Lake

Prospect Creek

FR 380

To
Platoro

Montezuma Peak
13,150 ft.

Continental Divide Trail 813

FR 242

To Platoro

FR 242

Treasure   Creek

Summit Peak
13,300 ft.

Trail 571

San Juan
Stock Driveway

Little Blanco
Trail 572

Adams Fork Trail 713

Adams Fork
Conejos River

Platoro
Reservoir

SOUTH
SAN JUAN
WILDERNESS
AREA

North Fork Trail 714

North Fork Conejos River

CONTINENTAL   DIVIDE

Hypsometry

	13,000
	12,500
	12,000
	11,500
	11,000
	10,500
	10,000
	9,500
	9,000
	8,500

(Elevation in Feet)

Lake
Ann

Middle Fork Trail 712

Middle Fork Conejos River

Gunsight
Pass

Divide for the first time. Expect tremendous views to nearly all of the South San Juan Wilderness and much of the Weminuche Wilderness.

The landscape is less rocky as you descend a moderate grade to a trail junction at 22.1 miles. Trail 726 heads southeast from here to Green Lake, Cañon Verde, and the South Fork Conejos River (see Hike 51 for more information). Stay on the CDT, heading northwest over open terrain. There are many tarns, stunted trees, and spectacular views, too. The trail crosses a wooded side slope with nice views into the deep realms of the East Fork Navajo River. You will reach the south end of Blue Lake and a junction with El Rito Azul Trail 718 at 26.5 miles.

Hike along the west end of the lake to a fork at 27 miles. Keep right and hike around the east, then north sides of a small pond. The trail steepens for about 0.4 mile but levels off somewhat as you approach the junction with Fish Lake Trail 574 at 28 miles. Look east from this point to views of Conejos Peak. (If you want to hike to Fish Lake, see Hike 41.)

The CDT heads north via an easy-to-moderate ascent, then winds west through the trees. Just before exiting the trees, you will see an unnamed lake to the south. A spur trail leads about 0.2 mile to the lake.

From here the CDT ascends at a steep grade and then eases somewhat. At 29.3 miles you'll reach a point on the ridge. If you're careful, you can peer over the edge and see lovely Conejos Falls and look up the Middle Fork drainage, where you are heading. Switchback down, mostly at a moderate grade with views galore, to a creek crossing at 31.5 miles. Look west to Gunsight Pass.

The CDT remains fairly level now and crosses a mostly open slope. You'll enter a pocket of forest before reaching an unmaintained trail at 32.5 miles. The trail leads past a waterfall to Lake Ann. It's approximately 0.5 mile to the top.

Continue through the drainage. You'll arrive at a post-marker for CDT 813 at 32.7 miles. Rock cairns and an occasional post-marker denote Middle Fork Trail 712, which intersects the CDT in this area (see Hike 57), though the trail can be difficult to see until you reach the tree line.

Climb out of the drainage via a moderate-to-steep traverse east, with grand views back to Gunsight Pass. You will level off at 33.9 miles, then wind around the south and west sides of a tarn to a saddle at 34.6 miles. The trail begins a moderate-to-steep drop to the northwest and enters the North Fork drainage, where there are several small streams. Lots of switchbacks make the descent more bearable. After 35.6 miles you'll reach a trail junction. Signs point the way to North Fork Trail 714 and the Conejos River.

Continue on the CDT and contour around the drainage, traveling north once again to a saddle at 38.1 miles. The trail leads across open slopes and an easy grade. There are two stream crossings. From the pass there are views west to Blackhead Peak and Nipple Mountain. You'll also get a good look into the rugged drainage called Rio Blanco.

From the saddle skirt around Peak 12,373 by traversing its south and east sides, then switching back to descend along the north side. The views to Summit Peak,

Montezuma Peak, and Long Trek are stupendous as you head west again. Switch-backs make life easier, but be prepared for intermittent ascents as you mostly descend to Adams Fork. The trail is marked, but it is sometimes difficult to follow as it nears Adams Fork. Dense willows complicate matters. Remember that the trail parallels the creek before reaching a post-marker and crossing at 41.2 miles. Look for cairns and posts as you climb to the junction with the Adams Fork Trail at 41.3 miles. (For more information on this trail, see Hike 55.)

From the Adams Fork junction, begin a mostly moderate climb to the head of Adams Fork. Along the way look for elk and deer, and enjoy the lofty views. Just before a signed junction to Trails 572 and 571, the CDT takes off through the wil-lows. Rock cairns mark the way, but they may be difficult to spot. Make sure that you turn before reaching the other two post-markers. (If you are interested in hiking Trails 571 and 572, see Hikes 38 and 40 for more information.)

From this point the CDT ascends easily to the northeast, crossing broad plateaus as it winds around the east side of Summit Peak—at 13,300 feet, the highest point in Archuleta County and in the wilderness. At 43.9 miles you will reach a junction with a trail that leads to Treasure Creek. Head northwest to the north side of Summit Peak and a beautiful lake at 44.6 miles. There are wonderful wildflowers here, too.

The trail climbs and descends as it makes its way north to the south side of Mon-tezuma Peak. Along the way it passes out of the wilderness at 45.7 miles. At this point the boundary follows the Continental Divide. Around the 46-mile mark, you'll top out at 12,648 feet—the highest point along the CDT in this wilderness. The trail continues east and then north, paralleling Long Trek Mountain before reaching a junction to Crater Lake Trail 707 at 48.9 miles. (For information on hiking to Cra-ter Lake, see Hike 59.) The CDT continues to the east (along with the Crater Lake Trail), cutting across the steep south slope of a peak that resembles a shark's fin. You'll reach another junction, this one providing access to Crater Lake trailhead, at 49.6 miles. Continue north on the CDT, entering the trees and skirting a meadow as you descend east to the trailhead at Elwood Pass at 51.4 miles.

WILDERNESS ANIMAL WATCH

Animals pervade the wilderness. In addition to reintroduced species, there are bald and golden eagles, Rocky Mountain elk, mule deer, mountain lions, and black bears. Some of my favorite animals are beavers, short-tailed weasels, white-tailed ptarmigan, and Swain-son's hawks. Beavers are adorable creatures that weigh up to sixty-six pounds. Short-tailed weasels are tireless hunters, not to mention cute and curious. White-tailed ptarmigan are camouflaged for life in the alpine tundra: In the summer they are gray-brown, just like the tundra; in the fall they are mostly white, ready to blend in with the winter snow. Swainson's hawks soar in the high alpine sky, but at the end of summer, they migrate south to Argentina.

View from the CDT with Summit Mountain in the background

Miles and Directions

0.0   Trailhead near Cumbres Pass.

5.8   Ridge northwest of logging road. GPS: N37 1.928' / W106 30.333'.

10.8 Flat Peak and wilderness boundary. GPS: N37 5.377' / W106 31.277'.

15.1 Dipping Lakes. GPS: N37 7.871' / W106 32.998'.

19.4 Junction with Trail 727. GPS: N37 9.561' / W106 35.121'.

26.5 Blue Lake and junction with El Rito Azul Trail 718. GPS: N37 14.266' / W106 37.684'.

32.5 Junction with trail to Lake Ann. GPS: N37 16.540' / W106 40.730'.

38.1 Saddle south of Peak 12,373. GPS: N37 18.879' / W106 39.920'.

44.6 Tarn north of Summit Peak. GPS: N37 21.284' / W106 41.866'.

51.4 Elwood Pass.

Hike Information

Local information: South Fork Chamber of Commerce, South Fork; (719) 873-5556; www.southforkcolorado.org. Chama Valley Chamber of Commerce, Chama, New Mexico; (575) 756-2306 or (800) 477-0149; www.chamavalley.com.

Local events/attractions: In South Fork attend the Little Britches Rodeo (June), Logger Days Festival (July), Rhythms of the Rio Music Festival (August), or Chili Cookoff (October).

Raft or fish the Rio Grande.

From Chama ride the Cumbres & Toltec Narrow Gauge Railroad; (888) 286-2737; www.cumbrestoltec.com.

Accommodations: Both South Fork and Chama have a number of private campgrounds and motels. Trujillo Meadows is the closest national forest campground to Cumbres Pass. There's a fee, but there are facilities. In addition, there is free camping (though no facilities except for an outhouse) near the trailhead at Cumbres Pass.

46 Red Lake Trail

If you like starting at high elevations and staying there, then this is the trail for you. It begins at 10,980 feet, reaches a high point at 11,735 feet, and then descends to Red Lake at 11,550 feet. Magnificent views, wildflowers, and animal life are a plus on this hike.

Start: Red Lake trailhead
Distance: 6 miles out and back
Hiking time: About 3 to 6 hours or overnight backpack
Difficulty: Moderate due to length and elevation gain of more than 750 feet
Canine compatibility: Dogs must be under control.
Nearest town: Chama, New Mexico
Fees and permits: Free trail registration at the trailhead

Maps: USGS Cumbres; Trails Illustrated South San Juan/Del Norte; DeLorme 3D TopoQuad CD-ROM; Maptech Terrain Navigator CD-ROM
Trail contact: Rio Grande National Forest, Conejos Peak Ranger District, La Jara; (719) 274-8971; www.fs.usda.gov/riogrande
Special considerations: Camping, campfires, and animal grazing are not allowed within 200 feet of Red Lake. In 2005 Search and Rescue rode ATVs on the trail. Scars will be visible for years; ATVs are no longer allowed.

Finding the trailhead: From CO 17, at a point about 28 miles from Antonito, Colorado, and 22 miles from Chama, New Mexico, travel northwest on FR 114 (gravel). You'll see a sign pointing the way to Red Lake Trail. Drive another 3.5 miles to the signed trailhead and a large parking area with hitching posts. *DeLorme: Colorado Atlas & Gazetteer:* Page 89 D6. GPS: N37 05.322' / W106 26.952'.

The Hike

Sign in at the register, and then hike Red Lake Trail 733. You'll start on an old logging road, traveling through the trees at an easy-to-moderate grade. Soon you'll reach the tree line and enjoy spacious views as you ascend to the wilderness boundary at 1.3 miles.

After 1.5 miles you'll see rock cairns heading west and northwest. These markers lead hikers and horseback riders on the La Manga Stock Driveway. To reach Red Lake follow the well-worn path and rock cairns northwest. You will top out at 11,735

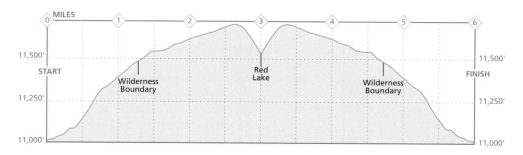

Red Lake Trail

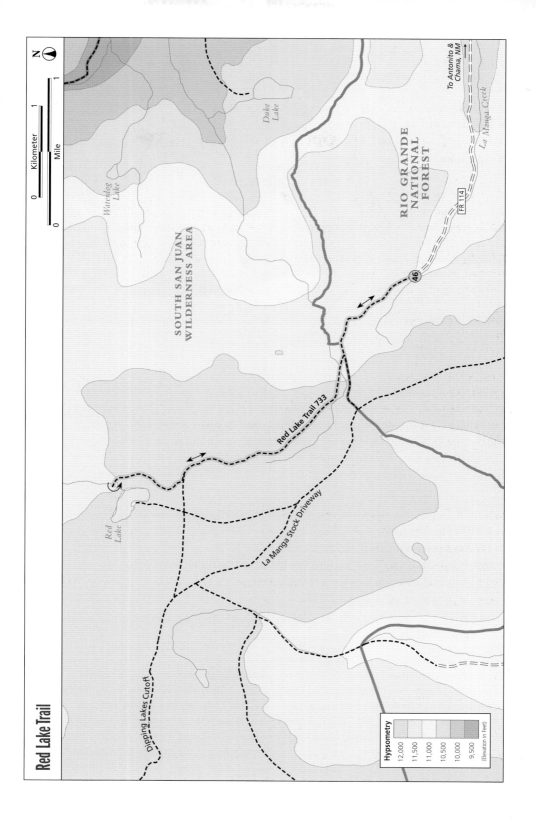

Golden-mantled ground squirrel (Callospermophilus lateralis)

feet before descending to the south end of Red Lake at 3 miles. There are many fine places to camp away from the lake, with trees for shelter. Views from this region are tremendous. Before descending to the lake, you'll see east to the San Luis Valley and the Sangre de Cristo Mountains. Look north for a stunning view of Conejos Peak and northwest for views of Summit and Montezuma Peaks. You'll see much of the South San Juan Wilderness from this area.

Miles and Directions

0.0 Red Lake trailhead.
1.3 Wilderness boundary.
1.5 Unmarked junction with La Manga Trail. GPS: N37 5.981' / W106 28.011'.
3.0 Red Lake. GPS: N37 7.017' / W106 28.709'.
6.0 Back to Red Lake trailhead.

Option: If you have time, hike the 1-mile loop around the lake, which is beautiful from all directions.

Hike Information

Local information: Chama Valley Chamber of Commerce, Chama, New Mexico; (575) 756-2306 or (800) 477-0149; www.chamavalley.com.
Local events/attractions: Ride the Cumbres & Toltec Narrow Gauge Railroad; (888) 286-2737; www.cumbrestoltec.com.

Accommodations: Chama has a number of private campgrounds and motels. Trujillo Meadows and Elk Creek are the closest national forest campgrounds to the trailhead. Both are fee areas with water and vault toilets. In addition, there are free places to camp en route to the trailhead.

47 Duck Lake Trail

The trail to Duck Lake is a wonderful hike for those who enjoy watching birds. Beaver ponds abound along the way and make for prime bird habitat. It's also a terrific place from which to watch for cute mammals. This trail is special in the fall, when the many aspens turn bright yellow and orange.

Start: Duck Lake trailhead
Distance: 7 miles out and back
Hiking time: About 4 to 6 hours or overnight backpack
Difficulty: Moderate due to length and elevation gain of more than 1,100 feet
Canine compatibility: Dogs must be under control.
Nearest town: Antonito

Fees and permits: Free registration at the trailhead
Maps: USGS Cumbres; Trails Illustrated South San Juan/Del Norte; DeLorme 3D TopoQuad CD-ROM; Maptech Terrain Navigator CD-ROM
Trail contact: Rio Grande National Forest, Conejos Peak Ranger District, La Jara; (719) 274-8971; www.fs.usda.gov/riogrande

Finding the trailhead: About 23 miles from Antonito, Colorado, and 27 miles from Chama, New Mexico, leave CO 17 to travel west on a paved road that doesn't have a name or number. It does have a sign pointing to Elk Creek Campground and the Duck Lake Trail. The road turns to gravel shortly after you make the turn. Follow signs, passing the turnoff to the Elk Creek Campground after 0.5 mile. After another 0.7 mile reach a fork leading right (north) to the Elk Creek trailhead via FR 1281C and left (southeast) via FR 128 to Duck Lake. You'll need a high-clearance vehicle to reach the Duck Lake trailhead in another 0.4 mile. There are many places to camp in this area. *DeLorme: Colorado Atlas & Gazetteer:* Page 89 D6. GPS: N37 06.955' / W106 22.951'.

The Hike

Sign the trail register, then from the trailhead for signed Duck Lake Trail 732, pass through the gate, making sure that you close it behind you. Cattle graze in the area, and you might see some of them on the trail. Hike up the trail; the grade is mostly moderate but sometimes a bit steep. The trail passes through a forest of evergreens mixed with aspens, so it's very colorful in the fall.

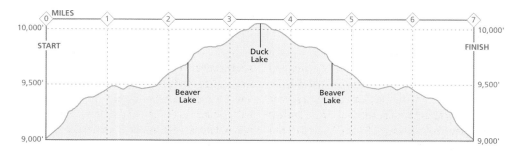

Duck Lake Trail

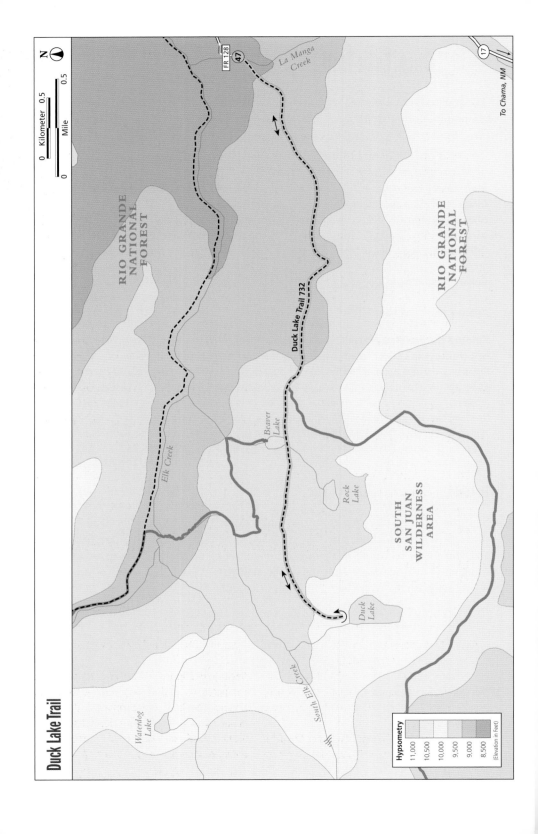

Eight switchbacks make the climb up the slope manageable. Once on top of an expansive bench at 0.6 mile, the trail follows a fairly level path, climbing again before reaching a series of beaver ponds at 2 miles. You'll pass four ponds, all of them home to many species of birds.

Continue west, entering the wilderness just before reaching Beaver Lake at 2.3 miles. The lake is a nice place for a lunch, though the beaver ponds are even better, as they seem blessed with more birdlife. Look for red-winged blackbirds, American coots, robins, a variety of ducks, and sapsuckers. The trail steepens as you proceed west; after 2.5 miles you'll see an unmarked trail junction for Rock Lake. It's a mere 0.2 mile to the lake, where there is supposed to be good fishing.

American beaver (Castor canadensis)

You will reach another beaver pond at 2.9 miles; be sure to stop and take a look. Continue to 3.4 miles and an unsigned junction near a small pond. If you look west, you'll see two waterfalls, one close enough to hear and the other up the canyon. There's an unmaintained trail that leads 0.5 mile to the closest waterfall, along South Elk Creek.

The trail turns south, leading to Duck Lake at 3.5 miles. You'll find more evidence of beavers at the pond, plus there are nice places to camp.

Miles and Directions

0.0   Duck Lake trailhead.

2.3   Wilderness boundary and Beaver Lake.

2.5   Junction with trail to Rock Lake. GPS: N37 6.693' / W106 24.877'.

3.4   Junction with unmaintained trail to waterfalls. GPS: N37 6.583' / W106 25.749'.

3.5   Duck Lake.

7.0   Back to Duck Lake trailhead.

Hike Information

Local information: Antonito Chamber of Commerce, Antonito; (719) 376-2277; www.slvguide.com/ANTONITO/INDEX.HTM. Chama Valley Chamber of Commerce, Chama, New Mexico; (575) 756-2306 or (800) 477-0149; www.chamavalley.com.

Local events/attractions: Ride the Cumbres & Toltec Narrow Gauge Railroad from Chama to Antonito; (888) 286-2737; www.cumbrestoltec.com.

Accommodations: There are some private campgrounds and motels near Antonito and Chama. Elk Creek Campground is the closest national forest facility. It's a fee area; facilities include water and vault toilets. There are also primitive areas where you can camp.

48 Elk Creek/Valle Victoria Semiloop

This long semiloop is a real treasure and is especially gorgeous in the late summer and early fall, when the aspens are gold. Wildlife is abundant in the Elk Creek drainage; you may see bald eagles, beavers, elk, and other species. Up high, on the Continental Divide Trail (CDT), there are see-forever views, and as you descend the Rough Creek drainage, there are endless meadows and dark forests.

Start: Elk Creek trailhead
Distance: 35.1-mile semiloop
Hiking time: 4- to 6-day backpack
Difficulty: Strenuous due to length and elevation gain of more than 4,000 feet
Canine compatibility: Dogs must be under control.
Nearest town: Antonito
Fees and permits: Free registration at the trailhead

Maps: USGS Cumbres, Spectacle Lake, and Victoria Lake; Trails Illustrated South San Juan/Del Norte; DeLorme 3D TopoQuad CD-ROM; Maptech Terrain Navigator CD-ROM
Trail contact: Rio Grande National Forest, Conejos Peak Ranger District, La Jara; (719) 274-8971; www.fs.usda.gov/riogrande
Special considerations: Some of the loop leads through very boggy areas. Wear waterproof boots and expect to get wet, especially in the spring and after rain- or snowstorms.

Finding the trailhead: About 23 miles from Antonito, Colorado, and 27 miles from Chama, New Mexico, leave CO 17 to travel west on an unnamed paved road. You'll see a sign pointing to Elk Creek Campground and the Duck Lake Trail. The road turns to gravel shortly after you make the turn. Follow signs, passing the turnoff to the Elk Creek Campground in 0.5 mile. After another 0.7 mile reach a fork leading right (north) to the Elk Creek trailhead via FR 1281C. Drive another 0.1 mile to the trailhead. There are many places to camp in the area. Amenities include a vault toilet and hitching posts. *DeLorme: Colorado Atlas & Gazetteer:* Page 89 D6. GPS: N37 07.197' / W106 22.590'.

The Hike

After signing in at the trail register, begin hiking Elk Creek Trail 731. Descend to Elk Creek and cross it via a sturdy bridge. The trail turns and travels west soon after the crossing. (You'll see a trail to the right that leads about 0.5 mile to the Elk Creek Campground.)

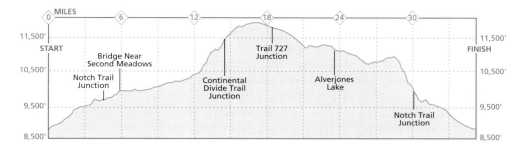

Mike Vining backpacking the Valle Victoria Trail

The path gradually (and sometimes moderately) ascends, with intermittent descents, across forested slopes of ponderosa pine, aspen, and various conifers. After 0.6 mile you'll come to a gate and paths heading straight (north) and left (west). Be sure to head west and continue paralleling Elk Creek. You will reach your first view of the beautiful realms of First Meadows at 2.6 miles. Pass a wilderness boundary sign at 2.8 miles. The trail heads northwest.

Although maps will show you next to the creek, in reality you are above it for much of the first portion of the hike. Switchbacks do lead down to a flat area along the way. Farther up the trail, at 4.5 miles, you'll reach the signed junction for Notch Trail 729. This is where the loop officially begins and ends. You will have to rehike the first 4.5 miles of trail to return to the trailhead.

From the junction head west. Cross to the south side of Elk Creek via a bridge at 5.6 miles, and cross back to the north side at 5.9 miles. Just beyond there is a lovely view northwest up the Second Meadow drainage.

The trail skirts northwest along the north edge of the long expanse of Second Meadows as it continues to climb gradually. Although the trail leads through an occasional stand of trees, most of the time it traverses through one meadow after another. It eventually travels southwest to 11.9 miles and the end of fairly flat terrain. (Along the way beaver activity is obvious, with many lodges, dams, and cut trees. There are also some talus slopes to cross—look for pikas as you hike.)

Elk Creek/Valle Victoria Semiloop

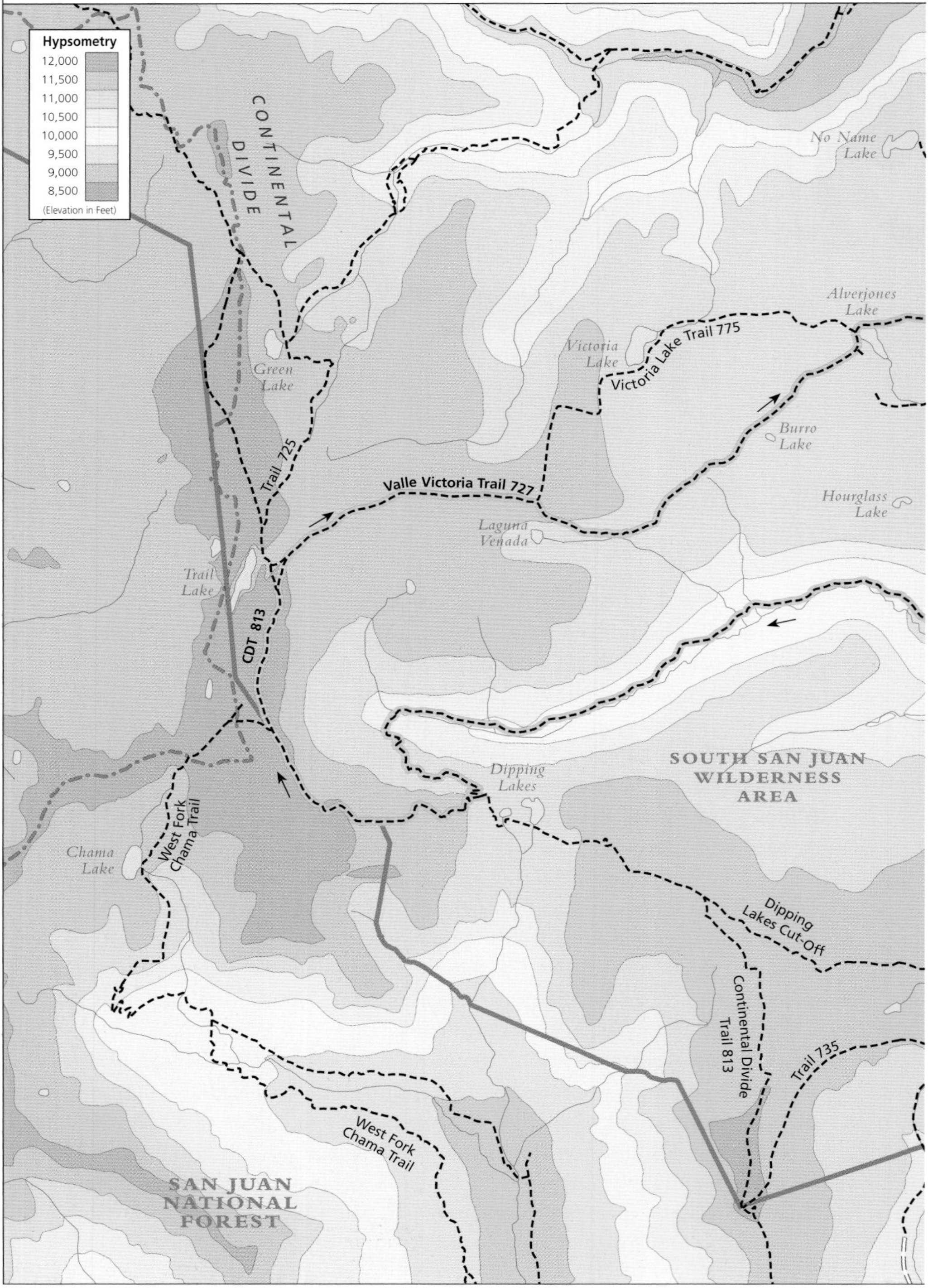

Hypsometry

12,000	
11,500	
11,000	
10,500	
10,000	
9,500	
9,000	
8,500	

(Elevation in Feet)

CONTINENTAL DIVIDE

No Name Lake

Alverjones Lake

Victoria Lake

Victoria Lake Trail 775

Burro Lake

Hourglass Lake

Green Lake

Trail 725

Valle Victoria Trail 727

Laguna Venada

Trail Lake

CDT 813

SOUTH SAN JUAN WILDERNESS AREA

Dipping Lakes

Chama Lake

West Fork Chama Trail

Dipping Lakes Cut-Off

Continental Divide Trail 813

Trail 735

West Fork Chama Trail

SAN JUAN NATIONAL FOREST

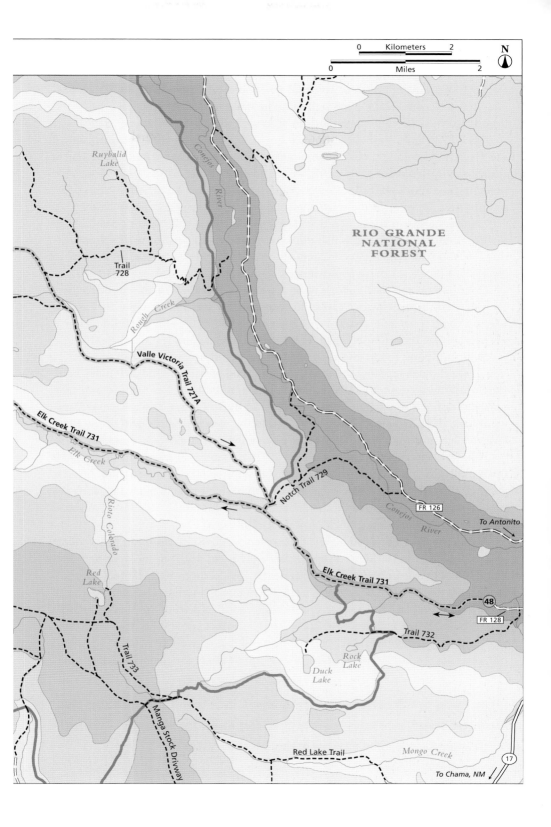

Ruybalid
Lake

RIO GRANDE
NATIONAL
FOREST

Trail
728

Conejos River

Rough Creek

Valle Victoria Trail 721A

Elk Creek Trail 731

Elk Creek

Notch Trail 729

Conejos River

FR 126

To Antonito

Rioto Colorado

Elk Creek Trail 731

Red
Lake

48

FR 128

Trail 732

Rock
Lake

Duck
Lake

Trail 733

Manga Stock Driwway

Red Lake Trail

Mongo Creek

17

To Chama, NM

Travel west and then circle around to the southeast, traveling through the trees as you climb moderately up and out of the drainage. Cross a stream and avalanche chute at 13.9 miles, and continue east to a trail junction at 14.4 miles. The Elk Creek Trail ends here at Continental Divide Trail 813. The trail south leads to Dipping Lakes and beyond to Mexico, while the trail north leads to Trail Lake and Canada.

CDT 813 climbs west above the tree line and across open, rocky plateaus, where the views are stunning. Look for ptarmigan in this part of the country. The trail is always easy to follow, as rock cairns are abundant and easy to see. You will reach a junction near Trail Lake at 18.3 miles. Although you won't see the lake at this point (it's just over the ridge to the west), there are two small lakes near the junction.

Follow the sign marked 727, descending gradually on Valle Victoria Trail 727 to the east. Enormous rock cairns mark the way, so there's no need to worry about getting lost. You will reach a signed trail junction at 18.8 miles. A sign points the way to Trail 725, which leads north approximately 2 miles and down 400 feet to Green Lake.

Continue on the Valle Victoria Trail. Descend across the vast mesa, where there are views north to Conejos Peak, a thirteener that is the highest point in Conejos County. You'll reach an unmarked trail junction at 20.4 miles. The trail heading north is Victoria Lake Trail 775 (see Hike 50 for more information).

From this point follow the rock cairns right (southeast) and descend moderately. You'll hike through meadow and forest, passing Laguna Venada around 20.9 miles. Look back to the west to see this lake. Continue through the trees, heading east and then northeast through an open meadow. You will find Burro Lake at 22.6 miles and Alverjones Lake at 23.7 miles. The trail skirts around the west and north ends of the latter. Post-markers at the north end of the lake point the way to Trails 775 (west) and 727A.

Hike east and then southeast on Trail 727A to another marked junction at 24.9 miles. Trail 728 continues to the east, but you want to hike south on Trail 727A. It descends through meadows and subalpine forest, crossing a couple of streams along the way. Please note that the trail can be difficult to follow in some areas, but if you look closely, you can usually find a rock cairn to mark the way.

After a stream crossing at 26.2 miles, the trail descends to the southeast past a couple of ponds. At 28.3 miles there's an especially lovely pond that is in the open and on a high bluff, with views west to the Continental Divide. From here the trail descends moderately (but sometimes at a very steep grade) through forest and aspens to a small pond at 29.7 miles. Climb a ridge shortly after, and then descend to Notch Trail 729 at 30.1 miles. A sign indicates that Cow Camp is 2 miles east and Elk Creek is 1 mile west. In reality, switchbacks lead 0.5 mile to the Elk Creek Trail at 30.6 miles. Travel east, covering the first 4.5 miles of the hike as you return to the trailhead at 35.1 miles.

When you are at high elevations, look for krummholz. These twisted, gnarled conifers have been bent, abused, and stunted by severe winds, deep snows, a short growing season, and frigid temperatures. Dwarfed trees may be hundreds of years old.

Rocky Mountain elk (Cervus elaphus nelsoni) *(cow)*

Miles and Directions

0.0   Elk Creek trailhead.

0.6   Gate. GPS: N37 7.206' / W 106 23.115'.

2.8   Wilderness boundary.

4.5   Notch Trail junction. GPS: N37 8.236' / W106 26.523'.

5.9   Bridge near Second Meadows. GPS: N37 8.500' / W106 27.711'.

14.4   Continental Divide Trail junction. GPS: N37 8.063' / W106 33.401'.

18.3   Valle Victoria Trail 727 junction. GPS: N37 9.605' / W106 35.108'.

20.4   Victoria Lake Trail 775 junction. GPS: N37 10.086' / W106 33.080'.

24.9   Trail 728 junction. GPS: N37 11.010' / W106 29.510'.

30.1   Notch Trail junction. GPS: N37 8.263' / W106 26.282'.

35.1   Back to Elk Creek trailhead.

Hike Information

Local information: Antonito Chamber of Commerce, Antonito; (719) 376-2277; www .slvguide.com/ANTONITO/INDEX.HTM. Chama Valley Chamber of Commerce, Chama, New Mexico; (575) 756-2306 or (800) 477-0149; www.chamavalley.com.

Local events/attractions: Ride the Cumbres & Toltec Narrow Gauge Railroad from Chama to Antonito; (888) 286-2737; www.cumbrestoltec .com.

Accommodations: There are some private campgrounds and motels near Antonito and Chama. Elk Creek Campground is the closest national forest facility. It's a fee area; facilities include water and an outhouse. There are also primitive places to camp in the area.

49 Ruybalid Lake via Ruybalid Trailhead

The climb up to Ruybalid Lake is a tough one, but as you're ascending remember that the trail was even steeper at one time. You'll see remnants of the old trail as you climb through the trees. Aspens grace the path, so it makes a nice fall hike.

Start: Ruybalid trailhead
Distance: 10.2 miles out and back
Hiking time: About 6 to 10 hours or overnight backpack
Difficulty: Strenuous due to length and elevation gain of more than 2,600 feet
Canine compatibility: Dogs must be under control.
Nearest town: Antonito

Fees and permits: Free registration at the trailhead
Maps: USGS Spectacle Lake; Trails Illustrated South San Juan/Del Norte; DeLorme 3D TopoQuad CD-ROM; Maptech Terrain Navigator CD-ROM
Trail contact: Rio Grande National Forest, Conejos Peak Ranger District, La Jara; (719) 274-8971; www.fs.usda.gov/riogrande

Finding the trailhead: From the junction of CO 17 and FR 250, about 22 miles from Antonito, Colorado, and 28 miles from Chama, New Mexico, travel north on FR 250. The road begins as paved, but quickly turns to gravel and can be pretty bumpy at times. Drive 7.5 miles to Rocky Mountain Lodge. Here you'll find a small group of cabins, an RV park, and gasoline, propane, and groceries for sale. Make a left onto Record Ridge Road, drive over the Conejos River via a bridge, and meet up with North and South Riverview Roads in 0.2 mile. You'll see places to park here at the junction and signs pointing the way to both Ruybalid Trail 855 and Rough Creek Falls. *DeLorme: Colorado Atlas & Gazetteer:* Page 89 C6. GPS: N37 11.225' / W106 26.968'.

The Hike

Begin hiking Ruybalid Trail 855, ascending the mostly steep grade past ponderosa pines, white and Douglas firs, and aspens. You will enter the wilderness at 0.2 mile and see a trail leading south at 0.8 mile. If you look closely, you'll see the word FALLS written on a stump. It points the way to Rough Creek Falls, which are a mere 0.3 mile off the main trail. Don't miss seeing the falls—they are awesome. On this short side trip you will gain 50 feet and descend 120 feet.

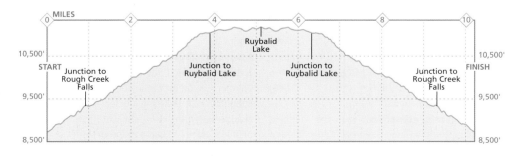

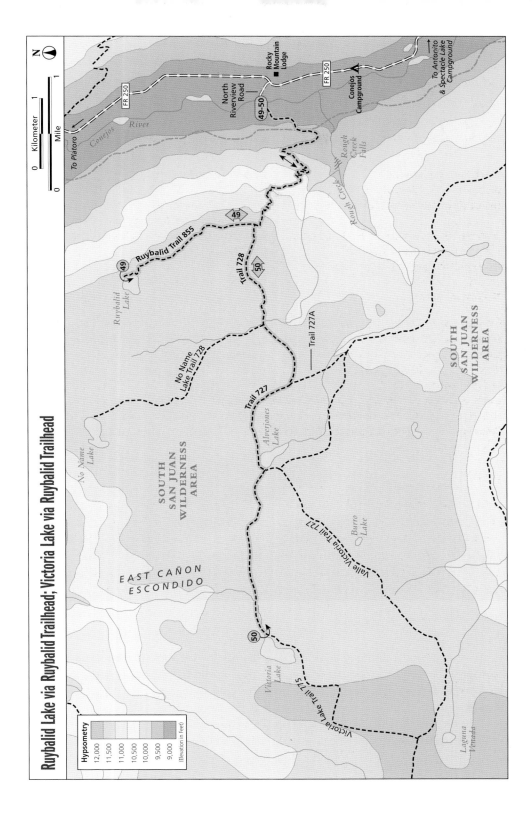

Ruybalid Lake via Ruybalid Trailhead; Victoria Lake via Ruybalid Trailhead

Hypsometry

	(Elevation in Feet)
12,000	
11,500	
11,000	
10,500	
10,000	
9,500	
9,000	

N

0   1   Kilometer
0   1   Mile

To Platoro

Conejos River

FR 250

North Riverview Road

Rocky Mountain Lodge

49-50

FR 250

Conejos Campground

To Antonito & Spectacle Lake Campground

Rough Creek Falls

Rough Creek

49

Ruybalid Trail 855

49

Ruybalid Lake

Trail 728

50

Trail 727A

No Name Lake Trail 728

No Name Lake

Trail 727

SOUTH SAN JUAN WILDERNESS AREA

Alverjones Lake

EAST CAÑON ESCONDIDO

Burro Lake

Valle Victoria Trail 727

50

Victoria Lake

Victoria Lake Trail 715

SOUTH SAN JUAN WILDERNESS AREA

Laguna Venada

Rough Creek Falls

As you continue climbing, look back to the east to see various cabins and the resort area. The trail provides for a gorgeous hike in the fall as you look out over the Conejos River Valley with its many shades of gold, orange, and red. You'll climb quickly until mile 3.6 and then get a break as the terrain levels off. Nearly thirty switchbacks help, but the trail is still a hump. (Please note that the trail takes a different path than in the past, so other maps may show it in a different place.)

PRIMORDIAL PINES

Bristlecone pines are the oldest known tree species on earth. The Colorado or Rocky Mountain bristlecone pine (*Pinus aristata*) is found in Colorado, northern New Mexico, and northern Arizona; it can live for up to 3,000 years. The Great Basin or Intermountain bristlecone pine (*Pinus longaeva*) is found from Utah to Nevada and eastern California; it can live for nearly 5,000 years. The oldest tree—age 4,900 years and counting—is in the White Mountains of California (its exact location is not disclosed to protect it). Bristlecone pines are relatively easy to identify. Their needles are crowded and clumped together, resembling bottlebrushes. The needles are in bundles of five, about 1 inch long, and they are usually curved. While the cones are developing, they are a deep purple; two years later they mature and become brown. Bristlecone pines derive their name from the clawlike bristle on the end of each cone scale.

At 3.8 miles you will reach a signed junction for Ruybalid Lake. Continue hiking Trail 855, traveling a gentle up-and-down grade through subalpine forest to the lake, which sits near the edge of a ridge at 5.1 miles. Walk to the eastern edge of the forested ridge for views of the San Luis Valley, the Sangre de Cristo Mountains, the Conejos River drainage, and Bennett Peak. Groves of bristlecone pines can be seen on the rocky ridge near the lake.

Miles and Directions

0.0 Ruybalid trailhead.
0.2 Wilderness boundary.
3.8 Trail junction to Ruybalid Lake. GPS: N37 11.302' / W106 28.147'.
5.1 Ruybalid Lake.
10.2 Back to Ruybalid trailhead.

Hike Information

Local information: Antonito Chamber of Commerce, Antonito; (719) 376-2277; www .slvguide.com/ANTONITO/INDEX.HTM. Chama Valley Chamber of Commerce, Chama, New Mexico; (575) 756-2306 or (800) 477-0149; www.chamavalley.com.

Local events/attractions: Ride the Cumbres & Toltec Narrow Gauge Railroad from Chama to Antonito; (888) 286-2737; www.cumbrestoltec .com.

Accommodations: There are some private campgrounds and motels in or near Antonito and Chama. Two national forest facilities— Conejos and Spectacle Lake Campgrounds—are nearest to the trailhead. Both are fee areas with water and vault toilets. If cabins are more to your liking, check out Rocky Mountain Lodge, located near the trailhead; (719) 376-5597.

50 Victoria Lake via Ruybalid Trailhead

The climb up to Ruybalid Lake is tough, but it provides the shortest access to Victoria Lake, which sits on a broad plateau to the west. Hike to this area, and you'll have the opportunity to make a side trip to No Name Lake and the Valle Victoria Trail.

See map page 221
Start: Ruybalid trailhead
Distance: 15.8 miles out and back
Hiking time: Overnight backpack
Difficulty: Strenuous due to length and elevation gain of more than 2,900 feet
Canine compatibility: Dogs must be under control.
Nearest town: Antonito
Fees and permits: Free registration at the trailhead

Maps: USGS Spectacle Lake and Victoria Lake; Trails Illustrated South San Juan/Del Norte; DeLorme 3D TopoQuad CD-ROM; Maptech Terrain Navigator CD-ROM
Trail contact: Rio Grande National Forest, Conejos Peak Ranger District, La Jara; (719) 274-8971; www.fs.usda.gov/riogrande
Special considerations: Some of the areas on this trail can be boggy. Expect to get wet; waterproof hiking boots are best.

Finding the trailhead: At the junction of CO 17 and FR 250, about 22 miles from Antonito, Colorado, and 28 miles from Chama, New Mexico, travel north on FR 250. The road is paved for a short distance, then turns to gravel and can be bumpy at times. Drive 7.5 miles to Rocky Mountain Lodge, which consists of some cabins and an RV park. They also sell gasoline, propane, and groceries. Make a left onto Record Ridge Road, drive over the Conejos River via a bridge, and meet up with North and South Riverview Roads in 0.2 mile. You'll see places to park here at the junction and signs pointing the way to both Ruybalid Trail 855 and Rough Creek Falls. *DeLorme: Colorado Atlas & Gazetteer:* Page 89 C6. GPS: N37 11.225' / W106 26.968'.

The Hike

Begin hiking Ruybalid Trail 855, ascending the mostly steep grade past pines, firs, and aspens. Enter the wilderness in 0.2 mile. At 0.8 mile you'll see a trail taking off to the south. If you look closely, you'll see the word FALLS written on a stump. It points the way to Rough Creek Falls, which is a mere 0.3 mile off the main trail.

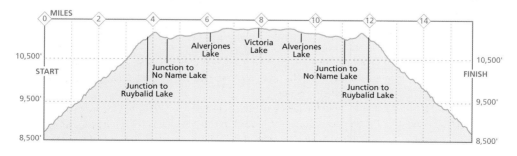

Don't miss the falls—they're awesome. On this short side trip you will gain 50 feet and descend 120 feet.

Back on the trail you'll climb quickly until mile 3.6 and then get a break as the terrain levels off. Nearly thirty switchbacks help, but the trail is still a hump. (Please note that the trail takes a different path than in the past, so other maps may show it in a different place.)

At 3.8 miles you'll reach a signed trail junction for Ruybalid Lake (see Hike 49 for more information). Head west, traveling an easy grade through trees and meadows. You'll reach a trail junction to No Name Lake at 4.6 miles. It's a three-way affair, with all three signs pointing the way to Trail 728. The sign to the north also refers to No Name Lake (see Option 1).

Proceed west to another junction at 5.3 miles. There are two signs and routes for Trail 727: One leads straight ahead (south) down Rough Creek and eventually to Elk Creek (see Hike 48 for more information). The other travels to the right (northwest), the way to Victoria Lake. Hike northwest and ascend gradually to Alverjones Lake at 6.2 miles. The lake is home to ducks and coots. Elk abound, as do deer, and you might even see a raptor or two.

From Alverjones Lake there are two trails (at times) leading west and up the drainage to the west. It doesn't matter which one you follow. Rock cairns and post-markers dot the way. The area just north of Alverjones Lake is very marshy and boggy at times; thus hikers have made a trail at the edge of the trees to the west of the lake. You'll reach Victoria Lake at 7.9 miles.

Miles and Directions

0.0 Ruybalid trailhead.

0.2 Wilderness boundary.

3.8 Trail junction to Ruybalid Lake. GPS: N37 11.302' / W106 28.147'.

4.6 Trail junction to No Name Lake. GPS: N37 11.218' / W106 28.881'.

6.2 Alverjones Lake. GPS: N37 11.261' / W106 30.334'.

7.9 Victoria Lake. GPS: N37 11.164' / W106 32.039'.

15.8 Back to Ruybalid trailhead.

Option 1: From the No Name Lake junction at mile 4.6, go northwest through open meadow and climb gently. You'll reach subalpine forest and a high point along the trail at 1.6 miles. Descend from here, hiking through woods to the lake at 1.9 miles.

Option 2: Although the trail actually follows Victoria Lake along its southeast side and then across the south end of the lake, at the post-marker Trail 775 sign (GPS: N37 11.227' / W106 31.931'), you can head right (northwest) and hike around the north and west ends of the lake. You'll find an unmaintained trail at times. The areas south of Victoria Lake can be boggy, so traveling around the north end is best when it is wet.

Whatever route you choose, from the lake you'll see a rocky slope to the southwest. Head in that direction (note that the trail seems to cease to exist in this area) and pick up the trail, which heads west and just to the north of the rocky slope, at 0.7 mile. At this point you're at the western edge of the valley, just below the rocky slope. Ascend west up the moderate-to-steep grade, past rocks that are home to many pikas. The trail eventually skirts around the west end of the rock pile and emerges into the open. Rock cairns mark the way to the unsigned junction at 1.9 miles. This is where the Valle Victoria Trail merges with the Victoria Lake Trail. From here there are spectacular views of Conejos Peak to the north. (See Hike 48 for more information on hiking all of the Valle Victoria Trail.)

Hike Information

Local information: Antonito Chamber of Commerce, Antonito; (719) 376-2277; www .slvguide.com/ANTONITO/INDEX.HTM. Chama Valley Chamber of Commerce, Chama, New Mexico; (575) 756-2306 or (800) 477-0149; www.chamavalley.com.

Local events/attractions: Ride the Cumbres & Toltec Narrow Gauge Railroad from Chama to Antonito; (888) 286-2737; www.cumbrestoltec .com.

Accommodations: There are some private camp-grounds and motels in or near Antonito and Chama. Two national forest facilities—Conejos and Spectacle Lake Campgrounds—are nearest to the trailhead. Both are fee areas with water and outhouses. If cabins are more to your liking, check out Rocky Mountain Lodge, located near the trailhead; (719) 376-5597.

51 South Fork/Roaring Gulch Semiloop

Although you can hike this semiloop in either direction, I describe the clockwise route. On this trip you'll enjoy wonderful views, colorful wildflowers, and much in the way of forest and alpine scenes. The foliage is especially beautiful in the fall.

Start: South Fork trailhead
Distance: 22.5-mile semiloop
Hiking time: 3- to 4-day backpack
Difficulty: Strenuous due to length and elevation gain of approximately 4,300 feet
Canine compatibility: Dogs must be under control.
Nearest town: Antonito
Fees and permits: Free registration at the trailhead

Maps: USGS Spectacle Lake, Victoria Lake, Platoro, and Red Mountain; Trails Illustrated South San Juan/Del Norte; DeLorme 3D TopoQuad CD-ROM; Maptech Terrain Navigator CD-ROM
Trail contact: Rio Grande National Forest, Conejos Peak Ranger District, La Jara; (719) 274-8971; www.fs.usda.gov/riogrande
Special considerations: Camping, campfires, and animal grazing are not allowed within 200 feet of Green and Blue Lakes.

Finding the trailhead: From the junction of CO 17 and FR 250, about 22 miles west of Antonito, Colorado, and 28 miles northeast of Chama, New Mexico, drive northwest and then north on FR 250 for 11.1 miles. FR 250 starts out as paved, but quickly becomes gravel and can be bumpy at times. There's a sign, a trail register, some hitching posts, and plenty of parking at the South Fork trailhead. *DeLorme: Colorado Atlas & Gazetteer:* Page 89 C6. GPS: N37 13.886' / W106 27.840'.

The Hike

Post-marker 724 points the way to the trail, which descends a moderate-to-steep grade past an old cabin. There's an unsigned trail junction at 0.3 mile. The trail to the north leads 0.5 mile to the South Fork Primitive Camp area, where there is an outhouse and room to camp. Continue due west and cross the Conejos River via a footbridge at 0.5 mile. Signs point the way right (northwest) to the South Fork and Roaring Gulch Trails. Stay on the trail, and be sure to keep gates closed as you hike through a mixed forest of aspens and evergreens.

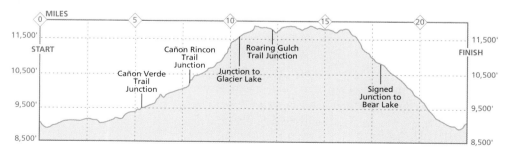

You'll reach a junction at 1.1 miles. South Fork Trail 724 heads left (west) from here, whereas Roaring Gulch Trail 720 goes straight (north). Although you can hike the semiloop in either direction, I think the clockwise route is best; it's certainly the easiest way to go. Hike left on Trail 724; you will enter the wilderness shortly thereafter. (Although some maps show Trail 724 along the South Fork Conejos River, at this point the trail is north of it.)

The trail ascends and descends but mostly climbs through trees. An abundance of aspens makes this a nice fall hike. There are open meadows, too, which means you might find cattle in the area.

At 3.2 miles cross Hansen Creek as you head into Cañon Escondido. Now you'll parallel the South Fork, though you're often way above it. Continue up and down, traveling the easy-to-moderate trail to a junction at 5.8 miles. Post-markers show the way to Trails 726 and 724. Trail 724 continues straight (west); Cañon Verde Trail 726 goes left (south). See Option 1 for information on a hike to Green Lake and the Continental Divide Trail.

From the junction climb the moderate-to-steep trail, heading a good distance above the river. The trail will ease up, alternately passing through subalpine forest, aspens, and open slopes. As you proceed you'll see many washouts and obvious avalanche chutes along the steep side drainages. Ford Cañon Rincon at 7.6 miles, then climb moderate-to-steep switchbacks to a junction at 7.8 miles. Although the semiloop will continue north on Cañon Rincon Trail 722, you can make a side trip west on Trail 724. A sign claims that it is 5 miles to Blue Lake, but the actual distance is closer to 3.8 miles (see Option 2 for more information).

Head north on Trail 722, ascending a steep grade that eases up every now and then. It's worth the effort, as the trail travels through a beautiful mix of forest and open slopes, where animal life and wildflowers are abundant. You will reach a point near the head of the drainage and a trail junction at 10.6 miles. Although the semiloop continues north to the Twin Lakes and beyond, this junction provides access to Glacier Lake Trail 711, which leads 1 mile west to Glacier Lake. This is also the junction to Timber Lake, which is southeast of this point (see Option 3).

Continue northeast, watching for rock cairns that lead the way to the easternmost of the Twin Lakes at 11 miles. The trail is easy to see as it heads northeast. From Twin Lakes the trail climbs steeply and then descends across an open plateau with views of Conejos Peak—at 13,172 feet, the highest point in Conejos County. You'll cross the head of Hansen Creek at 12.1 miles; there is a trail junction immediately after. From here you can ascend to Conejos Peak on a trail that heads to the northeast. (If you're interested in a trek to Conejos Peak and Glacier Lake, see Hike 53.)

The semiloop continues east as you travel the Roaring Gulch Trail. You will enter thick woods, hike up a steep grade, and then emerge in the open, where the views are grand and the terrain is flatter. You'll cross a very small stream at 12.7 miles. There is an unsigned trail junction here; it can be difficult to see, so pay close attention. The path going left (northeast) leads to Saddle Creek, whereas the path going right (east) continues the semiloop via Roaring Gulch.

South Fork/Roaring Gulch Semiloop

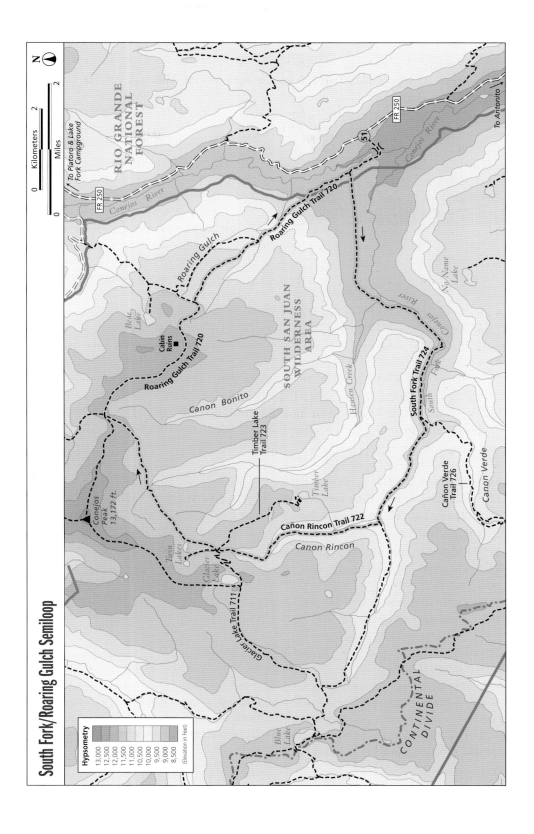

Hypsometry

13,000
12,500
12,000
11,500
11,000
10,500
10,000
9,500
9,000
8,500

(Elevation in Feet)

N

Kilometers
0   2

Miles
0   2

To Platoro & Lake
Fork Campground

FR 250

Conejos River

RIO GRANDE
NATIONAL
FOREST

Roaring Gulch

Roaring Gulch Trail 720

Bear Lake

Cabin Ruins

Roaring Gulch Trail 720

Cañon Bonito

Timber Lake
Trail 723

SOUTH SAN JUAN
WILDERNESS
AREA

Hansen Creek

Conejos River

South Fork

South Fork Trail 724

No-Name Lake

51

FR 250

To Antonito

Conejos Peak
13,172 ft.

Twin Lakes

Glacier Lake

Glacier Lake Trail 711

Timber Lake

Cañon Rincon Trail 722

Cañon Rincon

Cañon Verde
Trail 726

Cañon Verde

Blue Lake

CONTINENTAL DIVIDE

Colorado columbine (Aquilegia coerulea)

The trail meanders across open slopes and plateaus with wide views of much of the wilderness. It eventually leads through pockets of trees before descending to the remains of an old cabin at 15.8 miles. Look north, and you'll see a high ridge. Bear Lake is just over that ridge, on the north side. An unmaintained trail that is sometimes difficult to follow starts near the cabin remains and leads to the Roaring Gulch Trail and the trail to Bear Lake. (For a shortcut to Bear Lake, see Option 4.)

Continuing on the semiloop, you'll travel east and enter the forest at 16 miles. The descent can be steep at times, but moderate switchbacks make the trip much easier.

Cross a stream at 18.2 miles. You'll see a sign pointing the way to Bear Lake. From this junction it's 2.4 miles and a 940-foot elevation gain away. To finish the hike, continue descending what is now the Roaring Gulch Trail. Moderate switchbacks eventually lead you down through aspens. You'll reach a wilderness sign and gate at 20.9 miles. Hike another 0.5 mile, and you'll be back at the junction you faced on the first day of the hike (at mile 1.1). Retrace your steps to the trailhead at 22.5 miles.

Miles and Directions

0.0 South Fork trailhead.

5.8 Junction with Cañon Verde Trail. GPS: N37 13.050' / W106 32.469'.

7.8 Junction with Cañon Rincon Trail. GPS: N37 3.549' / W106 34.234'.

10.6 Junction with Glacier Lake and Timber Lake Trails. GPS: N37 15.656' / W106 34.696'.

12.7 Unsigned junction with trail to Saddle Creek. GPS: N37 16.601' / W106 33.304'.

15.8 Five-foot cairn and unsigned junction with trail to Bear Lake. GPS: N37 15.502' / W106 31.235'.

18.2 Signed junction with trail to Bear Lake. GPS: N37 15.162' / W106 29.626'.

20.9 Wilderness sign and gate.

22.5 Back to South Fork trailhead.

Option 1: From the junction of Trails 724 and 726 (mile 5.8), Cañon Verde Trail 726 descends to and crosses the South Fork Conejos River at 0.2 mile. The trail travels through pine, fir, and spruce trees and an occasional open meadow; although there are some moderate switchbacks, sometimes the trail is just plain steep. You will reach alpine country just before Green Lake, a popular place to fish, at 4.4 miles. A trail continues north from here, traveling on the east side of the lake and then northwest to a junction with Continental Divide Trail 813 at 5.3 miles. Gorgeous views abound, including a look at the Sangre de Cristo Mountains.

Option 2: From the junction of Trails 722 and 724 (mile 7.8), travel west on South Fork Trail 724. It's an easy-to-moderate climb through a mix of subalpine forest and open slopes. Look for deer and elk. The trail steepens somewhat as you travel into the head of the drainage. You'll cross small side streams along the way, but you won't cross the South Fork Conejos River until 3 miles. Proceed 100 yards west to a signed trail junction and the end of the trail. Turning left (west) onto Glacier Lake Trail 719 will take you 0.8 mile to Blue Lake; turning right (northeast) will lead you 2.4 miles to Glacier Lake.

Option 3: At the junction of Trails 722, 711, and 723 (mile 10.6), a post-marker and rock cairns connect to a well-defined, easy trail to Timber Lake. Timber Lake Trail 723 leads past a number of ponds, through scattered trees, and past slopes that were burned years ago. You will reach an overlook of Timber Lake at 1.5 miles. You can see to the Continental Divide and a peak near Trail Lake from this point. From above the lake, which looks as though it is sitting on the edge of the world, you also can view the San Luis Valley and the Sangre de Cristo Mountains. Switchbacks drop 200 vertical feet to the lake at 2 miles.

Option 4: To take a shortcut to Bear Lake from mile 15.8, continue east to a stream crossing in 100 yards. About 100 feet past the stream, you'll see a huge, 5-foot-high rock cairn. More rock cairns and some post-markers lead 1.4 miles northeast to an unsigned trail junction. You'll gain 320 feet in elevation en route. At the junction keep left (north) for 0.4 mile to another junction, then hike 0.2 mile west to Bear Lake. (See Hike 52 for a more detailed map and a different route to the lake.)

Hike Information

Local information: Antonito Chamber of Commerce, Antonito; (719) 376-2277; www .slvguide.com/ANTONITO/INDEX.HTM. Chama Valley Chamber of Commerce, Chama, New Mexico; (575) 756-2306 or (800) 477-0149; www.chamavalley.com.

Local events/attractions: Ride the Cumbres & Toltec Narrow Gauge Railroad from Chama to Antonito; (888) 286-2737; www.cumbrestoltec .com.

Accommodations: There are some private campgrounds and motels in or near Antonito and Chama and numerous campgrounds along FR 250. Lake Fork Campground, a national forest facility with water and vault toilets, is the closest to the trailhead. Primitive camping is available 0.2 mile and 2.7 miles north of the South Fork trailhead. There are cabins and rooms in Platoro, an old mining town about 11 miles north. Call Skyline Lodge (719-376-2226) or Conejos Cabins (877-376-2547). If you like great big scrumptious burgers and mountains of fries, check out the restaurant at Skyline Lodge!

52 Bear Lake Trail

Bear Lake Trail provides wonderful access for those who enjoy nice views and a high alpine lake. The fishing is supposed to be good at the lake, and the wildflowers are awesome, too. Hike in the fall, and you'll see plenty of gold, orange, and red leaves as you walk the trail. Two side trips make nice day hikes from a base camp at the lake.

Start: Bear Lake trailhead
Distance: 6 miles out and back
Hiking time: About 4 to 6 hours or overnight backpack
Difficulty: Moderate due to length and elevation gain of approximately 1,700 feet
Canine compatibility: Dogs must be under control.
Nearest town: Antonito
Fees and permits: Free registration at the trailhead

Maps: USGS Platoro and Red Mountain; Trails Illustrated South San Juan/Del Norte; DeLorme 3D TopoQuad CD-ROM; Maptech Terrain Navigator CD-ROM
Trail contact: Rio Grande National Forest, Conejos Peak Ranger District, La Jara; (719) 274-8971; www.fs.usda.gov/riogrande
Special considerations: Camping, campfires, and animal grazing are not allowed within 200 feet of Bear Lake.

Finding the trailhead: From the junction of CO 17 and FR 250, about 22 miles west of Antonito, Colorado, and 28 miles northeast of Chama, New Mexico, travel northwest and then north on FR 250. FR 250 begins as a paved road, but quickly turns into gravel and can be a bit rough at times. Go 16.4 miles to the junction of FR 250 and FR 105. Head left (west) on FR 105 for 2 miles to the signed trailhead on the left (south) side of the road. There are ample parking spaces, a trail register, and hitching posts. (Please note that some maps show the trailhead at a hairpin turn in the road; the trailhead is actually past that point.) *DeLorme: Colorado Atlas & Gazetteer:* Page 89 B6. GPS: N37 17.447' / W106 29.787'.

The Hike

From the trailhead, which is just off the road, sign the register and begin hiking Trail 721. It descends about 80 feet amid evergreens to Saddle Creek. Cross the creek via a bridge, and begin ascending the steep slope. Fourteen moderate switchbacks

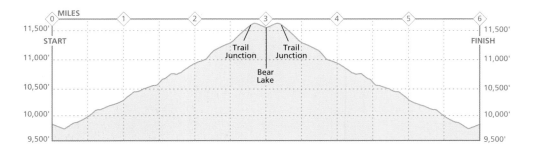

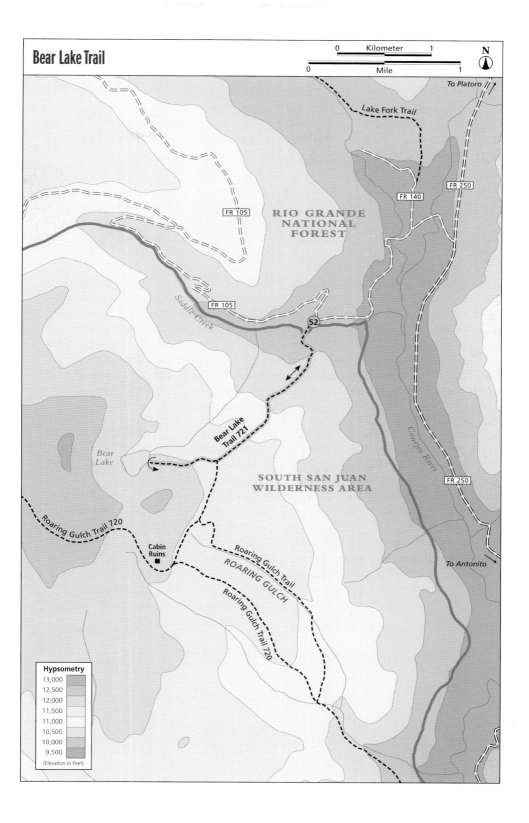

Bear Lake Trail

0 Kilometer 1

0 Mile 1

N

To Platoro

Lake Fork Trail

FR 250

FR 140

FR 105

RIO GRANDE
NATIONAL
FOREST

Saddle Creek

FR 105

52

Bear Lake
Trail 721

Bear
Lake

SOUTH SAN JUAN
WILDERNESS AREA

Conejos River

FR 250

Roaring Gulch Trail 720

Cabin
Ruins

Roaring Gulch Trail

ROARING GULCH

To Antonito

Roaring Gulch Trail 720

Hypsometry

| 13,000 |
| 12,500 |
| 12,000 |
| 11,500 |
| 11,000 |
| 10,500 |
| 10,000 |
| 9,500 |

(Elevation in Feet)

make the climb easier. Most ascend through subalpine forest, although the uppermost switchbacks cross an open slope, where there are views into the valley below.

You'll be back in the trees, then on the edge of them when you reach 2.8 miles and an unsigned junction (see Options for destinations from this point). Travel west through the trees to reach Bear Lake at 3 miles. The lake is nearly surrounded by steep, 1,000-foot-high cliffs. If you like wildflowers, explore the east and northeast ends of the lake to see many varieties of them.

Miles and Directions

0.0   Bear Lake trailhead.
2.8   Junction with unsigned trail. GPS: N37 16.530' / W106 30.614'.
3.0   Bear Lake.
6.0   Back to Bear Lake trailhead.

Options: From the unsigned junction at 2.8 miles, hike south for 0.4 mile to another unsigned trail junction (GPS: N37 16.231' / W106 30.488'). You can go right (southwest) or left (southeast). The unmaintained trail going southwest will take you 1.4 miles to an old cabin and the Roaring Gulch Trail. Although the path can be difficult to follow, rock cairns and post-markers serve as guides. There's a great view of Bear Lake from the saddle south of the lake and north of the cabin ruins. The trail going southeast from the 0.4-mile mark follows Roaring Gulch and crosses the stream after 1.2 miles. It reaches a junction with the Conejos Trail after another 0.6 mile; the total loss in elevation is 940 feet (see Hike 51 for more information).

Hike Information

Local information: Antonito Chamber of Commerce, Antonito; (719) 376-2277; www .slvguide.com/ANTONITO/INDEX.HTM. Chama Valley Chamber of Commerce, Chama, New Mexico; (575) 756-2306 or (800) 477-0149; www.chamavalley.com.

Local events/attractions: Ride the Cumbres & Toltec Narrow Gauge Railroad from Chama to Antonito; (888) 286-2737; www.cumbrestoltec .com.

Accommodations: There are some private campgrounds and motels in or near Antonito and Chama and numerous campgrounds along FR 250. Lake Fork Campground is the closest national forest facility to the trailhead; it is a fee area with water and vault toilets. There are cabins and rooms in Platoro, an old mining town about 11 miles north. Call Skyline Lodge (719-376-2226) or Conejos Cabins (877-376-2547). If you like great big scrumptious burgers and mountains of fries, check out the restaurant at Skyline Lodge!

53 Conejos Peak Semiloop

If you like being up high, then this is the trail for you. About one hour from the trailhead, you'll reach 12,000 feet, and you'll stay at or above the tree line for the duration of the hike. Look for wildflowers and wildlife, including weasels and ptarmigan, as you ascend Conejos Peak, the highest point in Conejos County.

Start: Twin Lakes trailhead
Distance: 14.5-mile semiloop
Hiking time: 2-day backpack; spend 3 days or more if you want to include a side trip to Blue Lake.
Difficulty: Strenuous due to length and elevation gain of approximately 3,000 feet
Canine compatibility: Dogs must be under control.
Nearest town: Antonito
Fees and permits: Free registration at the trailhead

Maps: USGS Platoro and Victoria Lake; Trails Illustrated South San Juan/Del Norte; DeLorme 3D TopoQuad CD-ROM; Maptech Terrain Navigator CD-ROM
Trail contact: Rio Grande National Forest, Conejos Peak Ranger District, La Jara; (719) 274-8971; www.fs.usda.gov/riogrande
Special considerations: Camping, campfires, and animal grazing are not allowed within 200 feet of Blue Lake.

Finding the trailhead: From the junction of CO 17 and FR 250, about 22 miles west of Antonito, Colorado, and 28 miles northeast of Chama, New Mexico, travel northwest and then north on FR 250. Although you'll begin on pavement, FR 250 quickly turns to gravel and can be quite bumpy at times. Go 16.4 miles to the junction of FR 250 and FR 105. Drive west on FR 105 for 6.1 miles to the signed trailhead on the left (west) side of the road. Park on the right (east) side of the road. *DeLorme: Colorado Atlas & Gazetteer:* Page 89 B5. GPS: N37 17.750' / W106 32.330'.

The Hike

From the trailhead, which is just off the road to the east, begin hiking signed Trail 720, which is just across the road to the west. The moderate-grade trail starts in subalpine forest. You soon will reach a fork and the wilderness boundary. The trail to the right (northwest) links up with the trail to Tobacco Lake (see Hike 54 for more information).

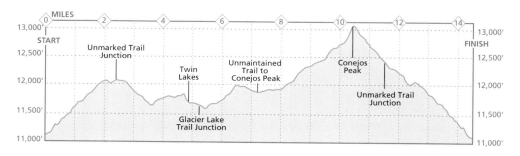

Mike Vining hiking up the southeast ridge of Conejos Peak

Keep to the left (southwest), and ford Saddle Creek at 0.7 mile. Long switchbacks will help as you climb through the trees. Once you are above the tree line, enjoy clear views of the Sangre de Cristo Mountains, the San Luis Valley, and much of the South San Juan Wilderness. You will reach a saddle at 2.3 miles and 12,040 feet.

Continue climbing to an unmarked junction at 2.4 miles. The ridge to the west will be your return route on this semiloop. Although the unmaintained trail up the ridge isn't marked at this point, it is easy to follow.

Follow the defined trail southwest, descending moderately across the open plateau. After 3.2 miles you will reach another unsigned junction. Trail 720 leads left (southeast) to Roaring Gulch (see Hike 51 for more information). Stay straight (east), eventually descending steeply through the forest to a signed trail junction at 3.8 miles. The trail leading across the headwaters of Hansen Creek travels northeast and reaches the east flank of Conejos Peak in 1 mile. If you're camping in the area, this is a nice route up Conejos Peak; the summit is a mere 2.2 miles from this point.

To continue the semiloop, cross the stream and head southwest. You'll ascend a plateau, climb a ridge, and then drop down what is sometimes a steep grade to Twin Lakes at 4.9 miles.

From Twin Lakes travel south, descending via an easy grade to a trail junction at 5.3 miles. Three trails take off from this point: You can travel to Timber Lake, descend Cañon Rincon, or head west to Glacier Lake. Continue west on Glacier Lake Trail 711 and cross Cañon Rincon, then climb moderate switchbacks to Glacier Lake at 6.5 miles. There are awesome views of Conejos, Summit, and Montezuma Peaks, plus Gunsight Pass and much more.

Continue west across the expansive plateau dotted with tarns. After 7.2 miles you'll reach a junction. The sign for the unmaintained trail heading northeast to

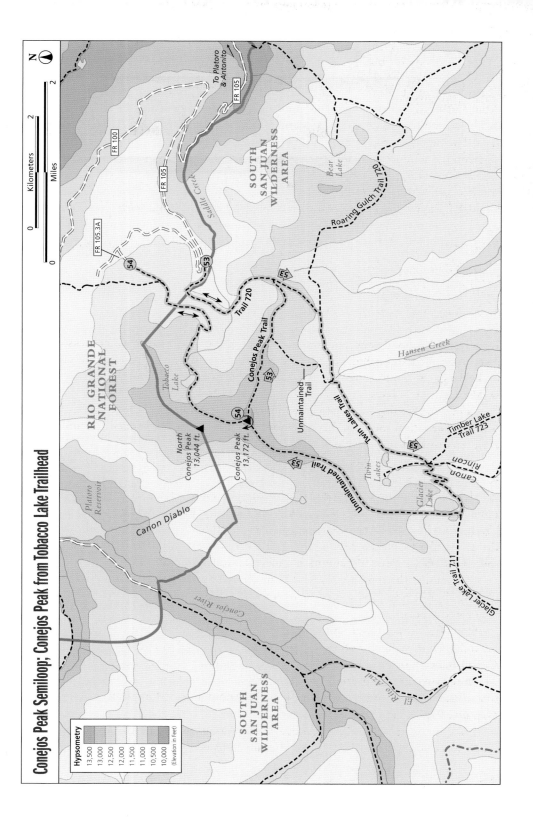

Conejos Peak Semiloop; Conejos Peak from Tobacco Lake Trailhead

Conejos Peak is missing, but another sign points the way to Blue Lake and the Conejos River (see Options). Follow an abundance of rock cairns and a post-marker or two as you travel northeast and then north to Conejos Peak at 10.3 miles. There are grand 360-degree views from the summit, including faraway vistas to the Weminuche, La Garita, and Sangre de Cristo wilderness areas, Great Sand Dunes National Park, and New Mexico to the south.

From the summit a trail leads north to North Conejos Peak and then to Tobacco Lake. If you are not interested in that side trip, hike down the east flank of Conejos Peak. Follow rock cairns to 11.5 miles and an unmarked junction with a trail leading southwest. Stay on the Conejos Peak Trail, following the ridge and what is sometimes only a faint or invisible path back to the saddle you enjoyed near the beginning of the hike (at 2.3 miles). Retrace your steps to the trailhead at 14.5 miles.

Miles and Directions

0.0 Twin Lakes trailhead.

2.3 Saddle at 12,040 feet.

5.3 Junction to Glacier Lake and Timber Lake Trails. GPS: N37 15.656' / W106 34.696'.

6.5 Glacier Lake.

7.2 Junction with trail leading to Conejos Peak. GPS: N37 15.253' / W106 35.895'.

10.3 Conejos Peak.

11.5 Unmarked junction with trail leading southwest.

14.5 Back to Twin Lakes trailhead.

Options: From the junction at 7.2 miles, the trail to Blue Lake continues to the west. It crosses a stream and then heads southwest through scattered trees to a trail junction at 1.8 miles. A post-marker points the way to Trail 724, which leads to the South Fork Conejos trailhead (see Hike 51 for more information). Continue west, and you will reach a signed trail junction for El Rito Azul Trail 718 at 2.5 miles. Keep left (west) to reach Blue Lake in another 0.2 mile. You can connect with the Continental Divide Trail on the south end of the lake; you also can hike northeast to Three Forks trailhead (see Hike 56 for more information).

Hike Information

Local information: Antonito Chamber of Commerce, Antonito; (719) 376-2277; www.slvguide.com/ANTONITO/INDEX.HTM. Chama Valley Chamber of Commerce, Chama, New Mexico; (575) 756-2306 or (800) 477-0149; www.chamavalley.com.

Local events/attractions: Ride the Cumbres & Toltec Narrow Gauge Railroad from Chama to Antonito; (888) 286-2737; www.cumbrestoltec.com.

Accommodations: There are some private campgrounds and motels in or near Antonito and Chama and numerous campgrounds along FR 250. Lake Fork Campground is the closest national forest facility to the trailhead; it is a fee area with water and vault toilets. There are cabins and rooms in Platoro, an old mining town about 11 miles north. Call Skyline Lodge (719-376-2226) or Conejos Cabins (877-376-2547). If you like great big scrumptious burgers and mountains of fries, check out the restaurant at Skyline Lodge!

54 Conejos Peak from Tobacco Lake Trailhead

This trail starts up high and stays high, making it the easiest route to the top of Conejos Peak—at 13,172 feet, the highest point in Conejos County. This is one of three beautiful routes to the summit; the views are tremendous as you ascend. Look for animal life and wildflowers.

See map page 237
Start: Tobacco Lake trailhead
Distance: 7.4 miles out and back
Hiking time: About 4 to 6 hours
Difficulty: Strenuous due to length
Canine compatibility: Dogs must be under control.
Nearest town: Antonito

Fees and permits: Free registration at the trailhead
Maps: USGS Platoro; Trails Illustrated South San Juan/Del Norte; DeLorme 3D TopoQuad CD-ROM; Maptech Terrain Navigator CD-ROM
Trail contact: Rio Grande National Forest, Conejos Peak Ranger District, La Jara; (719) 274-8971; www.fs.usda.gov/riogrande

Finding the trailhead: From the junction of CO 17 and FR 250, about 22 miles west of Antonito, Colorado, and 28 miles northeast of Chama, New Mexico, travel northwest and then north on FR 250. Though it starts out as a paved road, FR 250 quickly turns to gravel and can be bumpy at times. Go 16.4 miles to the junction of FR 250 and FR 105. Drive west on FR 105 for 7 miles to FR 105.3A. The road is quite rocky, so be prepared to drive slowly. Turn left (west), traveling another 0.5 mile on a bumpy dirt road to the signed trailhead. There are places to camp en route. *DeLorme: Colorado Atlas & Gazetteer:* Page 89 B5. GPS: N37 18.404' / W106 32.297'.

The Hike

From the trailhead begin hiking the Tobacco Lake Trail, traveling southwest. Although you will pass through a small section of trees, you'll mostly be above the tree line and able to see your surroundings. The trail is easy-to-moderate walking. After 0.7 mile you'll reach the wilderness boundary; continue to 1.1 miles and a post marking a trail to the west. It's easy to miss the junction if you aren't watching for it. If you start descending at a steep grade, you've gone too far. (If you descend, you'll be heading to the trailhead at Saddle Creek. From there you'll find another fine trail to the top of Conejos Peak. See Hike 53 for more information.)

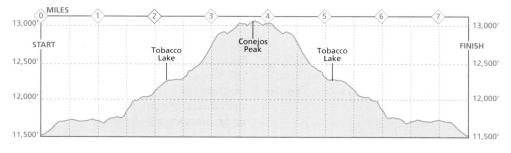

Mike Vining on top of North Conejos Peak

Hike west, climbing a moderate grade to Tobacco Lake at 2.2 miles. The lake is situated in a beautiful basin, with Conejos Peak visible to the southwest. Travel around the north end of the lake (some maps show a trail on the south end), and then climb the ridge to 3.1 miles and a saddle just south of North Conejos Peak. At 13,044 feet, North Conejos is a must-do for those collecting thirteener summits. Hike south along the ridge, reaching the top of Conejos Peak at 3.7 miles. Views from the summit are tremendous, with a sea of mountains visible in all directions.

Miles and Directions

0.0 Tobacco Lake trailhead.
0.7 Wilderness boundary.
1.1 Trail junction. GPS: N37 17.809' / W106 32.869'.
2.2 Tobacco Lake.
3.7 Conejos Peak.
7.4 Back to Tobacco Lake trailhead.

Hike Information

Local information: Antonito Chamber of Commerce, Antonito; (719) 376-2277; www .slvguide.com/ANTONITO/INDEX.HTM. Chama Valley Chamber of Commerce, Chama, New Mexico; (575) 756-2306 or (800) 477-0149; www.chamavalley.com.

Local events/attractions: Ride the Cumbres & Toltec Narrow Gauge Railroad from Chama to Antonito; (888) 286-2737; www.cumbrestoltec .com.

Accommodations: There are some private campgrounds and motels in or near Antonito and Chama and numerous campgrounds along FR 250. Lake Fork Campground is the closest national forest facility to the trailhead; it is a fee area with water and vault toilets. There are cabins and rooms in Platoro, an old mining town about 11 miles north. Call Skyline Lodge (719-376-2226) or Conejos Cabins (877-376-2547). If you like great big scrumptious burgers and mountains of fries, check out the restaurant at Skyline Lodge!

55 Adams Fork to Summit Peak

A hike up the Adams Fork of the Conejos River leads to one of the most beautiful glacier-carved valleys in all of the South San Juans. Adams Fork is also a mecca for animal life and wildflowers. Look for elk, deer, snowshoe hares, and birdlife galore. The region is a wonderful place for a base camp from which to explore. Summit Peak, the highest point in Archuleta County, offers 360-degree views to New Mexico, the San Juan Mountains, the La Garita Mountains, the San Luis Valley, and the Sangre de Cristo Mountains.

Start: Adams Fork trailhead
Distance: 17.8 miles out and back
Hiking time: 2- to 3-day backpack
Difficulty: Strenuous due to length and elevation gain of more than 3,200 feet
Canine compatibility: Dogs must be under control.
Nearest town: South Fork

Fees and permits: Free registration at the trailhead
Maps: USGS Platoro and Summit Peak; Trails Illustrated Weminuche Wilderness; DeLorme 3D TopoQuad CD-ROM; Maptech Terrain Navigator CD-ROM
Trail contact: Rio Grande National Forest, Conejos Peak Ranger District, La Jara; (719) 274-8971; www.fs.usda.gov/riogrande

Finding the trailhead: From South Fork head southwest on US 160 for 7.3 miles. Turn left (south/southeast) onto Park Creek Road (FR 380), which is gravel, and drive for 26.9 miles. FR 380 ends upon meeting up with FR 250, also gravel. FR 250 heads straight (east) to Alamosa or right (south) to Platoro. Drive south toward Platoro, traveling another 4.4 miles to a junction with Three Forks Road (FR 247). Keep right on FR 247, and drive south/southwest past Platoro Reservoir for 5.2 miles to the signed Adams Fork trailhead and a large parking area. There is plenty of room to camp at the trailhead. (If a national forest campground is more to your liking, from the junction of FR 250/247, drive south on FR 250 for another 1.1 miles to the turnoff for Mix Lake Campground. The quaint old mining town of Platoro is just beyond.) *DeLorme: Colorado Atlas & Gazetteer:* Page 89 B5. GPS: N37 19.111' / W106 35.742'.

The Hike

Hike northeast on Adams Fork Trail 713, then switchback and head mostly west/ northwest as you continue. The relatively easy grade has a few moderate sections as you travel through a mix of open slope and trees, mainly spruce and fir. There are several side stream crossings en route, which is a grand thing because although the trail parallels Adams Fork, it is usually above it. Enter the wilderness after 1.3 miles. The grade continues at an easy clip as you travel deeper into the glacier-carved basin, where elk and deer are plentiful.

Hike to 6.3 miles and a junction. The Adams Fork Trail officially ends where it meets up with Continental Divide Trail (CDT) 813; signs mark the spot. To finish out

Adams Fork to Summit Peak

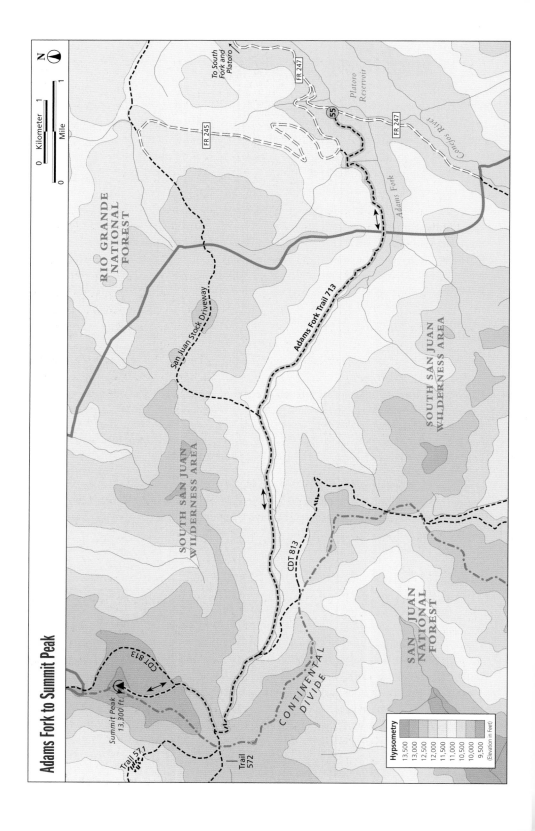

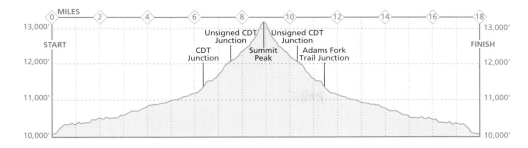

the hike, travel west and then north. You'll continue up a valley, where wildflowers are abundant in midsummer. There are many small waterfalls as well as you hike up the moderate grade.

At 7.5 miles you'll reach an unmarked junction for the CDT just below a saddle, where you'll see signs for Trails 571 and 572. Unfortunately, a sign is missing for CDT 813. To best find the CDT, look for it about 50 feet before the signs, just after you make a switchback. The CDT travels through thick willows in a northeasterly direction. Be aware that Trails 571 and 572 both head over the saddle and down the other side. (For more information on these trails, see Hikes 38 and 40.)

From the junction continue on the CDT to 8.1 miles. Now you'll see the top of Summit Peak, which is to the north. Hike off the trail, choosing the easiest slope, which is north/northwest. You'll reach the top of Summit Peak at 8.9 miles.

Miles and Directions

0.0 Adams Fork trailhead.

1.3 Wilderness boundary.

6.3 CDT junction. GPS: N37 19.824' / W106 41.386'.

7.5 Unsigned CDT junction near Trails 571 and 572. GPS: N37 20.185' / W106 41.386'.

8.9 Summit Peak. GPS: N37 21.036' / W106 41.808'.

17.8 Back to Adams Fork trailhead.

Hike Information

Local information: South Fork Chamber of Commerce, South Fork; (719) 873-5556; www.southforkcolorado.org.

Local events/attractions: Attend the Little Britches Rodeo (June), Logger Days Festival (July), Rhythms of the Rio Music Festival (August), or Chili Cookoff (October). Raft or fish the Rio Grande.

Accommodations: South Fork has a number of private campgrounds and motels. Mix Lake, a national forest campground, is located about 7 miles from the trailhead, near Platoro. It's a fee area with drinking water and vault toilets. You can also primitive camp near the trailhead. There are cabins and rooms in Platoro, an old mining town about 11 miles north. Call Skyline Lodge (719-376-2226) or Conejos Cabins (877-376-2547). If you like great big scrumptious burgers and mountains of fries, check out the restaurant at Skyline Lodge!

56 Blue Lake via Three Forks

The hike to beautiful Blue Lake, located in a high alpine setting, is just as stunning as the destination itself. First you'll hike through the lovely realms of the Conejos River drainage, then you'll cross the open meadows of the El Rito Azul drainage. Look for wildflowers and animal life.

Start: Three Forks trailhead
Distance: 11.8 miles out and back
Hiking time: About 6 to 8 hours or overnight backpack
Difficulty: Moderate due to length and elevation gain of approximately 1,500 feet
Canine compatibility: Dogs must be under control.
Nearest town: South Fork
Fees and permits: Free registration at the trailhead

Maps: USGS Summit Peak, Platoro, Elephant Head Rock, and Victoria Lake; Trails Illustrated South San Juan/Del Norte; DeLorme 3D TopoQuad CD-ROM; Maptech Terrain Navigator CD-ROM
Trail contact: Rio Grande National Forest, Conejos Peak Ranger District, La Jara; (719) 274-8971; www.fs.usda.gov/riogrande
Special considerations: Camping, campfires, and animal grazing are not allowed within 200 feet of Blue Lake.

Finding the trailhead: From South Fork head southwest on US 160 for 7.3 miles. Then travel south/southeast on Park Creek Road (FR 380), which is gravel, for 26.9 miles. FR 380 ends upon meeting up with FR 250, also gravel. FR 250 heads straight (east) to Alamosa or right (south) to Platoro. Drive south toward Platoro, traveling another 4.4 miles to a junction with Three Forks Road (FR 247). Keep right on FR 247, and drive south/southwest for 6.3 miles to the end of the road and the signed Three Forks trailhead. There's a large parking area here and an outhouse. There are plenty of places to camp en route to the trailhead. *DeLorme: Colorado Atlas & Gazetteer:* Page 89 B5. GPS: N37 18.126' / W106 36.333'.

The Hike

From the trailhead head southwest along the Conejos River via Three Forks Trail 712. You'll travel through trees at times, but mostly you'll be in a wide-open meadow. It's an easy hike to 1.9 miles and a spot called Three Forks, where the North and Middle Forks of the Conejos River come together with El Rito Azul.

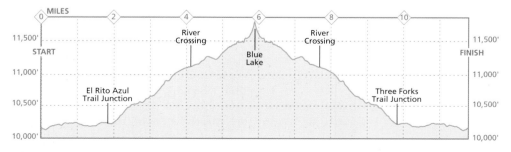

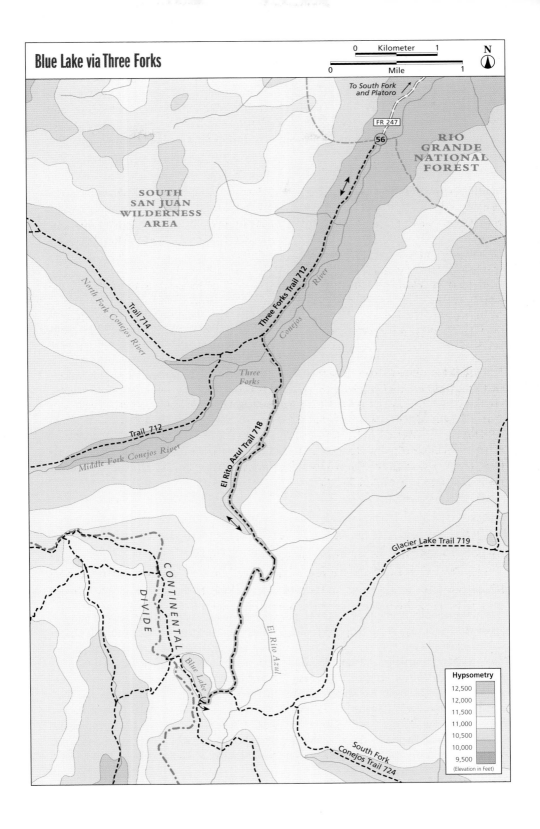

Blue Lake via Three Forks

0   Kilometer   1

0   Mile   1

N

To South Fork
and Platoro

FR 247

56

RIO
GRANDE
NATIONAL
FOREST

SOUTH
SAN JUAN
WILDERNESS
AREA

North Fork Conejos River

Trail 714

Three Forks Trail 712

Conejos River

Three
Forks

Trail 712

Middle Fork Conejos River

El Rito Azul Trail 718

Glacier Lake Trail 719

CONTINENTAL

DIVIDE

El Rito Azul

Blue Lake

South Fork
Conejos Trail 724

Hypsometry

12,500	
12,000	
11,500	
11,000	
10,500	
10,000	
9,500	

(Elevation in Feet)

Old man of the mountain (Hymenoxys grandiflora), *at Blue Lake*

At the junction you'll see a sign for Blue Lake and El Rito Azul Trail 718. Follow the trail south, and cross the Conejos River. You'll probably have to take off your shoes for this one. The trail follows the west side of El Rito Azul through subalpine forest to 2.7 miles, where you will cross the river. Follow the river on the east side, traveling through forest and meadow to 4.1 miles and a final river crossing. (All of the El Rito Azul crossings can be made by stepping on rocks or logs.) This time you'll stay on the west side of the stream, skirting a large meadow and hiking through more trees before reaching 5.7 miles and a marker for Trail 724 (see Hike 51 for more information on this trail). Another sign points the way to Blue Lake and reminds hikers to camp 200 feet away from it.

Continue west to lovely Blue Lake, 11,465 feet in elevation and a popular place for fishing and enjoying beautiful scenes. You'll reach the lake at 5.9 miles.

Miles and Directions

- **0.0**   Three Forks trailhead.
- **1.9**   Three Forks junction. GPS: N37 16.773' / W106 37.260'.
- **5.9**   Blue Lake. GPS: N37 14.267' / W106 37.684'.
- **11.8**   Back to Three Forks trailhead.

Options: If you'd like to connect with the Continental Divide Trail (CDT), continue 0.1 mile to the south end of Blue Lake. You'll see a marker for Trail 813. You can head south on the CDT from here. Also, about 300 feet to the west is another CDT marker and the remains of an old kiln. If you're going north on the CDT, take off from this point (see Hike 45 for more information).

Hike Information

Local information: South Fork Chamber of Commerce, South Fork; (719) 873-5556; www.southforkcolorado.org.

Local events/attractions: Attend the Little Britches Rodeo (June), Logger Days Festival (July), Rhythms of the Rio Music Festival (August), or Chili Cookoff (October). Raft or fish the Rio Grande.

Accommodations: South Fork has a number of private campgrounds and motels. Mix Lake, a national forest campground, is located about 7 miles from the trailhead, near Platoro. It's a fee area with drinking water and vault toilets. You can also primitive camp en route to the trailhead. There are cabins and rooms in Platoro, an old mining town about 11 miles north. Call Skyline Lodge (719-376-2226) or Conejos Cabins (877-376-2547). If you like great big scrumptious burgers and mountains of fries, check out the restaurant at Skyline Lodge!

57 Conejos River Semiloop

Hike this loop, and you're bound to feel as though you've seen it all. There's everything from the beautiful Conejos River drainage to Conejos Falls, a hike on the Continental Divide Trail (CDT), and views from more than 12,000 feet in elevation. In addition, you'll see abundant wildlife and wildflowers.

Start: Three Forks trailhead
Distance: 14.7-mile semiloop
Hiking time: About 8 to 10 hours or 2- to 3-day backpack
Difficulty: Strenuous due to length and elevation gain of approximately 2,200 feet
Canine compatibility: Dogs must be under control.
Nearest town: South Fork

Fees and permits: Free registration at the trailhead
Maps: USGS Platoro and Summit Peak; Trails Illustrated South San Juan/Del Norte; DeLorme 3D TopoQuad CD-ROM; Maptech Terrain Navigator CD-ROM
Trail contact: Rio Grande National Forest, Conejos Peak Ranger District, La Jara; (719) 274-8971; www.fs.usda.gov/riogrande

Finding the trailhead: From South Fork head southwest on US 160 for 7.3 miles. Then travel south/southeast on Park Creek Road (FR 380), which is gravel, for 26.9 miles. FR 380 ends upon meeting up with FR 250, also gravel. FR 250 heads straight (east) to Alamosa or right (south) to Platoro. Drive south toward Platoro, traveling another 4.4 miles to a junction with Three Forks Road (FR 247). Keep right on FR 247, and drive south/southwest for 6.3 miles to the end of the road and the signed Three Forks trailhead. There's a large parking area here and an outhouse. *DeLorme: Colorado Atlas & Gazetteer:* Page 89 B5. GPS: N37 18.126' / W106 36.333'.

The Hike

From the trailhead head southwest along the Conejos River via Three Forks Trail 712. You'll travel through trees at times, but mostly you'll be in a wide-open meadow. It's an easy hike to 1.9 miles and a spot called Three Forks, where the North and Middle Forks of the Conejos River come together with El Rito Azul. At this point Trail 712 is officially called Middle Fork Trail 712. Proceed 0.3 mile to a junction with the North Fork Conejos River and North Fork Trail 714, your return route.

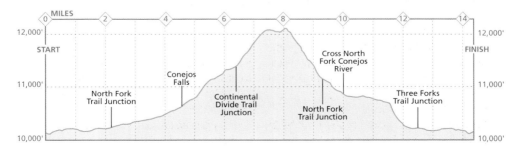

Conejos River Semiloop

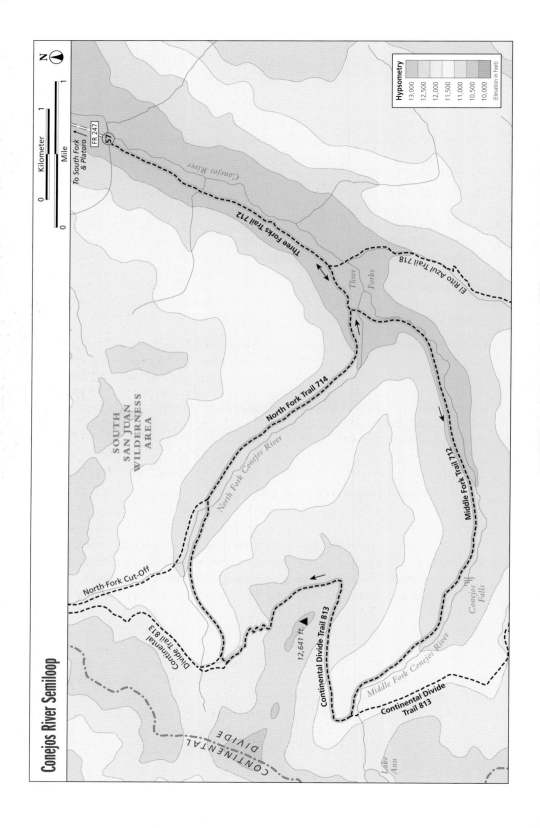

Junction of the Middle Fork Trail and the CDT

Continue hiking Trail 712 along the Middle Fork Conejos River. There are some steep sections leading through the forest, but you will always head back into the drainage, where the views get better and better as you hike up the river. You'll hear Conejos Falls after a total of 4.7 miles. Be sure to take one of the side trails to the waterfall, but be careful, as some lead down at a very steep grade. The waterfall flows over a basalt cliff and drops about 80 feet.

You'll hike mostly through the trees until 5.8 miles, when you'll emerge into the head of the basin, a scenic area blessed with wildflowers in summer. Continue up the trail to meet the CDT at 6.4 miles. (Notice the cascading waterfall flowing down from Lake Ann, which is tucked away to the west. If you want to visit Lake Ann, a good place for fishing, climb the steep trail on the north side of the stream. It's about 0.5 mile to the lake, elevation 11,910 feet. Please note that the lake is above the timberline and offers little protection during inclement weather.)

To continue on the semiloop, turn right (north) and hike the CDT as it leads east across a steep slope. It tops out at 12,100 feet; this is a good spot for lunch if thunderclouds aren't present. The views are grand from here, with Conejos Peak visible to the east.

Contour around to the north and northwest. Many switchbacks descend into the North Fork Conejos River drainage, where you'll see a trail junction at 9.3 miles. North Fork Trail 714 (your return route) is hard to find here, but if you descend, you'll see that it follows the river to the east. Be sure not to miss the river crossing around mile 10; watch closely for a post that marks the trail on the north side. Descend switchbacks en route to the junction with Three Forks Trail 712 at 12.5 miles. Go back the way you came, reaching the trailhead at 14.7 miles.

Miles and Directions

0.0 Three Forks trailhead.

2.2 North Fork Trail 714 junction. GPS: N37 16.652' / W106 37.493'.

6.4 Continental Divide Trail junction. GPS: N37 16.658' / W106 40.751'.

9.3 North Fork Trail 714 junction.

12.5 Three Forks Trail 712 junction.

14.7 Back to Three Forks trailhead.

Hike Information

Local information: South Fork Chamber of Commerce, South Fork; (719) 873-5556; www.southforkcolorado.org.

Local events/attractions: Attend the Little Britches Rodeo (June), Logger Days Festival (July), Rhythms of the Rio Music Festival (August), or Chili Cookoff (October).

Raft or fish the Rio Grande.

Accommodations: South Fork has a number of private campgrounds and motels. Mix Lake, a national forest campground, is located about 7 miles from the trailhead, near Platoro. It's a fee area with drinking water and vault toilets. You can also primitive camp en route to the trailhead. There are cabins and rooms in Platoro, an old mining town about 11 miles north. Call Skyline Lodge (719-376-2226) or Conejos Cabins (877-376-2547). If you like great big scrumptious burgers and mountains of fries, check out the restaurant at Skyline Lodge!

58 Montezuma Peak from Elwood Pass

The views from the top of Montezuma Peak and nearby Long Trek Mountain are both outstanding. From the summits look to the Weminuche Wilderness and see the Rio Grande Pyramid, the Grenadier Mountains, and the Needle Mountains. But wait, there's more: You'll also see to the La Garita Mountains, the Sangre de Cristo Mountains, the Spanish Peaks, and New Mexico.

Start: Continental Divide Trail at Elwood Pass
Distance: 11.2 miles out and back
Hiking time: About 6 to 10 hours (add 1 hour if you hike up and down Long Trek)
Difficulty: Strenuous due to length and high elevation
Canine compatibility: Dogs must be under control.
Nearest town: South Fork

Fees and permits: None
Maps: USGS Elwood Pass and Summit Peak; Trails Illustrated Weminuche Wilderness; DeLorme 3D TopoQuad CD-ROM; Maptech Terrain Navigator CD-ROM
Trail contact: Rio Grande National Forest, Conejos Peak Ranger District, La Jara; (719) 274-8971; www.fs.usda.gov/riogrande

Finding the trailhead: From South Fork head southwest on US 160 for 7.3 miles. Then travel south/southeast on Park Creek Road (FR 380), which is gravel, for 18.2 miles. At this point FR 380 continues straight (west); you need to make a right at the sign for Elwood Pass. The four-wheel-drive road is known as FR 667. It's 100 yards or so north to the trailhead. *DeLorme: Colorado Atlas & Gazetteer:* Page 89 A4. GPS: N37 24.333' / W106 38.656'.

The Hike

About 50 yards south of Elwood Pass, hike west off the four-wheel-drive road to unsigned Continental Divide Trail (CDT) 813. A raised trail leads over a boggy area before you enter the trees. The trail winds up a ridge before rising above the tree line, where the views are magnificent.

You'll reach a junction with Crater Lake Trail 707 at 1.8 miles. Here it merges with the CDT, and both head west to a junction at 2.5 miles. (See Hike 59 for more information regarding the hike to Crater Lake.) Continue south on the CDT, passing

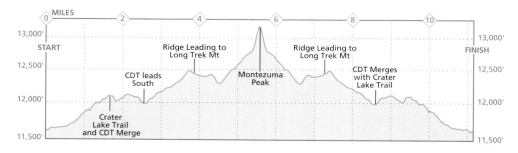

Montezuma Peak from Elwood Pass; Crater Lake Trail

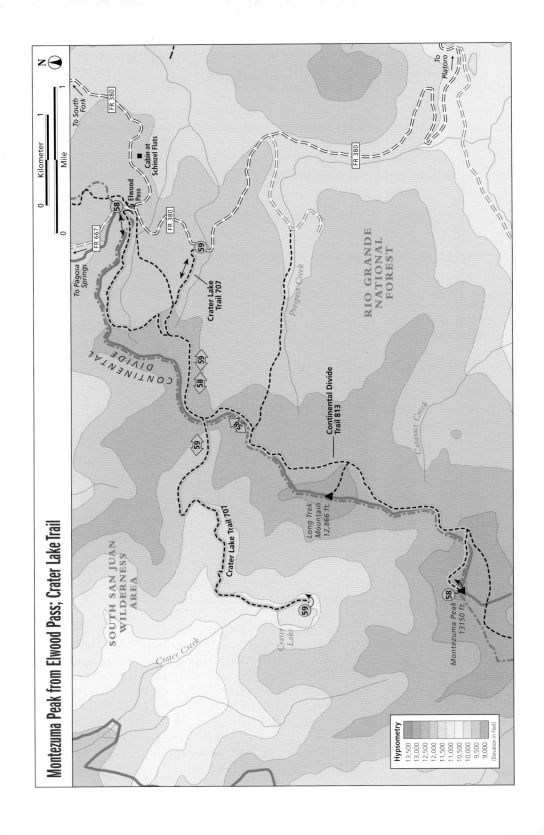

Long Trek, Montezuma, and Summit Peaks from the CDT

the Prospect Creek drainage en route. At 3.8 miles you'll see a good route up the southeast ridge to the top of Long Trek Mountain. Although it doesn't look like it, it's just over 400 feet to the summit (12,866 feet) via the southeast ridge. You'll hike 0.6 mile round-trip to the summit and back.

Continue south, passing the Cataract Creek drainage, where there's a pond on a little bench above the drainage. After a total of 5 miles, you'll reach the east side of Montezuma Peak. From here hike west and then northwest before climbing the steep northeast ridge. You'll reach the summit at 5.6 miles and in the process gain nearly 600 feet in elevation.

Miles and Directions

0.0 Elwood Pass.

1.8 Junction; Crater Lake Trail 707 and CDT merge.

2.5 Junction; CDT leads south. GPS: N37 23.885' / W106 40.260'.

5.0 East side of Montezuma Peak. GPS: N37 22.362' / W106 41.031'.

5.6 Montezuma Peak.

11.2 Back to Elwood Pass.

Hike Information

Local information: South Fork Chamber of Commerce, South Fork; (719) 873-5556; www .southforkcolorado.org.

Local events/attractions: Attend the Little Britches Rodeo (June), Logger Days Festival (July), Rhythms of the Rio Music Festival (August), or Chili Cookoff (October).

Raft or fish the Rio Grande.

Accommodations: South Fork has a number of private campgrounds and motels. Primitive campsites are numerous, so there are plenty of camping areas en route to the trailhead. There's also a cabin available at Schinzel Flats. Contact the Conejos Peak Ranger District at (719) 274-8971 for more information, or reserve it by calling the National Recreation Reservation Service at (877) 444-6777 or visiting the website www.recreation.gov.

59 Crater Lake Trail

Crater Lake is a wonderful destination, especially for those who enjoy high alpine lakes and the opportunity to fish them. The hike there and back is exciting; it includes some of the Continental Divide Trail (CDT). From the trail the views are tremendous, and there's a chance to see much in the way of wildlife and wildflowers.

See map page 252
Start: Crater Lake trailhead
Distance: 7.4 miles out and back
Hiking time: About 4 to 8 hours or overnight backpack
Difficulty: Strenuous due to elevation gain of almost 2,000 feet
Canine compatibility: Dogs must be under control.
Nearest town: South Fork

Fees and permits: None
Maps: USGS Elwood Pass; Trails Illustrated Weminuche Wilderness; DeLorme 3D TopoQuad CD-ROM; Maptech Terrain Navigator CD-ROM
Trail contacts: Rio Grande National Forest, Conejos Peak Ranger District, La Jara; (719) 274-8971; www.fs.usda.gov/riogrande. San Juan National Forest, Pagosa Ranger District, Pagosa Springs; (970) 264-2268; www.fs .usda.gov/sanjuan.

Finding the trailhead: From South Fork head southwest on US 160 for 7.3 miles. Then travel south/southeast on Park Creek Road (FR 380), which is gravel, for 19.1 miles. Although signed, the trailhead is easier to find if you look for the sign for Elwood Pass and continue 0.7 mile past it. There's room for only a few cars to park on the side of the road. *DeLorme: Colorado Atlas & Gazetteer:* Page 89 A4. GPS: N37 23.931' / W106 38.939'.

The Hike

Hike west from the trailhead, traveling Crater Lake Trail 707 through subalpine forest and spacious meadows to an unmarked junction at 0.7 mile. Here Trail 707 and the CDT merge. The grade is moderate and the views are tremendous as you proceed above the tree line; in midsummer the wildflowers are gorgeous. Be sure to look for ptarmigan, as they enjoy this region.

Continue traveling west; you will cross a steep side slope and then pass a small tarn. At 1.4 miles the CDT and Trail 707 split; proceed west on the latter. Instead of

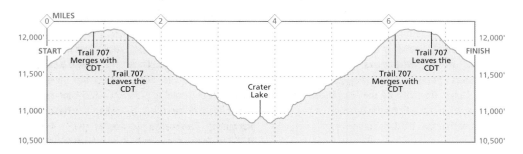

Crater Lake in the evening

climbing or contouring around, you'll descend a moderate slope and reach the wilderness boundary at 1.6 miles. Enter the trees (mostly fir and spruce), and hike downward to 3.5 miles and an unsigned trail junction. Both trails lead to Crater Lake. Take the right (southwest) fork to reach the north end of the lake. Take the left (southeast) fork to reach the northeast side; a trail drops to lake level and continues another 0.2 mile to the southeast end. Spaces for camping are limited, and the south and east sides of the lake are steep, so don't expect to camp there.

Miles and Directions

0.0 Crater Lake trailhead.
0.7 Crater Lake Trail 707 merges with the CDT. GPS: N37 23.942' / W106 39.616'.
1.4 Crater Lake Trail leaves the CDT. GPS: N37 23.885' / W106 40.260'.
1.6 Wilderness boundary.
3.7 Crater Lake.
7.4 Back to Crater Lake trailhead.

Hike Information

Local information: South Fork Chamber of Commerce, South Fork; (719) 873-5556; www.southforkcolorado.org.

Local events/attractions: Attend the Little Britches Rodeo (June), Logger Days Festival (July), Rhythms of the Rio Music Festival (August), or Chili Cookoff (October). Raft or fish the Rio Grande.

Accommodations: South Fork has a number of private campgrounds and motels. Primitive campsites are numerous, so there are plenty of camping areas en route to the trailhead. There's also a cabin available at Schinzel Flats. Contact the Conejos Peak Ranger District at (719) 274-8971 for more information, or reserve it by calling the National Recreation Reservation Service at (877) 444-6777 or visiting the website www.recreation.gov.

Trail Finder: Author's Favorites

Hikes for High-Altitude Scenery

1 Highland Mary Lakes Loop
4 Elk Park/Chicago Basin Shuttle Hike
6 Lime Mesa
7 Endlich Mesa/Burnt Timber Shuttle Hike
10 Cave Basin Trail
24 Highline Trail
25 Fisher Mountain
28 Ruby Lakes/Red Lakes Semiloop
31 The Window
33 Starvation Pass
34–37 The Continental Divide Trail in the Weminuche Wilderness
40 Little Blanco Trail from Junction of Quartz Lake Trail to Continental Divide
45 Continental Divide Trail (Cumbres Pass to Elwood Pass) Shuttle Hike
46 Red Lake Trail
48 Elk Creek/Valle Victoria Semiloop
51 South Fork/Roaring Gulch Semiloop
53 Conejos Peak Semiloop
54 Conejos Peak from Tobacco Lake Trailhead
55 Adams Fork to Summit Peak
58 Montezuma Peak from Elwood Pass

Hikes for Photography

1 Highland Mary Lakes Loop
4 Elk Park/Chicago Basin Shuttle Hike
6 Lime Mesa
7 Endlich Mesa/Burnt Timber Shuttle Hike
21 Hope Creek Trail
24 Highline Trail
28 Ruby Lakes/Red Lakes Semiloop
31 The Window
32 Ute Creek Semiloop
33 Starvation Pass
34–37 The Continental Divide Trail in the Weminuche Wilderness
40 Little Blanco Trail from Junction of Quartz Lake Trail to Continental Divide
45 Continental Divide Trail (Cumbres Pass to Elwood Pass) Shuttle Hike
46 Red Lake Trail
48 Elk Creek/Valle Victoria Semiloop
51 South Fork/Roaring Gulch Semiloop

52 Bear Lake Trail

53 Conejos Peak Semiloop

54 Conejos Peak from Tobacco Lake Trailhead

55 Adams Fork to Summit Peak

56 Blue Lake via Three Forks

58 Montezuma Peak from Elwood Pass

59 Crater Lake Trail

Hikes for Wildflowers

1 Highland Mary Lakes Loop

4 Elk Park/Chicago Basin Shuttle Hike

6 Lime Mesa

7 Endlich Mesa/Burnt Timber Shuttle Hike

24 Highline Trail

25 Fisher Mountain

26 Ivy Creek Trail to the Continental Divide

33 Starvation Pass

34–37 The Continental Divide Trail in the Weminuche Wilderness

41 Fish Lake Trail

43 Opal Lake Trailhead to Leche Creek Trail

45 Continental Divide Trail (Cumbres Pass to Elwood Pass) Shuttle Hike

53 Conejos Peak Semiloop

55 Adams Fork to Summit Peak

57 Conejos River Semiloop

58 Montezuma Peak from Elwood Pass

Hikes for Wildlife

4 Elk Park/Chicago Basin Shuttle Hike

8 Lake Eileen Trail

17 Fourmile Lake Loop

18 Turkey Creek Trail

24 Highline Trail

28 Ruby Lakes/Red Lakes Semiloop

29 Squaw Pass

34–37 The Continental Divide Trail in the Weminuche Wilderness

41 Fish Lake Trail

43 Opal Lake Trailhead to Leche Creek Trail

44 Navajo Peak/Leche Creek Trails Shuttle Hike

45 Continental Divide Trail (Cumbres Pass to Elwood Pass) Shuttle Hike

47 Duck Lake Trail

48 Elk Creek/Valle Victoria Semiloop

50 Victoria Lake via Ruybalid Trailhead

51 South Fork/Roaring Gulch Semiloop

53 Conejos Peak Semiloop
55 Adams Fork to Summit Peak
58 Montezuma Peak from Elwood Pass

Easy Day Hikes

6 Lime Mesa (to Dollar Lakes)
9 Vallecito Creek Trail (first few miles)
11 Pine River/Flint Creek Semiloop (first few miles)
16 Piedra Falls
20 South Fork/Archuleta Lake Semiloop (first few miles)
43 Opal Lake Trailhead to Leche Creek Trail (first few miles)
48 Elk Creek/Valle Victoria Semiloop (first few miles)
51 South Fork/Roaring Gulch Semiloop (first few miles)
55 Adams Fork to Summit Peak (first few miles)

Moderately Difficult Day Hikes

6 Lime Mesa
8 Lake Eileen Trail
21 Hope Creek Trail
30 Weminuche Pass Area
33 Starvation Pass
46 Red Lake Trail
47 Duck Lake Trail
52 Bear Lake Trail
56 Blue Lake via Three Forks

Long, Hard Day Hikes

1 Highland Mary Lakes Loop
10 Cave Basin Trail
15 Palisade Meadows
17 Fourmile Lake Loop
25 Fisher Mountain
31 The Window
38 Summit Peak via Quartz Creek
39 Little Blanco Trail to Quartz Lake
42 Flattop Mountain
57 Conejos River Semiloop
58 Montezuma Peak from Elwood Pass
59 Crater Lake Trail

First Overnight Hike in the Wilderness

9 Vallecito Creek Trail
11 Pine River Trail/Flint Creek Semiloop (first 5 to 6 miles)

23 Hunters Lake Loop
46 Red Lake Trail
59 Crater Lake Trail

Moderately Difficult Overnight Hikes

3 Crater Lake
6 Lime Mesa
26 Ivy Creek Trail to the Continental Divide
30 Weminuche Pass Area
52 Bear Lake Trail
54 Conejos Peak from Tobacco Lake Trailhead
56 Blue Lake via Three Forks
57 Conejos River Semiloop

Moderately Difficult Overnight Hikes of Two Nights or More

29 Squaw Pass
32 Ute Creek Semiloop
53 Conejos Peak Semiloop
55 Adams Fork to Summit Peak

Strenuous, Multiday Backpack Hikes

4 Elk Park/Chicago Basin Shuttle Hike
7 Endlich Mesa/Burnt Timber Shuttle Hike
11 Pine River/Flint Creek Semiloop
28 Ruby Lakes/Red Lakes Semiloop
34–37 The Continental Divide Trail in the Weminuche Wilderness
45 Continental Divide Trail (Cumbres Pass to Elwood Pass) Shuttle Hike
48 Elk Creek/Valle Victoria Semiloop
50 Victoria Lake via Ruybalid Trailhead
51 South Fork/Roaring Gulch Semiloop

Base Camp Options

3 Crater Lake
6 Lime Mesa
32 Ute Creek Semiloop
39 Little Blanco Trail to Quartz Lake
41 Fish Lake Trail
46 Red Lake Trail
53 Conejos Peak Semiloop
55 Adams Fork to Summit Peak

Appendix: For More Information

American Hiking Society
1422 Fenwick Ln.
Silver Spring, MD 20910
(800) 972-8608
www.americanhiking.org

American Trails
PO Box 491797
Redding, CA 96049-1797
(530) 547-2060
www.americantrails.org
trailhead@americantrails.org

Antonito Chamber of Commerce
PO Box 427
Antonito, CO 81120-0427
(719) 376-2277
www.slvguide.com/ANTONITO/
INDEX.HTM
info@conejoschamber.org

Bayfield Chamber of Commerce
PO Box 7
Bayfield, CO 81122
(970) 884-7372
www.bayfieldchamber.org

Chama Valley Chamber of Commerce
PO Box 306-RB
Chama, NM 87520
(575) 756-2306 or (800) 477-0149
www.chamavalley.com

Colorado Mountain Club
710 Tenth St., Ste. 200
Golden, CO 80401
(303) 279-3080
www.cmc.org
cmcoffice@cmc.org

Columbine Ranger District
San Juan National Forest
367 S. Pearl St.
Bayfield, CO 81122
(970) 884-2512
www.fs.usda.gov/sanjuan

Conejos Peak Ranger District
Rio Grande National Forest
15571 CR T5
La Jara, CO 81140
(719) 274-8971
www.fs.usda.gov/riogrande

Continental Divide Trail Society
3704 N. Charles St., #601
Baltimore, MD 21218
(410) 235-9610
www.cdtsociety.org
mail@cdtsociety.org

Creede & Mineral County
Chamber of Commerce
904 S. Main St.
Creede, CO 81130
(800) 327-2102
www.creede.com
office@creede.com

Cumbres & Toltec Scenic Railroad
(888) 286-2737
www.cumbrestoltec.com

Divide Ranger District
Rio Grande National Forest
13308 W. Highway 160
Del Norte, CO 81132
(719) 657-3321
www.fs.usda.gov/riogrande

Divide Ranger District (Creede Office)
Rio Grande National Forest
PO Box 270
Creede, CO 81130
(719) 658-2556
www.fs.usda.gov/riogrande

Durango Area Tourism Office
802 Main Ave.
Durango, CO 81301
(970) 247-3500 or (800) 525-8855
www.durango.org
visitorcenter@durango.org

Durango & Silverton Narrow Gauge
Railroad
479 Main Ave.
Durango, CO 81301
(970) 247-2733 or (877) 872-4607
www.durangotrain.com
info@durangotrain.com

Pagosa Ranger District
San Juan National Forest
180 Pagosa St.
Pagosa Springs, CO 81147
(970) 264-2268
www.fs.usda.gov/sanjuan

San Juan Mountains Association
PO Box 2261
Durango, CO 81302
(970) 385-1210
www.sjma.org

San Juan National Forest
15 Burnett Ct.
Durango, CO 81301
(970) 247-4874
www.fs.usda.gov/sanjuan

Sierra Club
Rocky Mountain Chapter
1536 Wynkoop St., 4th Floor
Denver, CO 80202
(303) 861-8819
www.rmc.sierraclub.org

Silverton Chamber of Commerce
414 Greene St.
Silverton, CO 81433
(970) 387-5654 or (800) 752-4494
www.silvertoncolorado.com
info@silvertoncolorado.net

South Fork Chamber of Commerce
29803 W. Highway 160
South Fork, CO 81154
(719) 873-5556
www.southforkcolorado.org
info@southforkcoloradochamber.com

Maps

DeLorme (Gazetteer and 3D TopoQuad)
Two DeLorme Dr.
PO Box 298
Yarmouth, ME 04096
(800) 561-5105
www.delorme.com

Maptech Terrain Navigator
One S. Broadway
Billings, MT 59101
(877) 587-9004
www.terrainnavigator.com

Trails Illustrated
www.natgeomaps.com/trailsillustrated.html

United States Geological Survey (USGS)
Box 25046 Denver Federal Center
Denver, CO 80225
(303) 202-4200
www.usgs.gov

HELP US KEEP THIS GUIDE UP TO DATE

Every effort has been made by the author and editors to make this guide as accurate and useful as possible. However, many things can change after a guide is published—trails are rerouted, regulations change, techniques evolve, facilities come under new management, and so on.

We would appreciate hearing from you concerning your experiences with this guide and how you feel it could be improved and kept up to date. While we may not be able to respond to all comments and suggestions, we'll take them to heart, and we'll also make certain to share them with the author. Please send your comments and suggestions to the following address:

Globe Pequot Press
Reader Response/Editorial Department
PO Box 480
Guilford, CT 06437

Or you may e-mail us at: editorial@GlobePequot.com

Thanks for your input, and happy trails!

About the Author

Donna Ikenberry loves to travel and enjoys the outdoors. A full-time photojournalist for more than thirty years, Donna started her career in 1983, when she was twenty-nine years old. That year she sold almost all of her belongings and started traveling full-time in an RV. She began writing guidebooks a few years later. Donna has written about all of the wilderness areas in Oregon and Colorado. She

The author; her husband, Mike Vining; and her late father, Donald Ikenberry (to whom this book is dedicated), on the island of Oahu in Hawaii

published a book on Utah's campgrounds, and she has written two bicycling guidebooks—one about riding the Atlantic Coast, the other about touring coast to coast, from Virginia to Oregon. Donna can happily say this is her thirteenth and last book. At least for now.

In addition to books, Donna has published nearly 5,000 photographs and more than 800 magazine and newspaper articles. Although she has spent most of her time traveling in the West, she has also explored Antarctica, her dream place. She has been there twice, and she hopes to return one day to photograph emperor penguins. Donna and her husband, Mike Vining, have also been to the High Arctic at Svalbard in Norway, and more recently to the equator to see and photograph the wildlife of the Amazon and the Galapagos Islands.

Donna met Mike on top of Guadalupe Peak—the highest point in Texas—in 1997. The following year the two were engaged on Mount Rainier, the highest point in Washington. It was no surprise to family and friends when they chose to get married on top of Mauna Kea, the highest point in Hawaii, on January 6, 1999. Mike retired from a thirty-year career in the US Army (he was in EOD and Delta Force) a few weeks after they were married and has been traveling with Donna ever since.

Today Donna and Mike have a home in South Fork, Colorado. Although they travel about half of the year, they enjoy each and every moment in their home state. They are avid mountain climbers, hikers, rock climbers, mountain bikers, kayakers, and both backcountry and downhill skiers. They also have a passion for high places and animal life. Donna and Mike are in the process of touching the tops of all of the state high points, as well as visiting as many zoos and national parks as they possibly can. Future travels will take them to see more of the United States, Canada, Mexico, High Arctic and Antarctica, as well as Australia, New Zealand, South Africa, and Europe.

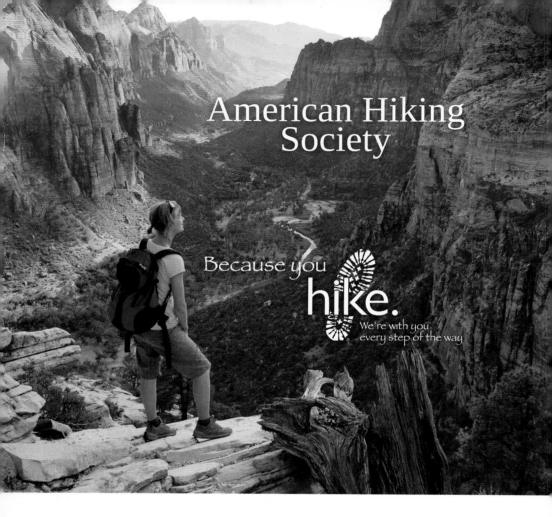

American Hiking Society

Because you hike.
We're with you every step of the way

As a national voice for hikers, **American Hiking Society** works every day:

- Building and maintaining hiking trails
- Educating and supporting hikers by providing information and resources
- Supporting hiking and trail organizations nationwide
- Speaking for hikers in the halls of Congress and with federal land managers

Whether you're a casual hiker or a seasoned backpacker, become a member of American Hiking Society and join the national hiking community! You'll enjoy great member benefits and help preserve the nation's hiking trails, so tomorrow's hike is even better than today's. We invite you to join us now!

American Hiking Society

iking.org